God's Plan for the Ages

The Blueprint of Bible Prophecy

Dr. David R. Reagan

LAMB & LION MINISTRIES

P.O. Box 919
McKinney, TX 75070
www.lamblion.com

Dedicated to

Jim and Darlene Bridges

in appreciation for their friendship, encouragement and support.

First edition, 2005

Copyright © 2005 by Lamb & Lion Ministries

ISBN: 0-945593-12-0

Library of Congress Control Number: 2005900774

Lamb & Lion Ministries
P.O. Box 919
McKinney, Texas 75070
lamblion@lamblion.com
www.lamblion.com

Cover design by Keith Fink of Master's Press
in Dallas, Texas.

All scripture quotations are from the New American Standard
Version, © 1995 by the Lockman Foundation.

Printed in the United States of America.

Contents

Part Three
Prophetic Views

**Part Four
Prophetic Signs**

About the Author

Dr. David R. Reagan is the senior evangelist for Lamb & Lion Ministries, a Bible prophecy ministry located in the Dallas, Texas area.

Before founding the ministry in 1980, Dr. Reagan served for 20 years as a university professor, teaching international law and politics. Throughout that time he was an ardent student of the Bible.

Since 1980 Dr. Reagan has taught Bible prophecy in meetings and seminars held all across America and around the world.

His weekly television program, "Christ in Prophecy," is broadcast throughout the United States.

He has made many trips to Israel and is considered an expert on Middle East politics and Israel in Bible prophecy.

Dr. Reagan has been gifted with the skill to communicate complex ideas in simple, understandable terms. He is the author of several books, including the only children's book ever published about end time Bible prophecy. It is entitled *Jesus Is Coming Again!* (Harvest House, 1992).

Dr. Reagan and his wife, Ann, live in a Dallas suburb. They are the parents of two daughters and have four grandchildren.

To secure a free catalogue of Dr. Reagan's tapes and publications, contact the ministry in one of the following ways:

- Write to Lamb & Lion Ministries, P.O. Box 919, McKinney, Texas 75070, U.S.A.

- Call the ministry at 1-800-705-8316.

- Access the ministry's website at www.lamblion.com.

Foreword

I'm tired of reading sensationalist prophecy books. Because Bible prophecy deals with the future, it attracts curiosity seekers, and that, in turn, motivates sensationalists to write titillating books that appeal to the flesh rather than minister to the spirit.

Journalistic Prophecy

The book titles in the prophecy section of any Christian bookstore often smack of the same flavor as the headlines in the tabloids:

"Babylon Rebuilt!"

"Ark of the Covenant Discovered!"

"Vultures Gathering in Israel!"

"Computer Beast in Belgium!"

"Is Gorbachev Gog?"

"Could King Carlos be the Antichrist?"

"The Mark of the Beast is Here!"

On and on it goes, *ad nauseam*.

Prophecy Rumors

A few years ago I received a letter from a radio listener who said her pastor had preached a whole sermon on a rumor he had heard from some prophecy teacher. The rumor, believe it or not, was that the building blocks of the next Jewish Temple have all been cut and numbered, and the blocks have been stored in K-Marts across the United States, waiting for the call to ship them to Jerusalem!

Bizarre rumors like this circulate constantly among prophecy buffs. It's enough to make anyone conclude that the whole field of Bible prophecy is nothing but a playground for fanatics. Unfortunately, many Christians have come to that conclusion and have written off prophecy as a fruitful field for study.

That is too bad, for prophecy, properly taught, can be green pastures for disciples.

Purposes of This Book

God has a plan for the future. He has had it from the foundation of the world. God proclaimed this truth through the prophet Isaiah (46:9-11):

9   "... For I am God, and there is no other;
I am God, and there is no one like Me,

10   Declaring the end from the beginning
And from ancient times things which have not
been done.
Saying, 'My purpose will be established,
And I will accomplish all My good pleasure'

11   ... Truly I have spoken; truly I will bring it
to pass.
I have planned it, surely I will do it."

The basic purpose of this book is to spell out the details of God's plan for the future as revealed in His Prophetic Word.

In the process, I will attempt to explain some of the basic concepts and issues in Bible prophecy in a non-sensationalist way. The purpose is not to stimulate the imagination but to feed the spirit.

Additionally, the book aims to use God's Prophetic Word to motivate Bible study, to generate greater hope about the future, to spur evangelism, to encourage a commitment to holiness, and to develop a deeper relationship with Jesus.

It is also written to create a sense of urgency about the soon return of Jesus — and, more than that, a sense of expectancy.

Prophetic Apathy

Because the proper study of Bible prophecy has been so ignored in the modern day Church, the average Christian is apathetic about the return of Jesus. The Bible says we are to yearn for the return of the Lord (2 Timothy 4:7-8). The Church today is yawning.

The proper Biblical yearning can be found today primarily among the Orthodox Jews worldwide who are earnestly expecting the coming of the Messiah any moment. They sense His soon coming because they know the prophecies of the Hebrew Scriptures — what we call the Old Testament.

The Church, by contrast, is generally ignorant of Old Testament prophecies and has ignored or spiritualized New Testament prophecy.

The resulting paradox is that whereas the Jews failed to recognize the First Coming of the Messiah, it is the Jews who are now attuned to the signs of the times while the Gentile Church seems blind.

As we will see in this book, God is currently performing one of His greatest miracles in history. The Jews fully recognize it. The Church seems oblivious to it.

A Prayer

I pray this book will challenge and transform your thinking about the future by driving you deeper into God's Prophetic Word than you have ever dared to venture.

I pray the book will give you an appreciation for the fact that God is in control of history, that He has a master plan and that He is capable of orchestrating its fulfillment.

I pray too that the book will thrill your soul with the marvelous blessings that God has promised His people in the future.

A Promise

I promise you that this study of prophecy will bless you. You may not agree with all I have to say, but you will be blessed by the promises of God that I will show you in the Scriptures.

The further you proceed in the book, the more you will come to fully appreciate the apostle Paul's statement in Romans 8:18 — "I consider that the sufferings of this present time are not worthy to be compared with the glory that is to be revealed to us."

Maranatha!

Dr. David R. Reagan
Allen, Texas
Winter of 2005

Fingertips and Noses

A song by Eddie Carswell & Oliver Wells

Up in the hills somewhere in Kentucky
Is a little old school way back in the nothing
Where special kids born with special needs
Are sent to learn life's ABC's

Their teacher, Mrs. Jones, tells them all about Jesus —
How in the twinkling of an eye
He's coming back to get us,
About streets of gold and pearly gates.
How they want to go, they just can't wait!
And she can't keep them in their seats.
They're all at the windows straining to see.

(Chorus)
And it's . . .
Fingertips and noses pressed to the windowpanes.
Longing eyes, expectant hearts,
For Him to come again.
All they know is that they love Him so,
And if He said He'd come, He's coming.
And they can't keep their windows clean
Back at the windows straining to see.

How will Jesus find us when He comes again?
Will we be like little children waiting just for Him,
With our fingertips and noses pressed to the windowpanes,
Longing eyes, expectant hearts,
For Him to come again?

God's Plan for the Ages

The Blueprint of Bible Prophecy

Introduction

The Gate to Prophecy

The Eastern Gate in the old walled city of Jerusalem has a very special place in my heart. The reason is that God used that gate to open my eyes to His Prophetic Word.

The year was 1967. The occasion was the Six Day War. As the fate of the new state of Israel hung in the balance, I searched the newspapers daily for any information I could find about the war.

The turning point came on June 7 when the Israeli army broke through the Lion's Gate and returned control of the ancient city of Jerusalem to the Jewish people for the first time in 1,897 years.

A Mysterious Remark

The next day I read a fascinating news account about one of the Jewish commando groups that had been involved in the assault on the city.

The article stated that some members of the group had suggested catching the Jordanian defenders of the city off guard by blowing open the sealed Eastern Gate. But the leader of the group, an Orthodox Jew, had vehemently protested the idea, stating that "the Eastern Gate can be opened only when the Messiah comes."

That statement caught my eye. I wondered what the fellow was talking about. I knew nothing about the Eastern Gate except that it was the only gate of the city that led directly onto the Temple Mount. I was not aware that it was sealed, nor did I know that its opening was in any way biblically linked to the return of the Messiah.

A Remarkable Prophecy

I decided to do some research on the matter, and that decision initiated my study of Bible prophecy. I had been attending church for 30 years, but like most Christians, I knew nothing about Bible prophecy. The topic was generally ignored by the preachers in my boyhood church.

My concordance quickly directed me to the passage that the Orthodox Jew had alluded to. I found it in Ezekiel 44. The context is a supernatural tour which the Lord is giving Ezekiel of the future Millennial temple (Ezekiel 40:1-3).

In chapter 43 the Lord gives Ezekiel a vision of God's glory entering the Millennial temple from the east, through the Eastern Gate. The Lord says to Ezekiel: "Son of Man, this is the place of My throne and the place of the soles of my feet where I will dwell among the sons of Israel forever" (Ezekiel 43:7).

The Lord then reveals to Ezekiel that the Eastern Gate will be closed and will not be reopened until the Messiah returns in glory (Ezekiel 44:1-3).

A Momentous Decision

The stage was set for the fulfillment of this prophecy more than 400 hundred years ago in 1517 when the Turks conquered Jerusalem under the leadership of Suleiman the Magnificent. He commanded that the city's ancient walls be rebuilt, and in the midst of this rebuilding project, for some unknown reason, he ordered that the Eastern Gate be sealed up with stones.

Legends abound as to why Suleiman closed the gate. The most believable one is that while the walls were being rebuilt, a rumor swept Jerusalem that the Messiah was coming. Suleiman called together some Jewish rabbis and asked them to tell him about the Messiah. They described the Messiah as a great military leader who would be sent by God from the east. He would enter the Eastern Gate and liberate the city from foreign control.

Suleiman then decided to put an end to Jewish hopes by ordering the Eastern Gate sealed. He also put a cemetery in front of the Gate, believing that no Jewish holy man would defile himself by walking through a Muslim cemetery.

A Prophetic Symbol

The gate has remained sealed since that time. The Muslim cemetery still blocks the entrance. The old walled city has eight gates, and the Eastern Gate, and it alone, is sealed — just as prophesied in Ezekiel 44. The world would call that an "amazing coincidence." I call it a "God-incidence."

The Eastern Gate is proof positive that the Bible is the Word of God. Its sealing is clear evidence that we are living in the end times. The Gate awaits the return of the Messiah. Then and only then, will it be opened.

A Vision

I have a vision of what that glorious day will be like. It is related to the Lord's First Coming. I believe Jesus is going to replay His triumphal entry into Jerusalem when He returns.

When He came the first time, Jesus rode a donkey from the Mt. of Olives down into the Kidron Valley and up to the Eastern Gate where He entered the Temple Mount for His last days of teaching. As He made that ride, the Valley of Kidron was filled with thousands of admirers who had heard about the resurrection of Lazarus. They waved palm branches and chanted, "Hosanna to the Son of David!" Within a few days that same fickle crowd was shouting, "Crucify Him!"

We are told in Revelation 19 that when Jesus returns He will come as a victorious military conqueror, riding through the air on a supernatural white horse. In Isaiah 61 we are told that He will come from the east, and in Zechariah 14 we are told that He will touch ground on the Mt. of Olives from which He ascended into Heaven.

Revelation 19:14 says that all the Redeemed will come with the Lord. Think of it! Those of us who are saved will be there to witness the Lord's return. Zechariah 14 says He will speak a word that will supernaturally destroy the Antichrist and his forces.

Then, I believe we will witness a replay of the Lord's triumphant entry into Jerusalem. With angels hovering above and millions of the Redeemed filling the Kidron Valley, Jesus will ride up to the Eastern Gate on His white horse, and as He approaches the Gate, it will open supernaturally. He will then enter the City of David, and to the triumphant shouts of "Hosanna to the Son of David," He will be coronated the King of kings and the Lord of lords.

I believe that's what Psalm 24:7-10 is all about when it says:

> 7   Lift up your heads, O gates,
>   And be lifted up, O ancient doors,
>   That the King of glory may come in!
>
> 8   Who is the King of glory?
>   The Lord strong and mighty,
>   The Lord mighty in battle.
>
> 10 Who is the King of glory?
>   The Lord of hosts,
>   He is the King of glory.

An Invitation

I invite you to enter the fascinating and spiritually enriching world of Bible prophecy with me. Allow me to be your guide to an overview of God's master plan for the future.

And as we proceed, remember to be a good Berean by testing everything I have to say against the Scriptures (Acts 17:10-11).

Part One

Prophetic Significance

"We have the prophetic word made more sure,
to which you do well to pay attention,
as to a lamp shining in a dark place."
2 Peter 1:19

The Importance of Prophecy   1

Is it just pie in the sky?

Although prophecy constitutes almost one-third of the Bible, its importance is constantly downplayed by those who dismiss it as having no practical significance or by those who object to it on the grounds that it is a "fad" that takes people's eyes off Jesus.

Revelation 19:10 says that "the testimony of Jesus is the spirit of prophecy." Thus, if prophecy is properly taught, there is no reason for it to divert anyone's attention away from Jesus. In fact, it should serve to emphasize the centrality of Jesus.

Is prophecy practical? Consider that all the New Testament writers testify to the fact that the study of prophecy will motivate holy living. What could be more practical than that?

Prophecy does not have to be either faddish, other-worldly, or impractical if taught properly. Nor does it have to be a playground for fanatics. It can and should be green pastures for disciples.

Reasons for Study

1) Quantity — Between one-fourth and one-third of the Bible is prophetic in nature. When thinking of prophetic literature, most people consider only the Major and Minor Prophets of the Old Testament. But there is much more than that. For example, the psalms are saturated with prophecies, and there are prophecies scattered throughout the historical books of the Old Testament. In the New Testament, one out of every twenty-five verses relate to the Lord's Second Coming. There are lengthy passages of end time prophecy, like Matthew 24 and 2 Peter 3. Additionally, there are entire books devoted to prophecy, like 1 & 2 Thessalonians and Revelation. The bottom line is that if you are going to ignore Bible prophecy, then you are going to deprive yourself of a significant portion of God's Word.

2) Uniqueness — The Bible is the only book in the world that contains detailed, specific prophecies that have been fulfilled in history. There are no fulfilled prophecies in the sayings of Buddha or Confucius. Nor are there any fulfilled prophecies in the Hindu Vedras, the Qur'an, or the Book of Mormon. In contrast, the Bible is filled with both spiritual and secular prophecies that have been fulfilled in history. A good example is the one I mentioned in the introduction — namely, the closing of the Eastern Gate which is prophesied in Ezekiel 44.

3) Validator of Scripture — Fulfilled prophecy is one of the best evidences I know of that the Bible is the inspired Word of God. The Bible contains hundreds of fulfilled secular prophecies pertaining to cities, nations, empires, and individuals. Jeremiah predicted the Babylonian captivity would last 70 years (Jeremiah 25:11-12). Isaiah stated that the children of Israel would be sent home from Babylon by a man named Cyrus (Isaiah 44:28; Ezra 1:1). Daniel predicted the precise order of four great Gentile empires (Daniel 2 and 7). The destruction of Babylon was foretold by a number of the Hebrew prophets (Isaiah 13). In the New Testament, Jesus predicted the complete destruction of Jerusalem 40 years before it actually occurred (Luke 21:6).

4) Validator of Jesus — The Bible contains more than 300 prophecies about the First Coming of Jesus, all of which were literally fulfilled. Every aspect of the life of Jesus was prophesied — the place of His birth, the nature of His birth, the quality of His ministry, the purpose of His life, and the agony of His death. Consider, for example, the prophecy in Psalm 22:16 that the Messiah's hands and feet would be pierced. That prophecy was written by David about a thousand years before the birth of Jesus. It was written 700 years before the Romans perfected crucifixion as a form of execution. The literal fulfillment of so many prophecies in the life of one individual transcends any mere coincidence and serves to validate that Jesus was who He said He was — the divine Son of God.

5) Revealer of the Future — Prophecy serves to tell us some things that God wants us to know about the future (Deuteronomy 29:29; Amos 3:7). God does not want us to know everything about the future, but there are some things we must know if we are to have a dynamic hope. Thus, prophecy assures us that Jesus is coming back, that He will resurrect us, and that He will take us to live forever with Him and God the Father. In this regard, Peter likens prophecy to "a lamp shining in a dark place" (2 Peter 1:19). Paul makes the same point in 1 Corinthians chapter 2. He begins by observing that no eye has seen, no ear has heard, nor has the mind of man conceived, what God has prepared for those who love Him. But in the next verse Paul says those things have been revealed to us by God through His Spirit (1 Corinthians 2:9-10).

6) Tool of Evangelism — Prophecy can be used as a very effective tool of evangelism, as illustrated in the story of Philip and the Eunuch (Acts 8:26ff). Philip used Isaiah's great suffering lamb passage (Isaiah 53) to teach that Jesus is the lamb who was slain for the sins of the world. Matthew and Peter both used fulfilled prophecy in the life of Jesus as one of their basic evangelistic tools. In fact, Peter referred to prophecy constantly in his first gospel sermon on the Day of Pentecost (Acts 2:14-39). He preached that Jesus had been crucified and resurrected in fulfillment of Hebrew prophecies. Later, Peter referred to fulfilled prophecy as one of the greatest evidences that Jesus was truly the Son of God (2 Peter 1:16-19).

7) Tool of Moral Teaching — People often overlook the fact that the Hebrew prophets were forthtellers as well as foretellers. In fact, the prophets spent most of their time using God's Word to spotlight societal problems. They called their listeners to repentance, true worship, social justice, and personal holiness. One of the great recurring themes of the prophets is that "obedience is better than sacrifice" (1 Samuel 15:22 and Hosea 6:6). That statement means that in God's eyes, obedience to His commands is more important than outward religious practices such as offering sacrifices. Prophecy is thus a great repository of moral teaching, and those moral principles are still relevant today. (See Amos 5:21-24; Micah 6:8; and Isaiah 58:3-9.)

8) Generator of Spiritual Growth — Prophetic knowledge encourages patient waiting (James 5:7-8); provokes earnest watching (Matthew 24:36,42); inspires dedicated work (2 Timothy 4:7-8); and enhances our hope (Titus 2:11-14). The result is holy living. Paul exhorts us to "behave properly as in the day," because the time is at hand when the Lord will return (Romans 13:12-13). Likewise, Peter calls us to gird up our minds and be sober and holy as we look forward to the revelation of Jesus (1 Peter 1:13-15).

Advice and Counsel

In 2 Timothy 3:16-17 Paul writes that all of God's Word is "profitable for teaching, for reproof, for correction, and for training in righteousness." That includes God's Prophetic Word. In 1 Thessalonians 5:20 the apostle Paul pleads with us to treat prophecy with respect.

Peter warns us in his second epistle, that one of the signs of the end times will be the appearance of "scoffers" who will cast scorn and ridicule on the promise of our Lord's return (2 Peter 3:3ff). The great tragedy of our day is that many of the loudest scoffers are religious leaders who profess to follow Christ. Such leaders crucified Jesus the first time He came. They now scoff at His promise to return.

A good example of what I'm talking about is the "Jesus Seminar" that operated throughout the 1990's. It was composed of forty New Testament "scholars" from a great variety of Christian seminaries in America. The seminar met every six months to vote on the sayings of Jesus as recorded in the four gospels. Their purpose was to produce a new version of the gospels in which the sayings of Jesus would be color-coded: red, if He said it; pink, if He may have said it; grey, if He probably did not say it; and black, if He definitely did not say it.

When they voted on the sayings of Jesus regarding His Second Coming, they voted that all the sayings were spurious and had probably been "made up" by His disciples. What apostasy!

Spiritual Food

God's Prophetic Word is food for our spiritual growth. We need to take it off the shelf. We need to open it up and feast upon it, and we need to do so with believing hearts.

The book of Revelation promises blessings to those who read it (or hear it read) and who obey it (Revelation 1:3). It is the only book of the Bible to promise such a specific blessing, but all God's Word is designed to bless us spiritually (Psalm 119), and that includes the Prophetic Word.

Key Scriptures about Prophecy

Before we get to the meat of our study, let's remind ourselves what the Word of God itself says about the value of prophecy. In this way we can be assured that the effort we expend in looking at the prophetic Scriptures will be time extremely well spent.

> "The secret things belong to the Lord our God; but the things that are revealed belong to us and to our sons forever." (Deuteronomy 29:29)

> "Surely the Lord God does nothing, unless He reveals His secret counsel to His servants the prophets." (Amos 3:7)

> "I am God, and there is no other; I am God, and there is no one like Me, declaring the end from the beginning and from ancient times things which have not been done. . . I have spoken; truly I will bring it to pass. I have planned it, surely I will do it." (Isaiah 46:9-11)

> "[Jesus said] 'Do not think that I have come to abolish the Law or the Prophets; I did not come to abolish, but to fulfill.'" (Matthew 5:17)

> "[Jesus] said to them, 'These are My words which I spoke to you while I was still with you, that all things which are written about Me in the Law of Moses and the Prophets and the Psalms must be fulfilled.'" (Luke 24:44)

"Of Him [Jesus] all the prophets bear witness that through His name everyone who believes in Him receives forgiveness of sins." (Acts 10:43)

"The prophets who prophesied of the grace that would come to you made careful search and inquiry, seeking to know what person or time the Spirit of Christ within them was indicating as He predicted the sufferings of Christ and the glories to follow." (1 Peter 1:10-11)

"But know this first of all, that no prophecy of Scripture is a matter of one's own interpretation, for no prophecy was ever made by an act of human will, but men moved by the Holy Spirit spoke from God." (2 Peter 1:20-21)

"The testimony of Jesus is the spirit of prophecy." (Revelation 19:10)

As these passages clearly indicate, Bible prophecy is to be held in high esteem and is to be taken seriously. But, as we shall see, it has been terribly abused.

The Abuse of Prophecy   2

Does it deserve the contempt it receives?

L et's face it — Bible prophecy is held in contempt by most people. Non-Christians scoff at the very idea of supernatural knowledge about the future. The ironic thing is that in doing so they fulfill
a prophecy of Peter: "In the last days mockers will come with their
mocking, following after their own lusts, and saying, 'Where is the
promise of His coming?'" (2 Peter 3:3-4).

The Apostates

The real tragedy concerning God's Prophetic Word is that so
many Christians share this same scoffing attitude. Apostate Christian seminaries have pretty well rejected the whole concept of prophecy. Most now teach that prophecy is really history written after
the fact but written like prophecy to make it more interesting.

This rejection of prophecy on the part of apostate Christians is a
natural outgrowth of their worship at the man-made altar of what
theologians call "historical criticism."

This despicable methodology rejects the Bible as God's revelation to Man, arguing instead that it represents Man's faltering search
for God. Its proponents have concluded that the Bible is full of
myth, superstition, and legend.

Since they have rejected the supernatural, these people cannot
accept the idea of prophecy as revealed pre-knowledge of history.
This is the reason the book of Daniel has been a focus of their scorn
and ridicule. It is not at all unusual to hear one of their scholars say,
"The book of Daniel is just too accurate. It had to be written after
the events it claims to prophesy." This is nothing but blatant unbe-

lief which calls into question our Lord's own acceptance of Daniel as authentic (Matthew 24:15).

This attitude is also a fulfillment of prophecy, for Jesus said that in the end times there will be a great apostasy within the professing Church (Matthew 24:10-12). As Paul put it, the end times will be marked by men "holding to a form of godliness, although they have denied its power" (2 Timothy 3:5).

The Spiritualizers

Prophecy has also suffered abuse at the hands of those who have specialized in spiritualizing it. Liberals and conservatives both have been guilty of this practice.

When I speak of "spiritualizing," I am referring to the methodology which holds that prophecy does not mean what it says. In practice this always leads to a symbolic interpretation of prophecy. The plain sense meaning of prophecy is denied, and prophetic books like Revelation are treated like they were adult Alice in Wonderland books with a vague, general message but no specific meaning.

This spiritualization of prophecy on the part of liberals is easy to understand. It is a natural extension of their tendency to spiritualize all of Scripture. They have spiritualized the miracles of God in the Old Testament and the miracles of Jesus in the New Testament, so why should they accept the plain sense meaning of prophecy, especially when it teaches a supernatural consummation of history?

It's the conservative spiritualizers who are such a perplexing mystery to me. They accept the Bible as the Word of God. They agree that the Bible contains supernatural revelations about the future. They interpret virtually all non-prophetic passages literally. They even interpret the First Coming prophecies literally. But for some strange inexplicable reason, they insist upon spiritualizing all the Bible's prophecies concerning the Second Coming.

Thus, they deny the coming reality of the Tribulation, the Millennial Reign, and the New Earth. They take a passage like Zechariah 14, which says Jesus will return to the Mount of Olives and reign on the earth, and they spiritualize it to mean that when you accept Jesus as Lord and Savior, He comes into your heart (the

Mount of Olives) and begins to reign in your life (the reign on earth). Such people should be granted Ph.D.'s in imagination!

If the prophecies concerning the First Coming of Jesus were all fulfilled in some literal way in their plain sense meaning, then why shouldn't the Second Coming prophecies be fulfilled the same way?

The Fanatics

Even some of the friends of Bible prophecy have been guilty of abusing it. I have in mind the fanatics who use it as a playground for their fanciful speculations.

They usually are obsessed with date setting or speculating about whether or not a person like Henry Kissinger is the Antichrist.

They are often rumor mongers who spread wild stories about vultures gathering in Israel, Belgian computers taking over the world, the Jews collecting building blocks for the Temple, the Social Security Administration stamping numbers on people's hands, and Bill Clinton's name having the numerical equivalent of 666!

The Apathetic

Finally, there are those Christians who are simply apathetic about prophecy. They couldn't care less.

Many of these Christians think prophecy has no practical relevance to their daily lives, so they ignore it. They have never read the Major Prophets. They couldn't even find the Minor Prophets. And they certainly aren't going to waste their time with that "Chinese puzzle" called the Book of Revelation.

My own church heritage fits this description. Our apathetic attitude was motivated by the peculiar belief that all Old Testament prophecy had been fulfilled and therefore the study of prophecy was a waste of time.

"It's too complicated."

Some Christians have washed their hands of prophecy because they contend it is too complex. "You have to have a doctorate in hermeneutics to understand it!" they exclaim.

This attitude is often prompted by the specialized vocabulary of prophecy. When people hear technical terms like "premillennial," "postmillennial," and "amillennial," their eyes usually roll back in their heads and they space out, concluding that prophecy is a field of study for experts only. But that, of course, is not true. As we shall see in this book, what is necessary is the in-dwelling power of the Holy Spirit and a conviction that prophecy can be understood.

"It's too ethereal."

Others ignore Bible prophecy because they consider it to be too "other-worldly." A lot of pastors have this attitude. "It's all pie-in-the-sky," they argue. And they usually add, "It just has no relevance to the present."

As we shall see, this contention is false. Bible prophecy has the power to transform lives here and now by calling us to holiness and motivating us to evangelism.

Satan used to defeat me all the time by constantly reminding me of my past sins. But my study of Bible prophecy has given me a new weapon to fight Satan with. Now, every time he reminds me of my past, I remind him of his future! He responds by sulking away in defeat.

"It's too contentious."

Some pastors ignore Bible prophecy because they consider it to be divisive. This is a legitimate concern because it can be it if it is not taught properly.

Many prophecy teachers seem intent on trying to prove that everyone else is wrong. They come across as attack dogs, and in the process, they alienate and divide. But if Bible prophecy is presented with a loving attitude and with the focus on Jesus, it can only be edifying.

"It's too gruesome."

And then there are those who consider Bible prophecy to be scary. As a person put it to me in a letter, "I don't like prophecy because it's all about blood and gore and beasts and things that go bump in the dark!" Again, there is some truth in this statement. There is a lot of bad news in Bible prophecy, but it is all for unbelievers. For those who have put their trust in Jesus, there is only good news.

Consider Malachi 4:1-2. In verse one the prophet speaks of how unbelievers will be burned like chaff at the Lord's Second Coming. But in verse two, he says that believers will rejoice and be blessed when they see the Son returning. In fact, he says they will be so joyful that they "will go forth and skip about" like calves released from a stall!

A Satanic Conspiracy

I believe that Satan himself has inspired all this abuse of God's Prophetic Word. Satan does not want anyone studying prophecy, because prophecy contains the revelation of Satan's ultimate and total defeat. The message of prophecy is that "Believers win in the end!" Satan does not want anyone to know that message.

The book of Revelation begins with the words, "The revelation of Jesus Christ." The book of Revelation, like the rest of prophecy, is meant to reveal the future. It is meant to be understood. God wants to build our hope in the midst of a dark and troubled world by revealing to us the great victories that lie ahead in His master plan.

I exhort you to stand firm against Satan in his attempt to convince you that God's Prophetic Word is not to be taken seriously. Do not abuse it. Do not ignore it. The apostle Paul commanded us to respect prophecy (1 Thessalonians 5:20). The apostle Peter likewise urged us "to pay attention" to prophecy "as to a lamp shining in a dark place" (2 Peter 1:19).

The Range of Prophecy   3
What are the varieties?

Hebrews 1:1 says that God spoke through the prophets "in many portions and in many ways." Have you ever stopped to think about the variety of people and ways which God used?

Writing Prophets

Of course, the method that immediately comes to mind is the written form. The prophets who wrote down their messages are the ones we know best — people like Isaiah, Jeremiah, Ezekiel, Daniel, and the so-called "Minor Prophets" like Habakkuk and Zephaniah. In the New Testament the writing prophets include Paul, Peter, and John.

But to lump all these writing prophets together into one broad category is misleading, for there is a great variety of people and styles among them.

As to people, the variety is astounding. The prophets range from uneducated farmers like Amos to sophisticated poets like Isaiah, from reluctant spokesmen like Jonah to men of great courage like Daniel, from the little known like Joel to the famous like King David.

There is an equal variety in the styles of writing. Some, like Ezekiel, Daniel, Haggai, and the New Testament prophets, primarily used a prose style. Others, like David, Isaiah, Joel, and Micah, expressed their ideas in poetic form. And then there are the preachers whose books are mainly collections of sermons — prophets like Jeremiah, Amos, and Zechariah.

Most were given direct revelations — "Thus says the Lord."

Others received their insight through dreams and visions. Some, like Hosea and Jonah, simply recorded their experiences.

Speaking Prophets

Some of the most important prophets wrote nothing at all, at least nothing that has been preserved. We know about them because others wrote about their revelations, pronouncements, and exploits. Elijah and his successor, Elisha, fall into this category, as does Samuel.

So does the greatest prophet who ever lived — the Prophet foretold by Moses (Deuteronomy 18:15-18). I'm speaking, of course, of Jesus Christ (Matthew 21:11). The only writings of Jesus that we have are His seven letters to the seven churches of Asia, recorded by John in Revelation 2 and 3. The bulk of Jesus' prophecies, like His Olivet Discourse (Matthew 24, Mark 13, and Luke 21), were written by His disciples. Jesus was an oral prophet.

Most of the oral prophets are not well known. Only a few are mentioned in the New Testament — like the four daughters of Philip (Acts 21:9) and Agabus, the prophet who counseled Paul (Acts 21:10).

But the Old Testament is full of oral prophets. There is Nathan, who confronted David (2 Samuel 12); Micaiah, who saw the Lord sitting on His throne (1 Kings 22); Ahijah, who condemned Jeroboam (1 Kings 14); Hananiah, the false prophet who spoke against Jeremiah (Jeremiah 28); and many nameless prophets like the "man of God from Judah" who prophesied the birth of Josiah (1 Kings 13).

Acting Prophets

My favorites are the prophets who were called upon by God to act out prophecies. Some were writing prophets; some were oral. The point is that God would tell them from time to time to stop writing or speaking and start acting.

God often used drama to get people's attention. For example, He told Isaiah to go barefoot and naked for three years (Isaiah 20:2ff). Yes, Isaiah was the original streaker! He used an unconventional method to get people's attention. The message was graphic and clear: Repent or be stripped naked like Isaiah.

Jeremiah was told to wear an oxen yoke on his neck to emphasize God's message that King Zedekiah should submit to Nebuchadnezzar (Jeremiah 27).

Ezekiel was called on to act many times. On one occasion the Lord told him to pack all his bags and carry them around Jerusalem in the sight of the people as a sign that if they did not repent, God would send them into exile (Ezekiel 12). On another occasion God ordered Ezekiel to play in a sand pile! God told him to label a brick, "Jerusalem," and to build dirt ramps around the brick to illustrate the coming siege of the city, if the people did not repent (Ezekiel 4).

The Prophetic Oscar

The greatest actor of all, the one who will undoubtedly win the prophetic Oscar for best performance, was the prophet Hosea.

God told him to find a prostitute and marry her. It must have been one of the hardest things God ever asked a righteous man to do. Hosea obeyed, and God told him to preach the message of his action.

The message was that Israel was like that prostitute when God selected the nation as His Chosen People. They were not selected for their beauty or wisdom or righteousness. They had no merit of their own. They were selected by grace.

This was an insulting message for the Jews. They did not understand what being "chosen" meant. They thought they were better than other peoples, and in their spiritual arrogance, they refused to listen to God's prophets who were calling for repentance.

When Hosea returned home from his preaching tour, he discovered that his wife had succumbed to her old passions. She had left the dignity and honor of his home and had returned to the streets, selling herself to the highest bidder. Hosea's heart was broken. God told him to preach the message of her action. The message was that — like Hosea's wife — Israel had been unfaithful to God, chasing after foreign gods. And like Hosea, God's heart was broken.

When Hosea returned home, God spoke to him again and asked him to do something incredible. God told him to swallow all his pride and go to the city square and bid for his wife when she offered herself for sale. He was instructed to pay all he had, if necessary, to redeem her from harlotry.

She didn't deserve it. She had not repented. But Hosea obeyed. He paid the price, and she was redeemed.

In this manner, God used an acting prophet to act out the story of what He would do for us at the Cross when He paid the price of His Son to redeem us from our unfaithfulness.

Symbolic Prophecy

A fourth type of prophecy is symbolic prophecy, or what is often referred to as "prophecy in type."

An understanding of prophetic types is essential to understanding the Old Testament. Jesus can be found on almost every page of the Old Testament, if you know how to look for Him. He is there symbolically in types. Looking for Him and finding Him in these types causes the Old Testament to come alive. I'm convinced that this is the kind of special teaching that Jesus gave His disciples during the 40 days between His resurrection and His ascension (Luke 24:45).

There are three kinds of prophetic types: individual lives; historical events; and inanimate objects.

Persons as Types

Almost all the major persons in the Old Testament are types of Christ in the sense that some events in their lives prophesied things that would happen to Jesus.

Take Joseph for example. He was rejected by his brothers. He was left for dead but was "resurrected" from the pit into which he had been cast. He took a Gentile bride and then redeemed his brothers from their famine.

Likewise, Jesus was rejected by his brethren (the Jews), experienced death and resurrection, is now taking a Gentile Bride (the

Church), and will soon return to save a remnant of His brethren from their spiritual famine.

Symbolic Events

Prophecies about Jesus are also symbolized in major historical events.

The seven feasts of Israel are a good example. Jesus was crucified on the Feast of Passover. He became our "unleavened bread" as His sinless body rested in the ground on that feast day. He arose from the dead on the Feast of First Fruits, and the Church was established on the Feast of Pentecost.

The three unfulfilled feasts (Trumpets, Atonement, and Tabernacles) must, in like manner, point to events that are yet to occur — most likely, the Rapture, the Second Coming, and the Millennial Reign of Jesus.

The history of the Jewish nation is the story of Jesus in prophetic type. The Children of Israel were born in Canaan, migrated to Egypt, came through the Red Sea (the baptism of Moses), endured testing in the wilderness, and then entered the Promised Land.

Likewise, Jesus was born in Canaan, was taken to Egypt, emerged publicly at His baptism, endured the wilderness temptations, and led the way to Heaven.

The Significance of Objects

Even inanimate objects like the Tabernacle and the robe of the High Priest are prophetic types pointing to Jesus.

Consider the Ark of the Covenant. Everything about it was symbolic of the Messiah. It was made of wood, indicating the Messiah would be human. It was overlaid with gold, signifying the Messiah would be divine. It contained three objects — the tablets of stone, a pot of manna, and Aaron's rod that budded. The tablets signified that the Messiah would have the law of God in His heart. The manna meant the Messiah would be the Bread of Life. The rod with blooms was a prophecy that the Messiah would arise from the dead.

The lid of the Ark was called the Mercy Seat. It had a golden angel at each end. The angels faced each other and their wings hovered over the lid. Once a year the High Priest sprinkled blood on the Mercy Seat and communed with the Shekinah glory of God which hovered above the angels.

The Mercy Seat pointed to the fact that through the work of the Messiah the mercy of God would cover the Law. The blood foreshadowed the fact that the Messiah would have to shed His own blood to atone for our sins.

Jesus fulfilled every prophetic type of the Ark. He was God in the flesh (John 10:30). He had the Law in His heart (Matthew 5: 17). He declared Himself to be the "Bread of Life" (John 6). He shed His blood on the Cross and was resurrected in power, atoning for our sins and covering the Law with Grace (Romans 3:21-26).

Mary saw the fulfillment of the Ark when she went to the tomb and discovered the body of Jesus missing. John 20:11-12 says she looked into the tomb and "beheld two angels in white sitting, one at the head, and one at the feet, where the body of Jesus had been lying." Do you understand what she saw? She saw the "mercy seat" where the blood had been spilled, with an angel at each end — exactly like the Mercy Seat that covered the Ark!

An Exhortation

As you can see, prophetic types bring the Old Testament alive and give us deep insight into New Testament events.

I encourage you to read the Bible with an attitude of always looking for Jesus. He is there on every page, waiting for you to discover Him in the symbols and types.

Pray for the guidance of the Holy Spirit as you read, and remember Revelation 19:10 — "The testimony of Jesus is the spirit of prophecy."

The Interpretation of Prophecy 4
Do you need imagination or common sense?

When I was about 12 years old, I stumbled across Zechariah 14. It was an amazing discovery.

You see, I grew up in a church where we were told over and over that "there is not one verse in the Bible that even implies that Jesus will ever set His feet on this earth again."

Simple Language

Well, Zechariah 14 not only implies that the Lord is coming back to this earth again, it says so point-blank! It says that the Lord will return to this earth at a time when the Jews are back in the land of Israel and their capital city, Jerusalem, is under siege. Just as the city is about to fall, the Lord will return to the Mount of Olives.

When His feet touch the ground, the mount will split in half. The remnant of Jews left in the city will take refuge in the cleavage of the mountain. The Lord will then speak a supernatural word, and the armies surrounding Jerusalem will be destroyed in an instant.

Verse 9 declares that on that day "the Lord will be king over all the earth."

Muddled Interpretations

When I first discovered this passage, I took it to my minister and asked him what it meant. I will never forget his response. He thought for a moment, and then He said, "Son I don't know what it means, but I'll guarantee you one thing: it doesn't mean what it says!"

For years after that, I would show Zechariah 14 to every visiting evangelist who came preaching that Jesus would never return to this earth. I always received the same response: "It doesn't mean what it says." I couldn't buy that answer.

Finally, I ran across a minister who was a seminary graduate, and he gave me the answer I could live with. "Nothing in Zechariah means what it says," he explained, "because the whole book is apocalyptic."

Now, I didn't have the slightest idea what "apocalyptic" meant. I didn't know if it was a disease or a philosophy. But it sounded sophisticated, and, after all, the fellow was a seminary graduate, so he should know.

A Discovery Experience

When I began to preach, I parroted what I had heard from the pulpit all my life. When I spoke on prophecy, I would always make the point that Jesus will never return to this earth. Occasionally, people would come up after the sermon and ask, "What about Zechariah 14?" I would snap back at them with one word: "APOCALYP-TIC!" They would usually run for the door in fright. They didn't know what I was talking about (and neither did I).

Then one day I sat down and read the whole book of Zechariah. And guess what? My entire argument went down the drain!

I discovered that the book contains many prophecies about the First Coming of Jesus, and I discovered that all those prophecies meant what they said. It suddenly occurred to me that if Zechariah's First Coming prophecies meant what they said, then why shouldn't his Second Coming promises mean what they say?

The Plain Sense Rule

That was the day that I stopped playing games with God's Prophetic Word. I started accepting it for its plain sense meaning. I decided that if the plain sense makes sense, I would look for no other sense, lest I end up with nonsense.

A good example of the nonsense approach is one I found several years ago in a book on the Millennium. The author spiritualized all of Zechariah 14. He argued that the Mount of Olives is symbolic of the human heart surrounded by evil. When a person accepts Jesus as Savior, Jesus comes into the person's life and stands on his "Mount of Olives" (his heart). The person's heart breaks in contrition (the cleaving of the mountain), and Jesus then defeats the enemy forces in the person's life.

Hard to believe, isn't it? When people insist on spiritualizing the Scriptures like this, the Scriptures end up meaning whatever they want them to mean.

Keys to Understanding

I believe God knows how to communicate. I believe He says what He means and means what He says. I don't believe you have to have a doctorate in hermeneutics to understand the Bible. The essentials, instead, are an honest heart and the in-dwelling of God's Spirit (1 Corinthians 2:10-16).

One crucial key is to approach the Scriptures with childlike faith. Dr. Henry Morris addresses this issue in his great commentary on Revelation, called *The Revelation Record*. He says, "Revelation is not difficult to understand. It is difficult to believe. If you will believe it, you will understand it."

For example, in Revelation 7 it says that at the start of the Tribulation God is going to seal a great host of Jews to serve as His special "bond-servants." The text specifies that the number will be 144,000, and that 12,000 will be selected from each of 12 specified tribes.

Now, I ask you: What would God have to do to convince us that He intends to set aside 144,000 Jews for special service during the Tribulation? The text is crystal clear. Yet, hundreds of commentators have denied the clear meaning and have spiritualized the passage to make it refer to the Church! This is reckless handling of God's Word, and it produces nothing but confusion.

The Meaning of Symbols

"But what about symbols?" some ask. Another crucial key is to keep in mind that a symbol stands for something, otherwise it would not be a symbol. There is always a literal reality or plain sense meaning behind every symbol.

Jesus is called "the rose of Sharon." He is not referred to as "the tumbleweed of Texas." The image that a rose conjures up is something beautiful; a tumbleweed is ugly.

The Bible is its own best interpreter as to the meaning of the symbols which it uses. Sometimes the symbols are clearly explained, as when God reveals to Ezekiel the meaning of the symbols in his vision of the valley of dry bones (Ezekiel 37:11-14). In like manner, the Apostle John was told the meaning of certain symbols which he saw in his Patmos vision of the glorified Lord (Revelation 1:20).

At other times, a simple search of the Scriptures will reveal the meaning of a symbol. Consider the statement in Revelation 12:14 where it says that the Jewish remnant will escape from the Antichrist into the wilderness "on the two wings of the great eagle."

Is this a literal eagle? Is it an air lift provided by the United States whose national symbol is an eagle?

A concordance search will show that the same symbolism is used in Exodus 19:4 to describe the flight of the children of Israel as they escaped from Egypt. The symbol, as Exodus 19 makes clear, is a poetic reference to the loving care of God.

The Importance of Context

Another key to understanding prophecy is one that applies to the interpretation of all Scripture. It is the principle that the meaning of words is determined by their context.

I ran across a good example of this problem recently in a book in which the author was trying to prove that Jesus is never coming back to reign upon this earth. Such a position, of course, required him to spiritualize Revelation chapter 20 where it says six times that there will be a reign of the Lord that will last one thousand years.

In this author's desperate attempt to explain away the thousand years, he referred to Psalm 50:10 where it says that God owns "the cattle on a thousand hills." He then asked, "Are there only one thousand hills in the world?" He answered his question, "Of course not!" He then proceeded to explain that the term is used figuratively. But then he made a quantum leap in logic by proclaiming, "therefore, the term, 'one thousand,' is always used symbolically."

Not so. It depends on context. In Psalm 50 the term is clearly symbolic. But in Revelation 20, it is not so. Again, the thousand years is mentioned six times. What would the Lord have to do to convince us that He means a thousand years? Put it in the sky in neon lights? Pay attention to context!

Reconciling Passages

An additional key to understanding prophecy is one that applies to all Scripture. It is the principle of searching out everything that the Bible has to say on a particular point.

Avoid hanging a doctrine on one isolated verse. All verses on a particular topic must be searched out, compared, and then reconciled.

Let me give you a prophetic example. Second Peter 3:10 says that when the Lord returns, "the heavens will pass away with a roar . . . and the earth and its works will be burned up." Now, if this were the only verse in the Bible about the Second Coming, we could confidently conclude that the heavens and earth will be burned up on the day that Jesus returns.

But, there are many other verses in both the Old and New Testaments, which make it abundantly clear that the Lord will reign over all the earth before it is consumed with fire. Those verses must be considered together with the passage in 2 Peter 3 in order to get the correct overall view.

Special Problems

There are some special problems related to prophetic interpretation. One is that prophecy is often prefilled in symbolic type before it is completely fulfilled.

In this regard, I feel certain that the Jewish people must have felt that Antiochus Epiphanes (215 - 164 BC) fulfilled Daniel's prophecies about a tyrannical leader who would severely persecute the Jews. But 200 years after Antiochus, Jesus referred to those prophecies of Daniel and told His disciples they were yet to be fulfilled.

Another example is the sign which Isaiah gave to King Ahaz to assure him that the city of Jerusalem would not fall to the Syrians who had it under siege. The sign was that a young woman would give birth to a son whose name would be called Immanuel (Isaiah 7:1-19). The passage certainly implies that such a boy was born at that time.

But hundreds of years later, Matthew, by inspiration of the Holy Spirit, reached back to Isaiah's prophecy and proclaimed that its ultimate fulfillment was to be found in the virgin birth of Jesus (Matthew 1:22-23).

Compressed Time

Another peculiar feature of prophetic literature is called "telescoping." This occurs when a prophet compresses the time interval between two prophetic events. This phenomenon is very common.

The reason for it has to do with the perspective of the prophet. As he looks into the future and sees a series of prophetic events, they appear to him as if they are in immediate sequence.

It is like looking down a mountain range and viewing three peaks, one behind the other, each sequentially higher than the one in front of it. The peaks look like they are right up against each other because the person viewing them cannot see the valleys that separate them.

In Zechariah 9:9-10 there is a passage with three prophecies which are compressed into two verses but are widely separated in time. Verse 9 says the Messiah will come humbly on a donkey. The first part of verse 10 says the Jewish people will be set aside. The second part of verse 10 says the Messiah will reign over all the nations.

These three events — the First Coming, the setting aside of Israel, and the reign of Christ — appear to occur in quick succession, but in reality, there were 40 years between the first two events, and there have been almost 2,000 years thus far between the second and third events.

Prophetic Gaps

Another way of viewing the phenomenon of telescoping is to focus on what are called "prophetic gaps." These are the time periods between the mountain peak prophetic events.

Because the Old Testament rabbis could not see the gap between the First and Second Comings of the Messiah, some theorized that there would be two Messiahs — a "Messiah ben Joseph" who would suffer and a "Messiah ben David" who would conquer. From our New Testament perspective we can see that the Old Testament prophets were speaking of one Messiah who would come twice. We can see the gap between the two comings.

A Challenge

I ask you: How do you treat Zechariah 14 — as fact or fiction? Are you guilty of playing games with God's Word in order to justify sacred traditions and doctrines of men?

I challenge you to interpret God's Word — all of it — for its plain sense meaning. As you do so, you are very likely to find yourself challenged to discard old doctrines and to adopt new ones. This will be a painful process, but it will be a fruitful one, for you will be blessed with the truth of God's Word.

> "If you abide in My word, then you are truly disciples of Mine; and you shall know the truth, and the truth shall make you free." — John 8:31-32

The Messiah in Prophecy   5
Does prophecy validate Jesus?

Was Jesus who He said He was? Was He really God in the flesh? Bible prophecy offers some of the strongest proof I know of that Jesus truly was divine.

Hundreds of Prophecies

The Old Testament contains more than 300 prophecies concerning the First Coming of Jesus. Some of these are repetitious, but when the repetition is accounted for, we are still left with at least 108 separate and distinct prophecies.

In addition to these specific texts, there are many more symbolic prophecies which point to various aspects of the First Coming.

Take the book of Ruth for an example. It does not contain any specific messianic prophecies. Yet, the book's story contains a beautiful prophetic type of Jesus. One of the central characters, Boaz, is a kinsman-redeemer who takes a Gentile bride — just as Jesus came as a redeemer to His people, the Jews, and is now taking a Gentile bride, the Church.

The lives of Joshua, Jeremiah and Daniel all give us insights about the faith, courage, and righteousness of the Messiah. Joshua and Jesus even had the same name, Yeshua, meaning "the salvation of God."

The life of Moses is a preview of many aspects of the life of Jesus. Moses tried to deliver his people from captivity and was rejected. In like manner, Jesus came to deliver His people from their spiritual bondage and was rejected by them. After his rejection, Moses took a Gentile bride. He then returned and was received by his people as a deliverer. Jesus is now taking a Gentile bride, the Church, and when He has completed that task, He will return and be received as Messiah by His own people, the Jews (Zechariah 12:10).

Every aspect of the life of Jesus was prophesied hundreds of years before He was born — the nature and place of His ministry, the nature of His death, and the triumph of His resurrection.

The very first prophecy in the Bible predicts that the Messiah will be born to a virgin. In Genesis 3:15 God says that the seed of the serpent (Satan) will be defeated by the seed of a woman (Jesus).

Genealogy in Prophecy

The entire lineage of the Messiah is prophesied in the Hebrew Scriptures. The prophets said the Savior would be born of the descendants of Abraham (Genesis 12:3), the heritage of Isaac (Genesis 17:21), the children of Jacob (Genesis 28:14), the tribe of Judah (Genesis 49:8), the family of Jesse (Isaiah 11:1), and the house of David (Jeremiah 23:5).

That's why the gospel of Matthew begins with such a long listing of Jesus' family tree. Matthew is trying to show his Jewish readers that the lineage of Jesus fulfills the predictions of the prophets.

Prophecy or Coincidence?

Some people shrug their shoulders at all these prophecies and say, "It's all a coincidence." Coincidence? The fulfillment of more than 100 prophecies?

"Well, He purposefully fulfilled them," says another. It is true that Jesus could have consciously fulfilled some of the prophecies about the Messiah. In fact, on one occasion it appears that Jesus did just that when He requested a donkey for His final ride into Jerusalem. Matthew says this was done to fulfill Zechariah's prophecy that the Messiah would come humbly, riding a donkey (Matthew 21:1-7).

But can a man purposefully fulfill prophecies concerning both his birth and death?

Micah prophesied 700 years before Jesus that the Messiah would be born in the little town of Bethlehem (Micah 5:2). Isaiah foretold that He would be born of a virgin (Isaiah 7:14). And Hosea said the Messiah would come out of Egypt (Hosea 11:1), the exact place the parents of Jesus took Him to after His birth.

Jesus was betrayed for 30 pieces of silver. The prophet Zechariah made that precise prophecy 500 years before Jesus was born! (See Zechariah 11:13.) David foresaw that the Messiah would be crucified (Psalms 22:16), and that was one thousand years before the birth of Jesus and 700 years before the extensive use of crucifixion by the Romans.

How could Jesus fulfill these prophecies purposefully? And could their fulfillment be just a "coincidence?"

Prophecy and Mathematics

Peter Stoner in his book, *Science Speaks* (Moody Press, 1963), has calculated the odds that just eight of the prophecies concerning Jesus could have been fulfilled accidently in the life of one man. The odds are one in ten to the seventeenth power! That's the number one with 17 zeros after it — 100,000,000,000,000,000 (one hundred quadrillion.)

To illustrate these mathematical odds, Stoner asks us to imagine filling the state of Texas knee-deep with silver dollars. A plane flies over and one silver dollar is dropped with a black checkmark on it. Thousands of bulldozers move in and mix the silver dollars thoroughly for several years. A man is then blindfolded and turned loose in this sea of silver dollars.

The odds that he would reach down and pick up the marked silver dollar on the first draw are the same as eight of the Bible's prophecies about the Messiah being fulfilled in the life of one man accidentally. You might as well argue that a Boeing 747 could be the accidental product of a tornado blowing through a junk yard!

Prophecy as Proof

The powerful testimony of fulfilled prophecy in the life of Jesus is the reason that the gospel writers constantly appeal to it in their writings to prove that Jesus was the promised Messiah. It is the reason Jesus appealed to it in His teachings to the masses (Matthew 5:17-18). It's also the reason Jesus emphasized it in His post-resurrection teachings to His disciples (Luke 24:25ff).

Likewise, the apostles constantly cited prophetic fulfillment in their sermons to verify the identity of Jesus. On the Day of Pentecost, Peter focused his remarks in that first gospel sermon on the prophecies of David which Jesus had fulfilled (Acts 2:24-36). Peter utilized prophecy again in his second sermon at the Temple (Acts 3:12-26) and in his sermon to Cornelius and his household (Acts 10).

In his first epistle, Peter refers to three cardinal evidences of the deity of Jesus. He first mentions that he was an "eyewitness of His majesty" — a reference to the Transfiguration. Then he mentions that he heard an "utterance from Heaven" in which God the Father proclaimed Jesus as His "beloved Son." Finally, he appeals to the testimony of prophecy, pointing to its fulfillment in the life of Jesus (2 Peter 1:16-19).

Phillip used a prophecy from Isaiah to convert the Ethiopian Eunuch (Acts 8). Paul also referred constantly to fulfilled prophecy in his preaching of the gospel (Acts 17:2-3). In fact, when Paul wrote his famous definition of the gospel in 1 Corinthians 15:1-4, he stressed that all the major events in the life of Jesus had happened "according to the Scriptures" (1 Corinthians 15:4).

Some Questions

How do you feel about the evidence of Bible prophecy? Are you going to try to explain it away? Are you going to flippantly write it off to "coincidence"? Are you simply going to ignore it?

God is not calling you to a blind faith that is based upon no evidence. Prophecy is evidence. It is evidence that demands a verdict. What is your verdict?

The Last Prophecy

I believe fulfilled prophecy proves that Jesus was who He said He was.

Fulfilled prophecy also proves that the last prophecy of the Bible, a prophecy yet to be fulfilled, is one that we can rely upon. It is contained in Revelation 22:20, and it was spoken by Jesus Himself: "Surely I am coming quickly."

Amen. Come, Lord Jesus!

Prophecy and Evolution 6

How do they relate?

During the first 30 years of my life, I didn't understand all the fuss over evolution. I couldn't see what difference it made whether God created instantly in a matter of a few days or gradually over millions of years. I was a theistic evolutionist — one who believes in evolution, but believes that it was God directed.

One of my problems was that I had grown up in a church that focused its study of the Bible almost exclusively on the New Testament. I had never really read and studied *all* of God's Word. When I did, I immediately dropped my flirtation with evolution.

A Matter of Integrity

The first reason I did so is because I discovered the integrity of God's Word is at stake on this issue. People dismiss the Genesis account of creation rather flippantly by saying, "The Bible is not a book of science."

But think for a moment: if we cannot trust what the Bible tells us about the creation of mankind and the universe, then what part of the Bible can we believe? Was there really a worldwide flood? Did a man named Abraham really exist? Did Jesus die on the Cross for our sins? If you start picking and choosing what part of the Bible you are going to believe, how are you going to determine what is true and what is false?

Symbolic Language?

I tried to deal with the Bible's creation account by arguing that it used symbolic language. But there is no basis for drawing that conclusion.

Adam and Eve are never dealt with as mythical figures by later biblical writers. And there is a passage in the book of Exodus that makes it very clear that the "days" of Genesis 1 and 2 are literal, 24 hour days (Exodus 20:8-11):

> Remember the sabbath day, to keep it holy. Six days you shall labor . . . but the seventh day is a sabbath to the Lord . . . in it you shall not work . . . for in six days the Lord made heaven and earth, the sea, and all that is in them, and rested the seventh day.

Good or Evil Creation?

Another problem I found with theistic evolution is that it demeans the character of God. The Bible says God created instantly and majestically and that the creation was "good."

Theistic evolution presents an entirely different picture. It holds that God used a very vicious and violent method of creation — "the survival of the fittest." In other words, creation occurred in a dog-eat-dog atmosphere that was anything but good.

The Origin of Death

Theistic evolution also makes a lie of what the Bible teaches about sin and its consequences. According to the Bible, sin came into the world through the rebellion of Adam and Eve against God's will. One of the results was physical death. Another was the curse which God placed upon nature.

Theistic evolution turns the biblical picture upside down, for it portrays all of creation as being involved in a death struggle *before* the evolutionary appearance of Man — and thus *before* Man could ever have sinned. Did death exist from the beginning of life, or was it the consequence of Man's sin, as God's Word says?

Tough Questions

When I decided to believe God's Word, I had to junk evolution in any form — both the theistic and scientific forms. That raised new and tough questions for me. Is the earth only six to seven thousand years old? What about the fossil record? What about stars that are so far away that it has taken millions of years for their light to reach the earth?

Fortunately for me, as I began to wrestle with these tough questions, I ran across the voluminous publications of the Institute for Creation Research, an organization of scientists who are Christians and who accept the Genesis account as literal. Through their writings I began to find answers to my new questions.

For example, they point out a simple but often overlooked truth: *special creation always carries with it the appearance of age*. Think about it. If I were to instantly create an adult man and then present him to you as my miraculous creation, you would respond by saying, "But, David, this man is 30 years old!"

The same would be true of a full grown tree. If I created it that way, I would have a tough time trying to convince you that it did not grow from a seed.

The same is true of our universe. When God created it, He created it in maturity. The light from the most distant stars did not have to travel hundreds of millions of miles over millions of years to reach the earth. The stars were created with their light already reaching the earth.

More Tough Questions

But what about the dating techniques that indicate a very ancient age for the earth? The fact is that all of them are based upon evolutionary assumptions to begin with, and thus they produce highly distorted, untruthful results that conform to their built-in evolutionary bias.

What about the fossil record? The truth is that evolutionists themselves do not like to talk about the fossil record any more. The reason is that despite the discovery of millions of fossils, they have not yet found even one that represents a transition form in the theorized evolutionary process. Dogs are still dogs in the fossil record. Cats are still cats. No one has yet found a "Dat."

Scientific Denial

One of the strangest things about the modern theory of evolution is that it denies one of the fundamental axioms of science! Consult any physics book and you will find what is called the Second Law of Thermodynamics. It holds that everything in the universe is running down — that everything is moving from order to disorder.

This law of physics is nothing but an expression of common sense. If you don't believe it, just look in a mirror! Your body is aging, and there is nothing you can do to stop it. You can camouflage it, but you can't stop it!

This law of physics is the reason we have to have maintenance programs for cars and buildings. If we don't maintain them, they will stop running or fall down.

Now, the point is this: evolution contends that all living things in the universe are moving in exactly the opposite direction — from disorder to order, from simplicity to greater complexity. Evolution contradicts one of the fundamental rules of science!

Logical Denial

Evolution also contradicts common sense. The complexity of the universe demands a designer. How could the human eye have developed by chance? To say it did is equivalent to saying that the faces on Mt. Rushmore are the accidental product of natural erosion.

Scientists tell us that the whole universe came into existence as the result of a "big bang." Again, this contradicts common sense. How many explosions have you ever witnessed that produced order instead of chaos?

Prophetic Fulfillment

The development of the theory of evolution is prophesied in Scripture as one of the signs of the end times. The prophecy is found in 2 Peter 3:3-7. It says that "scoffers will arise in the last days" and that they will mock the promised return of the Lord by saying, "Where is the promise of His coming? For ever since the fathers fell asleep, all things have continued as they were from the beginning of creation." Peter says that these people will deliberately ignore the fact that God created the world and then destroyed it with water.

The scientific principle prophesied in this passage is what is called uniformitarianism. It is one of the cornerstones of evolution. It is the idea that things have always been essentially the same, changing only minutely over billions of years.

This idea denies what the Bible teaches about special creation out of nothing. It also denies the Bible's historical record of a world-wide flood and the Bible's promise that one day God will destroy the earth again with fire.

Courting God's Wrath

The Bible says that God pours out His wrath on nations that "suppress the truth in unrighteousness" (Romans 1:18). We are doing that today in America. Our public schools are not allowed to teach children the true origin of the universe. Only the lie of evolution can be taught.

The same passage in the Bible says God's wrath is also poured out upon those nations whose people "serve the creature rather than the Creator" (Romans 1:25). The teaching of the theory of evolution has led this nation to the point where we are now worshiping the creation rather than the Creator. Our god is "Mother Earth," not Father God.

The Relationship

So, what is the relationship between Bible prophecy and evolution? Many Christian leaders today, even some Evangelicals, have adopted some form of theistic evolution. In doing so they have to spiritualize the biblical account of creation, arguing that it is not literal and therefore the six days of creation really represent hundreds of millions of years.

And that is exactly what the majority of Christendom has done with Bible prophecy. It has been spiritualized into meaninglessness. They argue that we are in the Millennium now, even though the Bible says that during the Millennium the earth will be flooded with peace, righteousness, and justice, as the waters cover the seas. They claim that Jesus is ruling now even though all the nations of the world are in rebellion against God and His Word. They claim that

Satan is now bound even though he continues to prowl about like a roaring lion, seeking whom he may devour.

When you start spiritualizing God's Word, you can make it mean whatever you desire. In the process, you become your own god.

To understand either the beginning or the end of history, we must accept the plain sense teaching of God's Word. Are you willing to do that?

Prophecy and Salvation 7

Is millennial belief essential?

What is the relationship of prophetic doctrine to salvation? Is it possible to be saved and yet reject the biblical teaching that the Lord is going to return to reign over all the world for a thousand years?

I raise this issue because differences in prophetic doctrine have been used by many denominational groups to draw lines of fellowship between Christians. Some have even gone so far as to make prophetic doctrine a condition of salvation!

A Personal Experience

I speak from painful personal experience regarding this point. I grew up in a denomination that was amillennial in its prophetic viewpoint. That means we rejected completely the idea that Jesus would ever return to this earth to reign.

Our church leaders felt so strongly about this issue that they made it a test of fellowship and a condition of salvation. Any person among us who developed a premillennial view (that Jesus would return to reign for a thousand years) was labeled "heretical" and was sooner or later (usually sooner) given the left foot of fellowship. They would then write off that person as one who had "fallen from grace."

Needless to say, I eventually became one of those brothers who was condemned and shunned because my study of the Word led me to adopt a premillennial interpretation of prophecy.

The Problem

The fundamental problem here has nothing whatsoever to do with prophecy. The problem is the erroneous concept of salvation.

Those who draw lines of fellowship over matters like prophetic interpretation are people who believe in salvation by perfected knowledge; that is, they believe that salvation is dependent upon being right about every doctrine.

I can still vividly recall a classic expression of this attitude several years ago at a prophecy conference I helped put together. We tried to arrange to have a speaker representing each of the major prophetic viewpoints.

The person who presented the amillennial view, a preacher from my childhood denomination, was asked after his presentation whether or not a premillennialist could be saved. His response was, "I couldn't be saved if I were premillennialist, because I know it's wrong." I wanted to jump up and stop the discussion on prophecy and spend the rest of the day discussing the real issue of salvation.

Are we saved by being right about prophecy? Can I really lose my salvation if I am wrong about my belief that Jesus is coming back to reign upon the earth?

If you and I can be lost by being wrong about prophecy, then we can be lost by being wrong about anything — such as the frequency of communion or the role of women in the Church. That means we really have no hope of salvation because none of us is right about everything.

The Certainty of Salvation

And yet the Bible says we can be confident of our salvation. Consider these words of the apostle John:

> "We know that we have passed out of death into life."
> — 1 John 3:14

> "These things I have written to you who believe in the name of the Son of God, in order that you may know that you have eternal life." — 1 John 5:13

"We know that we are of God." — 1 John 5:19

Over and over John says we can know that we are saved. But how can we ever have such assurance if our salvation depends upon our being right about everything? The answer is that we can't. And that is precisely why some conservative churches are filled with souls who seem sure of everything except the most important thing of all — namely, their salvation!

You can know with absolute certainty that you are saved, because Paul said you are saved by the grace of God, "as a gift" (Romans 3:24). You can also be certain about your salvation, because if you are saved, then you know your Savior, and you know He is trustworthy and that He meant it when He said: "I am the resurrection and the life; he who believes in Me shall live even if he dies" (John 11:25).

Our confidence is also assured by Paul's glorious proclamation, "There is therefore now no condemnation for those who are in Christ Jesus" (Romans 8:1).

The Essence of Salvation

This means that you and I can be wrong about a lot of things, but if we are right about one thing — Jesus Christ — then we can claim the promise of eternal salvation. It also means that although all truth is important, it is not all equally important.

Accordingly, whatever the truth may be about such things as instrumental music or communion or prophecy, these truths are as nothing compared to the truth that Jesus is Lord (1 Corinthians 12:3). That's why Paul wrote, "If you confess with your mouth Jesus as Lord, and believe in your heart that God raised Him from the dead, you shall be saved" (Romans 10:9).

The essence of salvation is not doctrinal perfection. Rather, it is a relationship with a person. Jesus put it this way: "This is eternal life, that they may know You, the only true God, and Jesus Christ whom You have sent" (John 17:3).

Does this mean that what you believe about prophecy is irrelevant? Not at all! It just means that it has nothing to do with your justification — that is, with your judicial standing before God. We are justified by our faith in Jesus as our Lord and Savior (Romans 3:21-26).

The Process of Salvation

Much of the problem here is due to the fact that many churches have never distinguished between justification, sanctification, and glorification. The result is that many Christians are ignorant of the fact that salvation is a process.

Justification is the starting point. It occurs when you put your faith in Jesus.

The salvation process continues with your sanctification. This is a lifelong process of dying to self and living more and more for Christ.

The process consummates in your glorification, when you are resurrected and given an immortal body. It is then that you will stand face-to-face with the Lord and be fully conformed to His image (Romans 8:29-30).

Justification results in your being born again spiritually. When you are justified, you put on the righteousness of Christ, and you stand guiltless before the judgment bar of God, washed clean in the blood of the Lamb (1 Corinthians 1:30). You receive the gift of the indwelling Holy Spirit as the guarantee of your eternal inheritance (Ephesians 1:13-14), and you begin your walk with the Lord.

The Meaning of Sanctification

It is true that you are sanctified when you are justified, because you are washed clean of your sins and are set apart from the world as God's sacred possession (1 Corinthians 6:11 and Hebrews 10:10). But the process of sanctification continues as you begin walking with the Lord.

Through the process of sanctification, God shapes your soul (your will, emotions, and personality) into the image of Christ. This takes place as you learn more and more about the Lord and His Word through Bible study, prayer, worship, and fellowship. This does not mean that sanctification is something you earn. Like justification, sanctification is a gift of God's grace through the power of His Holy Spirit working within you.

But whereas you are justified by responding to the truth of the gospel (the death, burial, and resurrection of Jesus — 1 Corinthians 15:1-4), you are sanctified by responding to the truths of Christian doctrine. This means that the quality of your walk with the Lord will be substantially affected by what you believe about such things as the Holy Spirit, the Church, discipleship, stewardship, miracles, prayer, and prophecy.

The Impact of Prophecy

To use another personal example: Before I came to a premillennial understanding of prophecy, I had little enthusiasm for the return of Christ. I certainly was not watchful for His return, and I felt that the only impact of His return on world history would be to bring it to an end.

Now I have a whole new perspective that has drawn me closer to the Lord and has strengthened my faith, deepened my love, and enhanced my hope.

I now look for the return of Christ with fervent expectancy as my "blessed hope" (Titus 2:13). My watchfulness has become a powerful motivator for holy living (Romans 13:11-14). I thrill to the thought of the triumph of Jesus over Satan (Revelation 20:1-2, 10). I look forward with joy to the establishment of the Lord's reign of perfect peace and righteousness here on earth (Micah 4:1-7). I rejoice that Jesus will soon be fully vindicated in history, just as He was humiliated in history (Isaiah 24:21-23).

I have been brought to the awe-inspiring realization that one of the greatest miracles of history is occurring before my very eyes — the regathering of the Jews (Jeremiah 16:14-15). Scripture passages concerning the Jews which never had any meaning at all to me have suddenly come alive (Jeremiah 23:5-8; Ezekiel 36 and 37; and Amos 9:14-15).

For the first time, I understand the meaning of Paul's writings in Romans 9-11 where he talks of God's grace for the Jewish people. I rejoice that a remnant of the Jews will come to know their Messiah

(Zechariah 12:10) and that they will be established as the prime nation of the world through whom all the nations will be blessed (Isaiah 60-62).

I praise God for the redemption that Jesus will bring to all the creation (Romans 8:18-23). And I look forward with great anticipation to an eternity in the presence of God upon this earth after it has been purged of its corruption and renovated to its previous glory (2 Peter 3:1-13 and Revelation 21:1-4).

I have a grasp of God's master plan of history that I never had before, and that has given me a sense of comfort and peace that serves as a sturdy anchor in such perilous times as these. I now know with certainty that God's Word is sure, that His promises are certain, that He is alive and well, that He still cares intensely about His creation, and that He still intervenes in marvelous and miraculous ways to direct and comfort His people while He orchestrates the evil deeds of Man to a climax that will bring eternal honor and glory to His holy name (Psalm 2).

A Call to Love

As you can see, what we believe about prophecy does make a difference in the quality of our Christian lives. That's why I always get a little annoyed when I hear a Christian saying, "I don't know anything about Bible prophecy, and I don't care, because what you believe about prophecy makes no difference." Not so. It makes a lot of difference.

But it should make no difference at all as to our attitude toward each other as brothers and sisters in Christ. I have Christian brothers and sisters who are premillennialists and amillennialists and post-millennialists, and I have some relatives in Christ who don't know the difference in a millennium and a millipede! I will spend eternity with some who have never even read the book of Revelation.

We need to stop playing God by drawing lines of fellowship which we have no right to draw over matters of opinion, and we need to start loving each other because we share a belief in the fundamental fact of history — namely, that Jesus is Lord.

I Can't Wait

(Pat Terry)

Just as the lightening comes from the east
And flashes even to the west,
So shall the coming of the Son of Man be.
Put on your Sunday best.
Put on your Sunday best.

I can't wait to see Jesus
In His glory as He bursts from the sky.
I can't wait to be held in His arms
And see the glimmer in His eyes.

Tell me how it's gonna be.
Read it from the Bible again.
I can't wait to see Jesus
'Cause Jesus is coming again!

I can't wait to hear trumpets
'Cause I know what they mean when they sound.
I can't wait to cast off my burdens
And feel my feet leave the ground

Tell me how it's gonna be.
Read it from the Bible again.
I can't wait to see Jesus
'Cause Jesus is coming again!

I can't wait to see Heaven
And to walk those streets of gold.
I can't wait to check into my mansion
And get my sleeping bag unrolled.

So, tell me how it's gonna be.
Read it from the Bible again.
I can't wait to see Jesus
'Cause Jesus is coming again!

Part Two

Prophetic Issues

The prophecies are "things
into which angels long to look."
1 Peter 1:10-12

The Jews in Prophecy 8
Have they been cast aside?

Few biblical studies are as exciting as an examination of the Jews in prophecy, for the Jews are one of the key focal points of Bible prophecy.

In fact, if you are anti-Semitic, you will hate Bible prophecy. That's because God's Prophetic Word makes it clear that He has a deep and abiding love for the Jewish people.

The Scriptures reveal the Jews as "the apple of God's eye" (Zechariah 2:8). Their land is described as "holy" (Zechariah 2:12). Their city of Jerusalem is termed the "center of the nations" (Ezekiel 5:5). They are pictured as the wayward wife of God (see Ezekiel 16 and the book of Hosea). And the Bible makes it clear that they will be the object of both God's wrath (Jeremiah 30:7) and His grace (Zechariah 13:1) in the end times.

The panorama of prophecy that relates to the Jews is breathtaking. It applies to the past, the present, and the future. It demonstrates God's love and grace as nothing else does except the Cross itself.

Paul was so overwhelmed by God's patient determination to bring a remnant of the Jews to salvation that he cried out in ecstasy: "Oh, the depth of the riches both of the wisdom and knowledge of God! How unsearchable are His judgments and unfathomable His ways!" (Romans 11:33).

Let's take a look at the incredible prophecies that pertain to the Jewish people, and let's begin with the prophecies that have already been fulfilled

Fulfilled Prophecies

1) Dispersion — The Jews were warned repeatedly that they would be dispersed worldwide if they were not faithful to their covenant with God. Consider the words of Moses: "The Lord will scatter you among all peoples, from one end of the earth to the other . . ." (Deuteronomy 28:64; see also Leviticus 26:33).

2) Persecution — The Lord also warned the Jews that they would be persecuted wherever they went. Again, the words of Moses are graphic in this regard: "Among those nations you shall find no rest, and there shall be no resting place for the sole of your foot; but there the Lord will give you a trembling heart, failing of eyes, and despair of soul" (Deuteronomy 28:65).

3) Desolation — God promised that after their dispersion, their land would become "desolate" and their cities would become "waste" (Leviticus 26:33). Moses put it more graphically when he said, "the foreigner who comes from a distant land . . .will say, 'All its land is brimstone and salt, a burning waste, unsown and unproductive, and no grass grows in it'" (Deuteronomy 29:22-23).

4) Preservation — But God in His marvelous grace promised He would preserve the Jews as a separate people during their worldwide wanderings. (See Isaiah 66:22 and Jeremiah 30:11; 31:35-37.) Isaiah puts it in a colorful way. He says the Lord could no more forget Israel than a mother could forget her nursing child (Isaiah 49:15). He then adds that God cannot forget Israel because He has them tattooed on the palms of His hands! (Isaiah 49:16)

Fulfillment

God has fulfilled all four of these prophecies during the past 2,000 years. In 70 A.D. the Romans destroyed the city of Jerusalem and took the Jewish nation into captivity, desolating the land and scattering the Jewish people across the face of the earth. As prophesied, everywhere they went they were persecuted, with their persecution culminating in the Nazi Holocaust of World War II.

But God also preserved the Jews, and the fulfillment of this prophecy has been one of the most remarkable miracles of history. No other people have ever been so dispersed and yet been able to retain their identity as a nation.

Current Prophecies

We are privileged to live in an age when God is fulfilling many promises to the Jews. What a testimony this is to the fact that God is alive and well, that God is on His throne and in control, and that God is faithful to His promises.

1) Regathering of the People — The Old Testament prophets promise repeatedly that the day will come when God will regather the Jews to the land of Israel (see Isaiah 11:10-12 and Ezekiel 36:22-28). This remarkable regathering of the Jews from the four corners of the earth has occurred in our life time. World War I prepared the land for the people as the control of Palestine was transferred from a nation that hated the Jews (the Turks) to a nation that was sympathetic to their return (Britain). The Holocaust of World War II prepared the people for the land by motivating them to return.

2) Re-establishment of the State — The prophets stated that when the people were regathered, the nation of Israel would be re-established (see Isaiah 66:7-8 and Zechariah 12:3-6). This occurred on May 14, 1948. This is the cornerstone prophetic event of our age. It is an event that prophetic scholars have pointed to for 400 years amid much scoffing and ridicule by those who did not believe that Israel would ever exist again as a nation.

3) Reclamation of the Land — God promised that with the re-establishment of the nation, the land would bloom again (Isaiah 35:1-7 and Joel 2:21-26). As Ezekiel put it, people would one day exclaim: "This desolate land has become like the garden of Eden!" (Ezekiel 36:35). And that is exactly what people exclaim today when they visit Israel, for it is once again a land of milk and honey. Over 300 million trees were planted during the 20th Century. Rainfall during that century increased 450 percent. The former malaria infested swamps have been converted into cultivated land. Water from the Sea of Galilee has been channeled to the deserts, causing them to bloom.

4) Revival of the Language — When the Jews were scattered worldwide in the First Century, they ceased speaking the Hebrew language. The Jews who settled in Europe developed a language called Yiddish (a combination of Hebrew and German). The Jews in the Mediterranean basin mixed Hebrew with Spanish to produce a language called Ladino. The prophet Zephaniah implied a time would come when the Hebrew language would be revived (Zephaniah 3:9). It has been. Today the Israelis speak biblical Hebrew. It is the only example in history of the resurrection of a dead language. The man God used to revive the language was Eliezer Ben Yehuda (1858-1922).

5) Re-occupation of Jerusalem — Jesus said that one of the surest signs of His imminent return would be the re-occupation of Jerusalem by the Jews (Luke 21:24). This occurred during the Six Day War in June 1967.

6) Resurgence of Military Strength — Zechariah prophesied that when the Jews were re-established in the land, their military strength would be overwhelming — like "a flaming torch among sheaves" — and that they would "consume" all the peoples around them (Zechariah 12:6). Need anything be said about the fulfillment if this prophecy?

7) Re-focusing of World Politics — Israel is always pictured as the focal point of world politics in the end times (Zechariah 12:3 and 14:1-9). This has been true since the Arab oil boycott in 1973. The West suddenly realized its dependence on Arab oil and began to line up behind the Arab obsession to annihilate Israel.

Future Prophecies

As we witness ancient promises to the Jewish people being fulfilled before our eyes today, we can be assured that God will one day fulfill all the remaining prophecies concerning the fate of Israel.

1) Tribulation — God will put the Jewish people through an unparalleled period of tribulation (Deuteronomy 4:30), during which two-thirds of the Jews will perish (Zechariah 13:8-9). The purpose will be to soften the hearts of a remnant so that they will accept Jesus as their Messiah.

2) Salvation — At the end of the Tribulation, a remnant of the Jews will "look upon Him whom they have pierced" and will accept Him as Lord and Savior (Zechariah 12:10 and Romans 11:1-6, 25-29). On that glorious day, the Bible says "a fountain of salvation will be opened for the house of David and the inhabitants of Jerusalem, for sin and for impurity" (Zechariah 13:1).

3) Primacy — At the Second Coming of Jesus, God will regather all the believing Jews to Israel where they will be established as the prime nation in the world during the Millennium. (See Deuteronomy 28:1, 13; 2 Samuel 7:9; Isaiah 60-62; and Micah 4:1-7.) God's blessings to the world will once again flow through the Jewish people, and thus, when a Jew walks by, ten Gentiles will grab his robe and say, "Let us go with you, for we have heard that God is with you" (Zechariah 8:23).

A Pernicious Doctrine

These prophecies concerning present day Israel and its glorious future make it clear that God has not washed His hands of the Jewish people, as many Christian denominations claim today.

One of the most pernicious doctrines that has infested the Church since about 400 A.D. is one called Replacement Theology. It contends that when the Jews rejected Jesus, God cast them aside permanently and replaced them with the Church. In the process, He transferred to the Church all the blessings that had been promised to Israel.

This doctrine directly contradicts the Old Testament prophecies concerning the future of Israel. It also violates the clear teaching of Paul in the book of Romans.

For example, in Romans 3:1-4, Paul presents a rhetorical question for thoughtful consideration. He asks, "Has God rejected His people because of their unbelief?" For almost two thousand years the Church has answered this question, "Yes!" But Paul answers, "May it never be!" Again, in chapter 11, Paul asks, "Has God rejected His people?" And once again, he answers his own question by asserting: "God has not rejected His people whom He foreknew" (Romans 11:1-2). He proceeds then to affirm the Old Testament promise that a great remnant of Jews will be saved in the end times (Romans 11:25-33; see also Romans 9:27).

God's Infinite Love

God set the Jews aside and put them under discipline because of their disobedience, but He did not cut them off from His grace.

He intends to bring His wayward wife home: "For the sons of Israel will remain for many days without king or prince . . . Afterward, the sons of Israel will return and seek the Lord their God . . . and they will come trembling to the Lord and to His goodness in the last days" (Hosea 3:4-5).

The lovingkindness and faithfulness of God in keeping His promises to the Jewish people should be a source of encouragement to all Christians. As we watch God fulfill promises which He made to the Jewish people thousands of years ago, we can be absolutely certain that He will be faithful to fulfill all the promises He has made to the Church.

God's Amazing Grace

The first time my wife heard me preach about the Jews in prophecy, she came to me and said, "When you talk about how much God loves the Jews, you make me want to be one."

I responded by saying, "No, Honey, you don't want to be a Jew because if you were, you would most likely have a veil over your heart and would refuse to believe in Jesus as your Messiah" (2 Corinthians 3:12-18).

I then stressed something to her that I hope you will never forget. I pointed out that everything God is doing for the Jews He is willing to do for you and me.

The Jewish people are witnesses of God's amazing grace. And that same grace is available to all of us, whether we be Gentiles or Jews.

The Arabs in Prophecy 9

Do they have any hope?

"**W**hy do you Bible prophecy guys spend all your time talking about the Jews? There's a whole lot more Arabs than Jews. Don't you think God also cares about the Arabs?"

It was a testy question during an open forum at one of my prophecy conferences. It was one I had heard many times before in various ways. It reminded me of a letter I had received in which a person asked, "Don't the Palestinians have rights too? Does God love only the Jews?"

There is no doubt that Bible prophecy teachers spend a lot of time speaking and writing about the Jewish people. It would be easy, therefore, to conclude that the Arab peoples are ignored in God's Prophetic Word. But, as we shall see, that is not the case. Bible prophecy focuses on the Jewish people because they are God's Chosen People. In the process, it does not ignore the Arabs.

The Significance of the Jews

God chose the Jews to give the world the Scriptures, and it was through the Jews that He provided the Messiah. The Jews also serve as God's prophetic time clock, for He points to future events in their history as the key to the timing of other important events.

For example, the timing of the First Coming of the Messiah was related to events in Jewish history. Daniel said the Messiah would come 483 years after an edict was issued for the rebuilding of Jerusalem (Daniel 9:25-26). In like manner, Jesus told His disciples that Jerusalem would one day fall to the Gentiles (which it did 40 years later in 70 AD) and that it would remain under Gentile control until it was time for Him to return to earth (Luke 21:24). In other words, Jesus said His Second Coming would occur when Jerusalem was back in the hands of the Jews (something that happened on June 7, 1967).

The Continuing Witness of the Jews

There is another key to the Jews significance. They continue to serve today as a chosen witness of God's grace. This is manifested in their very existence, for what other God would have tolerated for so long a people so stubborn and rebellious?

They also continue to be a witness of what it means to have a relationship with God. Their history reveals that when people are faithful to God's Word, He blesses; when they are unfaithful, He disciplines; and when they repent, He forgives, forgets, and starts blessing again. This is the constant cycle that is clearly patterned in the book of Judges.

The Primacy of the Jews

The Bible says that the Jewish people will continue to serve as the Chosen People — as His special witness — in the future.

At the end of the Tribulation, a great remnant of the Jews will be brought to the end of themselves and will turn to God in repentance and accept His Son as their Messiah (Zechariah 12:10 and 13:1). They will cry out, *"Baruch haba bashem Adonai!"* — that is, "Blessed is He who comes in the name of the Lord!" (Matthew 23:39). It is at this point that God's discipline will be lifted, and the Jewish people will start being blessed again.

Moses prophesied that when the Jewish remnant repents, they will be regathered from all over the world back to the land of Israel (Deuteronomy 30:1-5). Isaiah says that Israel will then serve as the prime nation of the world (during the Lord's millennial reign), and he spells out in detail all the incredible blessings that will be showered upon the nation and the city of Jerusalem (Isaiah 60-62).

But the Jews will not be just a repository of God's blessings. Zechariah says they will be a channel of blessings to the whole world (Zechariah 8:13), and he says that the attitude of the world toward the Jews will be radically changed. Anti-Semitism will be replaced by respect and admiration: "In those days, ten men from the nations will grasp the garment of a Jew, saying, 'Let us go with you, for we have heard that God is with you'" (Zechariah 8:23).

Do these promises to the Jews mean that God has no blessings for the multitudinous Arab peoples? Not at all. God has given them great blessings in the past, and He has great blessings reserved for them in the future.

Arab Identity

But before we look at those blessings, let's consider first the identity of the Arab peoples. Who are they?

A popular misconception is that Arab identity is determined by religion — that if you are a Muslim, then you are an Arab. That is not true.

The most populous Muslim nation in the world is Indonesia, an island nation in Southeast Asia. Indonesians are not Arabs. They are Malays. Likewise, the nation of Iran is composed of Muslims, but they are not Arabs. They are Persians.

There are also Christian Arabs scattered all across the Middle East. Until recently, the town of Bethlehem was dominated by Christian Arabs. Nazareth continues to be a town with many Christian Arabs.

Arab identity is not determined by religion. Most Arabs are Muslims, but not all; and all Muslims are certainly not Arabs.

Arab identity is determined by ethnic heritage. And the amazing thing is that all Arabs — like all Jews — are descended from the family of Abraham! That means the Arab-Israeli conflict is a family dispute — the longest running and most intense family squabble in history.

Arab Origins

It all began when Abraham decided to help God. That's a nice way of saying that he decided to run ahead of God. I'm referring, of course, to his impatience with God's promise that he would be given an heir.

As he and Sarah continued to advance in years without a child, they decided to "help" God by having Abraham conceive a child through Hagar, his wife's Egyptian handmaid. The child born of that union was named Ishmael. God made it clear that Ishmael would not be the child of promise through whom all the world would be blessed (Genesis 17:20-21), but God did make some great promises to Ishmael's mother.

God promised that He would make Ishmael fruitful and would multiply his descendants exceedingly, making of him a "great nation" (Genesis 17:20). He also gave Ishmael's descendants the land to the east of Canaan (Genesis 16:12).

God has been faithful to these promises. Today there are 22 Arab nations with a combined population of over 250 million people. The Arabs occupy a total area of 5.3 million square miles of oil rich land.

By contrast, there is only one Jewish state with a population of 5 million Jews who are squeezed into only 8,000 square miles of space. That's a population ratio of 50 to 1 and a land ratio of 662 to 1. The Arabs have truly been blessed.

Arab Tribes

Ishmael took an Egyptian wife (Genesis 21:21) and became the father of 12 tribes which are listed in Genesis 25:12-16. These tribes were to become the nucleus of the Arab peoples, a people with a mixture of Semitic and Egyptian blood.

Other Arab tribes trace their origin to the six sons of Abraham who were born to him by his second wife, Keturah. They are listed in Genesis 25:1-4. Finally, some Arab tribes were to emerge from the descendants of Esau, the twin brother of Jacob who sired the 12 tribes of Israel.

All the Arab tribes have been characterized historically by their impulsive and violent nature. They have been involved in endless wars among themselves and against both Jews and Christians.

It is interesting to note that their volatile nature is a fulfillment of prophecy. God told Hagar that her son, Ishmael, would be "a wild donkey of a man" and that "his hand will be against everyone"

(Genesis 16:12).

Arab Prophecies

Let's look now at what the Bible prophesies about the Arab peoples. First, it says they will claim the land of Israel which God gave to their brothers, the Jews. The prophet Ezekiel says this claim will be made in the end times (Ezekiel 35:5,10; 36:2,5).

This prophecy was fulfilled in the 20th Century. For over 1,900 years the Jews were dispersed from the land which God gave them, and during that long period of time there was never an Arab state in the area that the world called Palestine. The Arabs who lived in the land considered themselves Syrians. They had no consciousness as Palestinians, and no effort was ever made to create a Palestinian state.

When the Jews began returning at the beginning of the 20th Century, the Arabs gleefully sold them the land at inflated prices because it was considered worthless. It was World War I that changed the Arab viewpoint. The war resulted in the land of Palestine being transferred from the Turks to the British, and the British immediately proclaimed it to be a homeland for the Jews. Suddenly, the Arabs were confronted with the prospect of a Jewish state, and they began to dig in their heels, claiming the land as their own.

The British gave in to Arab pressure, and in 1922 they gave two-thirds of Palestine to the Arabs, creating the state of Jordan. This was land that they had implicitly promised to the Jews. But this action did not satisfy the Arab appetite. They wanted all the land God had given to the Jews, and they still covet it to this day, just as prophesied.

Arab Judgments

The Bible further prophesies that God will pour out judgment upon the Arab nations in the end times for their hostility toward the Jews and their attempt to claim the Jewish homeland as their own.

Consider Joel 3:19, for example. This passage has a clear end time context, and in that context it says, "Egypt will become a waste, and Edom will become a desolate wilderness, because of the violence done to the sons of Judah, in whose land they have shed innocent blood."

Keep in mind that Edom is often used as a symbolic term for all the Arab peoples, just as Israel is used as a term for all the Jewish tribes. Ezekiel says that "all Edom" will be dealt with in the end times because of its hatred against the Jews, and the result will be desolation (Ezekiel 35:10-11, 15). The book of Obadiah prophesies a similar fate for Edom in "the day of the Lord" (Obadiah 15-18).

Arab Promises

But the future for the Arabs is not all bleak. They must suffer for their sins just as the Jewish people will suffer during the Tribulation. And, like the Jews, a remnant of the Arabs will emerge from their suffering with their hearts turned to the one and only true God (Jeremiah 12:14-17).

The most remarkable prophecy concerning the future salvation of an Arab remnant is contained in Isaiah 19:16-25. Isaiah says that when the Lord strikes Egypt and Assyria, they will turn to Him and He will have compassion on them and "heal them." Isaiah then presents an incredible picture of Egypt, Assyria and Israel living together in peace, worshiping the same God!

Another remarkable prophecy concerns the Arabs who will be living in the land of Israel after the Lord returns. This prophecy relates to the fact that the territory of Israel will be greatly expanded when Jesus returns, incorporating many of the Arab nations that exist today. (The considerably expanded borders of Israel during the Millennium are detailed in Ezekiel 47:15-20.) Amazingly, Ezekiel says that the Arabs living in Israel at that time will be "allotted an inheritance" of the land together with the tribes of Israel! (See Ezekiel 47:21-23 and Isaiah 14:1-2.)

An Impartial God

There is no partiality with God (Romans 2:11). He chose the Jews, not to be a repository of His blessings, but to be a vehicle through whom He would bless all the nations of the world, including the Arabs. But the fundamental requirement to receive God's blessings — for both Jew and Arab, as well as all people — is to accept God's gift of love in Jesus by receiving Him as Messiah.

When I consider God's grace toward the Arab peoples, I am reminded of what Paul wrote when he considered God's grace toward his Jewish brethren: "Oh, the depth of the riches both of the wisdom and knowledge of God! How unsearchable are His judgments and unfathomable His ways!" (Romans 11:33).

Keep in mind that the amazing grace which God is displaying toward the Arabs and the Jews is available to you. The message of God's dealings with the physical descendants of Abraham is that there is no sin so great and dark that it can separate you from the love of God which He has expressed in Jesus.

The key to experiencing that grace is repentance. As Paul put it in his sermon in Athens: "God is now declaring to men that all everywhere should repent" (Acts 17:30).

Will the Roman Empire be revived?

> Let the name of the Lord be blessed forever
>   and ever,
> For wisdom and power belong to Him.
> It is He who changes the times and epochs;
> He removes kings and establishes kings . . .
> Daniel 2:20b-21a

Before the birth of the nation-state system, which has dominated world politics since the 1800's, mankind seemed enamored by the concept of empire, real or imagined.

At the dawn of history, the peoples of the earth tried to unite at Babylon to form a world empire that would "reach into the heavens," challenging even the sovereignty of God (Genesis 11:1-4). God put an end to that attempt by confusing the people's language (Genesis 11:6-9).

Biblical Empires

But before long, people were at it again. First came the Egyptian Empire (dating back to 3500 BC) and then the Assyrian (founded in 1810 BC). The conflicts between these empires and the ones that followed are chronicled in the history books of the Old Testament.

The reason the Bible contains so much information about them is because of the strategic location of ancient Israel. That tiny nation constituted a land bridge that connected Africa, Asia, and Europe. The result is that it often served as a battlefield for competing empires.

One of the empires that had a tremendous impact upon the Jewish people was the Babylonian. It existed only 73 short years, from 612 BC to 539 BC, but God worked through it to discipline the Jews for their idolatry. He allowed the Babylonians to conquer Jerusalem and ultimately to destroy it and the Jewish Temple.

A Remarkable Man

One of the many captives who were taken in the first siege of Jerusalem in 605 BC was a young man named Daniel. He rapidly came to the attention of the Babylonian leaders because of his ability to interpret dreams.

The event that catapulted him into the center of attention was a dream which God gave to the Babylonian king, Nebuchadnezzar. The king made an unusual request of his court magicians and sorcerers. Instead of just asking them to interpret his dream, he demanded that they first tell him the content of his dream! They were mystified and were about to be put to death, when Daniel sent word to the king that he could both reveal the dream and provide its interpretation (Daniel 2:14-16).

When King Nebuchadnezzar agreed to give Daniel an audience, the young man and his fellow prisoners went to their knees in prayer and cried out to God for understanding (Daniel 2:17-18). The mystery was immediately revealed to Daniel in a night vision (Daniel 2:19).

A Remarkable Dream

When Daniel was ushered into the king's presence, he began by revealing the details of the dream (Daniel 2:31-35). He declared that the king had seen a huge statue of a man that was both splendid and awesome in appearance. The statue was made of a succession of metals. It had a head of gold, a silver chest, thighs of brass, and legs of iron. It rested upon a precarious foundation — feet of iron mixed with clay.

As Nebuchadnezzar stared at the statue, admiring its beauty, the feet were suddenly struck by a supernatural stone ("a stone cut out without hands"). The statue collapsed, and the stone expanded rapidly into a mountain that engulfed the whole world (Daniel 2:31-35).

A Prophetic Interpretation

Daniel explained that the dream dealt with the future and extended even to the "latter days" (Daniel 2:28). He pointed out that the golden head was representative of the Babylonian empire. It would be succeeded by another empire represented by the silver chest, and it would, in turn, be overthrown by another empire symbolized by the thighs of bronze. The final empire was represented by the legs of iron (Daniel 2:36-40).

Later, God revealed to Daniel that the empire that would follow Babylon would be the Medo-Persian which, in turn, would be overthrown by the Greeks under Alexander the Great (Daniel 8:1-8, 20-21).

The empire represented by the iron legs was never specifically identified, but we know from history that it was the Roman Empire which eventually split into two parts, the Eastern and Western Empires.

Regarding the feet of iron mixed with clay, Daniel declared that this would be Mankind's final world kingdom and that it would be both strong as iron and brittle as clay. Daniel further asserted that this final kingdom of Mankind would be suddenly and totally destroyed when "the God of Heaven will set up a kingdom which will never be destroyed" (Daniel 2:44). That kingdom, represented by the stone, will encompass the whole world, will destroy all other kingdoms, and will "endure forever" (Daniel 2:44-45).

A Prophetic Gap

The prophecy evidently contains a time gap because there is nothing in history that corresponds to the empire represented by the feet of iron mixed with clay. Also, it must contain a time gap because the text specifically states that it relates to "the latter days."

Amillennialists (those who deny there will be a future reign of Jesus on the earth) object to the idea that the prophecy contains a time gap. They argue that the stone represents the kingdom of the Church which destroyed the Roman Empire and proceeded to expand all over the earth.

But Christianity served to unite and consolidate the Roman Empire rather than destroy it. And although the Church has spread all over the world, it certainly has not displaced the kingdoms of this world. Nor does the Bible teach that the Church Age will endure forever. In fact, the Bible teaches it will come to a screeching halt when the Church is raptured out of this world.

Further Revelations

In subsequent dreams and visions, the Lord revealed to Daniel that this kingdom of iron mixed with clay would be a loose confederation of ten rulers (Daniel 7:24). This confederation would arise out of the territory of the empire of iron — the Roman Empire (Daniel 7:7-8). Daniel was also shown that this revived European confederation would serve as the base for the construction of the last great Gentile world empire — namely, the empire of the Antichrist (Daniel 7:8, 24-26 and 8:19-27).

These revelations provide additional evidence of a time gap in the prophecy because history fails to show a ten nation European confederation expanding into a world empire and then being suddenly destroyed by a supernatural intervention of God. Nor has any such European confederation ever produced a leader equivalent to the Antichrist described in both Daniel and Revelation.

An Accurate Interpretation

Daniel's interpretation of Nebuchadnezzar's dream proved to be historically accurate to the minutest detail. Just as prophesied, the Babylonian Empire was overthrown by the Medo-Persian Empire in 539 BC. The Greeks, under Alexander the Great, conquered the Persians in 331 BC, and the Romans succeeded the Greeks. As one writer put it, "Daniel wrote history in advance better than any historian has ever written it after the fact."

The Roman Empire divided in 395 AD and proceeded into a long decline. By the 5th Century AD the empire was dead. But the idea of the empire would never die. The hope of reviving it continued to capture the imaginations of European leaders.

Revival Attempts

In 800 AD, Charlemagne, in conjunction with the Roman Catholic Church, laid the foundation for what came to be known as the Holy Roman Empire. It lasted until 1806, but it was never really a true empire. It mainly consisted of German states ruled by German kings who usually sought but did not always receive coronation as emperor by the popes in Rome.

It was an attempt to revive the old Roman Empire, but it existed primarily on paper and in the imaginations of its "emperors." Voltaire summed it up succinctly when he wrote, "It is neither Holy, nor Roman, nor an Empire."

The form of government that truly existed during the Middle Ages was feudalism in the form of tribal-states, city-states, and city-leagues. The nation-state system burst on the scene in the 1700's after the printing press and the spread of education made people aware of national groupings, fueling a desire for each national group to have its own state.

However, even the extreme nationalism of the nation-state system was not sufficient to kill the idea of reviving the old Roman Empire. Napoleon attempted to do it and almost succeeded. Hitler dreamed of accomplishing it, and in the process, he reduced Europe to a heap of ashes.

The Miracle Rebirth

But out of the ashes arose a renewed zeal to unite Europe. The zeal was motivated by desperation. Visionary European leaders realized that if they were ever going to rebuild Europe, they would have to put aside their national rivalries and integrate their economies.

They established the European Coal and Steel Community in 1951, encompassing six nations (France, Germany, Italy, the Netherlands, Belgium, and Luxembourg). In 1958 this organization was expanded in scope to cover all economic activities. It was renamed the European Economic Community. Between 1973 and 1993 six additional states were added to the community, including Great Britain.

The biggest and boldest step was taken in 1993 when the member nations decided to surrender their political sovereignty by agreeing to integrate themselves politically as well as economically. With this step, the European Union was born.

Today the European Union consists of 25 nations with a population of over 450 million people. Additional nations are poised to enter the union. There is little doubt that the EU will soon eclipse the United States as the world's greatest super power.

What mankind could never accomplish by war has become a reality peacefully through diplomacy over a period of 50 years. The reason, of course, is that it is now God's timing for the old Roman Empire to be reborn.

The Ten Nations

But what about the prophecy that the end time revival of the Roman Empire will consist of a confederation of ten rulers or nations? How does the EU with its 25 nations (and more to come) fulfill this prophecy?

We will have to wait and see, but the groundwork for its fulfillment is probably being laid at present through the EU's emphasis on de-nationalization. What this means is that the EU is doing everything possible to de-emphasize national identities and replace them with a common European identity. In other words, people are being encouraged to think of themselves not as Frenchmen or Germans or British but as Europeans.

Accordingly, passports have been changed to state first that the person is a member of the European Union and secondarily is a citizen of a particular state. But this is only a transitional step to a passport that will say nothing more than that the person is a citizen of the EU.

More significantly, nations as such are no longer represented in the European Parliament. Delegates represent sections of nations and are required to be seated in the Parliament by political ideology (liberal, moderate, or conservative) rather than by national origin. As more nations are added and the organization becomes more unwieldy, it seems likely that the EU will be divided into administrative units that will cut across national boundaries. It could very well be that there would be a total of ten such units, each headed up by its own ruler.

The Missing Element

The European Union now has a common parliament, court, bank, and currency. It is in the process of organizing an army. The main thing it lacks is a strong leader. Its executive currently consists of a committee, but Bible prophecy makes it clear that the committee will soon be replaced by a single individual.

Before long, some dynamic, charismatic political personality will emerge within the European Union who seems to have the answers to all the world's problems. He will take over the Union, and he will then venture forth to build a new world order, using both deception and force (Daniel 11:36-45 and Revelation 6:1-6).

The New World Order

This final empire will unite the whole world politically, socially, economically and spiritually. The Antichrist will be assisted by a False Prophet who will pull together the world's religions into an amalgamated, apostate super-church that will worship the Antichrist (Revelation 13:11-18).

The Bible makes it clear that this empire of the Antichrist will be history's one and only true world empire, for unlike all the other empires that have existed, this one will include "every tribe and people and tongue and nation" (Revelation 13:7).

The Fate of the Antichrist Empire

Mankind's final world empire will be a brutal one. One-half of humanity will die in the first three and a half years as the Antichrist unites the world through military power (Revelation 6-9). Then, utilizing modern technology, he will institute a totalitarian dictatorship that will control every aspect of life (Revelation 13:16-17).

Mercifully, his reign will be short. At the end of seven years of unparalleled tribulation upon the earth, God will pour out His wrath upon this last empire. Its overwhelming destruction by fire will take place in one hour (Revelation 18).

That's when Jesus will return to set up God's empire. It will be radically different from all the empires of mankind because it will result in a perfect world order. Jesus will reign from Mt. Zion in Jerusalem with a rod of iron, and the world will be flooded with peace, righteousness and justice (Psalm 2 and Micah 4).

A Warning

Do not be deceived by all the current talk about a "New World Order." It is the old world order dressed up in new clothes.

Satan is pulling together one last worldwide empire in his futile attempt to frustrate God's master plan. Most of the world will be deceived into believing that this "New World Order" will produce a utopia on earth. It will create, instead, a living hell.

The "New World Order" is doomed to failure, for it will be based on the wisdom of Man. Pray for the coming of the perfect world order that Jesus will establish when He returns. It will be based upon the Word of God.

Will there be a certain end time configuration?

> "He makes the nations great, then destroys them;
> He enlarges the nations, then leads them away"
>   Job 12:23

The interpretation of Bible prophecy cannot be dictated by world events. If the Bible says an event is going to occur in the future — like a Russian invasion of Israel — it is going to happen, regardless of trends in world politics.

When the Soviet Union collapsed in 1991, many people felt that was the end of any possible Russian invasion of Israel, as prophesied in Ezekiel 38 and 39. But the Russian invasion of Israel predicted in Bible prophecy has never been dependent upon Russia being a Communist state.

Believing What the Bible Says

When interpreting what the Bible says about the nations in the end times, we need to have the faith that was demonstrated by C. I. Scofield when he published his famous Study Bible in 1909. He interpreted Ezekiel 38 and 39 to mean that Russia would invade Israel in the end times. That interpretation was challenged and even mocked.

Scholars asked, "How can you possibly say that these chapters prophesy a Russian invasion of Israel? Russia is a Christian Orthodox nation, and Israel doesn't even exist! Nor is there any possibility that Israel will ever exist again."

Scofield's response was simple: "I don't understand it, and I can't explain it, but the Bible says it, and therefore I believe it."

Today, one hundred years later, Israel exists and Russia is anything but a Christian nation. The Russians are currently sporting a thin democratic veneer, but underneath is an ugly heritage of dictatorship, repression, and anti-Semitism. Furthermore, the society is wallowing in economic chaos and violence as former Communist officials now operate as Mafia thugs building regional empires that are immune to government control. Another thing to keep in mind is that the central Russian republics contain an enormous Islamic population that is vehemently opposed to the state of Israel.

The Key Nation

Russia is only one of several nations that are specifically mentioned in end time prophecies. The key nation is Israel because all end time prophecy revolves around the Jewish people.

Four hundred years ago, Puritan scholars began to preach that the nation of Israel would be re-established in the end times, right before the return of Jesus. A good example of this teaching can be found in a book by Increase Mather, *The Mystery of Israel's Salvation,* which was published in 1667.

The Puritan claim was scoffed at by most Christians. After all, the Jews had been scattered all over the world, and their homeland, called Palestine, was a part of the Ottoman Empire. There seemed to be no prospect whatever that the nation of Israel would ever exist again.

The Testimony of Scripture

But the Puritan claim was based on solid biblical evidence. Isaiah 11:10-12 plainly states that in the end times there will be a "second" regathering of the Jews (the first being from Babylon). The passage further says that this will be a regathering of Jews from all tribes, both the ten tribes of Israel and the two tribes of Judah (the return from Babylon included only Judah). Finally, the passage says that this regathering will be "from the four corners of the earth."

Another of the great end time regathering prophecies is found in Ezekiel 37. It is the famous prophecy of the valley of the dry bones. Ezekiel was brought by the Spirit of God to a valley strewn with bones. He was told to preach to the bones.

As Ezekiel began preaching, the bones began to come to life! They came back together, and muscles formed on them. As they resumed their human forms, breath came into them, and they stood up!

The astonished prophet was told by the Lord that the bones represented the Jewish people who had been scattered and seemed to have no hope. The Lord then assured Ezekiel that one day the "graves" of the Jewish people — the nations where they would be dispersed — would be opened, and the people would be brought back to the land of Israel (Ezekiel 37:11-12).

Again, Ezekiel asserts that this will be a regathering that will include both Israel and Judah: "Thus says the Lord God, 'Behold, I will take the stick of Joseph, which is in the hand of Ephraim, and the tribes of Israel, his companions; and I will put them with it, with the stick of Judah, and make them one stick, and they will be one in My hand'" (Ezekiel 37: 19). He also says this will occur right before the return of the Messiah to reign over the nations from Jerusalem (Ezekiel 37:24-28).

Similar prophecies can be found throughout the Hebrew Scriptures. In fact, the return of the Jews to their homeland in the end times is the most prolific prophecy in the Old Testament, mentioned more frequently than any other one.

Triggering the Prophecies

The Lord launched His fulfillment of these prophecies near the end of the 19th Century when He gave a Viennese journalist a vision for the re-establishment of the state of Israel. The man was an Hungarian Jew by the name of Theodor Herzl (1860-1904). Like most Jewish intellectuals of his time, Herzl believed that the Jews had been assimilated into European society. But in 1894 his attitude radically changed.

He went to Paris to cover the trial of a French army officer by the name of Alfred Dreyfus. The officer had been falsely accused of treason because he was Jewish. When Herzl arrived at the court house, he was astonished to see thousands of Parisians standing in the streets shouting, "Death to the Jews!"

This agonizing experience convinced Herzl that the only hope for the Jews was for them to form a state of their own. He expressed this sentiment very convincingly in 1896 in a pamphlet called, "Der Judenstaat" ("The Jewish State"). His pamphlet led to the convocation of the First Zionist Congress, held in Basel, Switzerland in August of 1897. Herzl wrote in his diary, "At Basel, I founded the Jewish state." He predicted that within 50 years people would see the truth of his statement.

Sure enough, 50 years later in November 1947 the United Nations authorized the creation of a Jewish state in Palestine. And on May 14, 1948 the state of Israel came into existence.

The Arab Threat

Once Israel is re-established, as it has been, the Bible prophesies that it will be threatened from all sides by a variety of nations. First and foremost, the very existence of Israel will be challenged by the surrounding Arab states.

Ezekiel prophesied that "at the time of the punishment of the end" (his term for the end times), God will pour out His wrath upon "Mount Seir" (his collective term for the Arab peoples) because they will covet the land which He has given the Jews (Ezekiel 35:5, 10-11). Isaiah had previously given the same prophecy when he stated that a time will come when God will pour out His wrath upon Edom (Isaiah's collective term for the Arabs) because of their mistreatment of the Jewish people (Isaiah 34:5-6).

The end time Arab conspiracy to destroy Israel is spelled out in detail in Psalm 83 where the psalmist says that the Arab nations of Jordan, Egypt, Lebanon, Gaza, Saudi Arabia, Syria, and Iraq will make a covenant to "possess for ourselves the pastures of God [the land of Israel]" (Psalm 83:5-12).

These prophecies have been fulfilled since the re-establishment of the Jewish state in 1948. The Arab nations surrounding Israel have launched six wars in a never-ceasing attempt to annihilate the Jewish state. Additionally, there have been several significant intifadas (Palestinian uprisings), climaxing with the one that began in September 2000.

The Russian Threat

The Arabs are not the only enemies of Israel prophesied for the end times. The Bible says another nemesis of the Jews will be Russia. In Ezekiel 38 and 39 we are told that a nation from "the remote parts of the north" will prove to be Israel's greatest enemy (Ezekiel 38:6,15).

All directions in the Bible are given in reference to Jerusalem. If you take a string and put one end of it on the city Jerusalem on a world globe and then place the other end on the North Pole, you will see that the string passes through Moscow, the capital of Russia. This is a good indication that Ezekiel is speaking of Russia as the nation in "the remote parts of the north."

There are other indicators. Ezekiel says this nation will comprise the land of Magog (Ezekiel 38:2) which the Jewish historian, Josephus, identified as the area occupied by the Scythians in south central Russia. It is also identified as the land ruled by "the prince of Rosh" (Ezekiel 38:2). Rosh is an ancient root word for Russia. The ruler is also identified as being in control of Meshech and Tubal — probably ancient names for Moscow and Tobolsk.

A Coalition of Nations

The Russians are pictured as invading Israel with a coalition of nations. Persia is named first (Ezekiel 38:5). At that time, Persia included modern day Syria, Iraq, Iran, and Afghanistan. Named also are Ethiopia, Put (Libya), and two areas — Gomer and Beth-togarmah — included in modern day Turkey (Ezekiel 38:5-6).

Ezekiel says the Russian invasion of Israel will occur at a time when the Jews are living in unwalled cities, as is the case today (Ezekiel 38: 11). He also says the purpose of the invasion will be "to capture spoil and to seize plunder" (Ezekiel 38:12). We will see later what this could be referring to.

As I stated earlier in this chapter, there is no nation on earth with a longer and more persistent anti-Semitic history than Russia. Russian rulers have used the Jews as their whipping boys throughout their recorded history, blaming all the ills of Russian society on "the international Jewish conspiracy." That demonic spirit of anti-Semitism remains firmly rooted in Russian society to this day.

The Role of Europe

As pointed out in the previous chapter, Europe is another big-time player in the Bible's end time scenario of events. The prophecies contained in Daniel and Revelation make it clear that in the end times, the Roman Empire will be revived and, out of it, the Antichrist will arise.

Nebuchadnezzar's dream, which we discussed in chapter 10, revealed a progression of future Gentile empires: Babylon, Medo-Persia, Greece, and Rome (Daniel 2:31-45). It also revealed that the final Gentile empire would be related to the Roman Empire and would consist of a loose confederation of ten nations or regions.

Daniel's vision of the same procession of empires, given to him 48 years later, also indicated the last Gentile empire of history would be a confederation of ten units that would be located in the area of the old Roman Empire (Daniel 7:1-8). Further, Daniel was shown that the Antichrist would rise out of this reconstructed Roman Empire, first taking over three of the units, and then the rest (Daniel 7:8-12, 23-26).

In chapter 9 of his prophecies, Daniel again asserts that the Antichrist will rise out of a revised Roman Empire. He states that the Antichrist will originate from among the people who would one day destroy the Jewish temple (Daniel 9:26). Those people proved, of course, to be the Romans in 70 AD.

New Testament Confirmation

The apostle John confirmed the message of Daniel's visions in the book of Revelation. In chapter 17 he sees a "woman sitting on a scarlet beast . . . having seven heads and ten horns" (Revelation 17:3). We know the beast is Satan because he is described with the same terminology in Revelation 12:3. The woman is symbolic of the apostate church which the Antichrist will use to inspire worldwide worship of himself (Revelation 13:12).

John explains that the seven heads of the beast represent "seven kings," five which had already fallen, one which existed at that time, and the seventh which was yet to come (Revelation 17:10). This appears to be a reference to a succession of Gentile world empires. The five fallen would be Egypt, Assyria, Babylon, Medo-Persia, and Greece. The one existing at that time was Rome. The one yet to come would be the end time European confederation, representing a revival of the Roman Empire. John then reveals that the revived Roman Empire will evolve into the eighth and final Gentile empire of history — namely, the worldwide empire of the Antichrist (Revelation 17:11-12).

A Persistent Dream

It is interesting to note that ever since the Roman Empire ceased to exist in 476 AD, repeated attempts have been made throughout history to revive it. In the Middle Ages the Pope attempted a revival through the creation of what was called the Holy Roman Empire. But it was an empire in name only. Napoleon and Hitler both tried to unite Europe through military power, and both failed because it was not God's timing.

Undoubtedly, all these attempts were inspired by Satan. He knows Bible prophecy (Revelation 12:12), and he therefore understands that he cannot raise up his false messiah, the Antichrist, until he is able to orchestrate the reunification of Europe.

The Impact of World War II

The turning point for the fulfillment of these prophecies came with World War II. Just as the War accelerated the re-establishment of Israel by motivating the Jewish people to go back home, it also motivated the movement toward European unity.

Europe was in ruins and was desperate. This desperation prompted European leaders to put aside ancient hatreds and jealousies in order to reach out to each other for mutual support and aid.

The result was a series of economic mergers which began in the 1950's and which ultimately led to political integration in the 1990's. Today, the European Union contains 25 nations with a combined population of over 450 million. The Union has developed into the super power prophesied by Daniel, and it will provide the base of operations for the Antichrist when he makes his move to take over the world.

The Likely Scenario

Now that the prophesied end time pattern of nations is in place for the first time, what is likely to be the outcome of international politics?

The Bible says that as we approach the threshold of the Tribulation, leading up to the day of the Lord's return, the world will become increasingly hostile to Israel. In fact, we are told that the whole world will come together against Israel over the issue of Jerusalem (Zechariah 12:2-3).

That is precisely where we are today in the end time scenario of events. The Arab nations are demanding sovereignty over Jerusalem. The European Union is insisting that the city be divided between the Arabs and the Jews. The United Nations would like to see the city internationalized, and the Vatican would like to see it put under its control. Even Israel's greatest ally, the United States, is pressuring the Jews to surrender a part of the city.

A War for Jerusalem

All of this international pressure is leading up to a major conflagration over the control of the city. When the war breaks out, the Israelis will win it quickly, prompting the Palestinians to send out a call for help to the Arab world. The Syrians are most likely the ones who will jump in first, due to their implacable hatred of the Jews. They will target both Tel Aviv and Haifa with missiles, and the only way Israel will be able to survive is to retaliate with its own missiles, possibly using nuclear warheads. This would explain the fact that Bible prophecy clearly states that Damascus, the capital of Syria, will cease to exist in the end times (Isaiah 17:1-14 and Jeremiah 49:23-27).

The whole Arab world will be thrown into a panic over the destruction of Damascus, and the Arab leaders will turn to their natural ally for help — Russia. The Russians will respond gleefully to the Arab invitation because they will see it as an opportunity not only to destroy Israel, but to seize the oil fields of the Middle East. This is the "plunder" that will draw them into the area (Ezekiel 38:12).

The Russian troops will be destroyed supernaturally on the hills of Israel. It will happen in such a way that even the Israelis will realize that the defeat came from God, and many Jewish hearts will be turned to the Lord (Ezekiel 39:1-6).

The Rise of the Antichrist

At this point the whole world will be thrown into a panic, and into that atmosphere will step a dynamic, charismatic political leader from Europe who will seem to have all the answers. He will broker an amazing settlement for the Middle East that will enable the Jews to truly live in peace and even to rebuild their temple.

He will use his success in the Middle East to take over the European Union, and he will use that empire as his base for launching a war to take over the world. He will be spectacularly successful, due to his ruthlessness. He will slaughter one-half of the world's population in a nuclear war that will enable him to become the first person in history to conquer all the nations of the world. He will combine them into the final Gentile empire of history which he will rule from Rome (Daniel 7:23-26, Daniel 8:23-26, and Revelation 6-9).

The Nagging Question

All of which brings us full circle to the most frequently asked question in Bible prophecy today: Where is the United States in these end time events? What role will we play? And if the Bible is silent about us, how is that to be explained? After all, we are the nation that dominates world politics at the very time when all the signs of the time point to a quick fulfillment of these end time prophecies.

For the answer to this question, let's go to chapter 12.

The United States in Prophecy   12
Will America play a central or peripheral role?

Where is the United States in Bible prophecy? It is a question I am asked wherever I go. It is only natural that we should wonder. Since the United States is not mentioned specifically by name in Bible prophecy, people have resorted to their imaginations to find our nation in the Scriptures.

A "tall and smooth people"?

Some have pointed to Isaiah 18 which speaks of a people "tall and smooth" who are "feared far and wide." The passage further states that this is a "powerful nation whose land the rivers divide." The chapter ends by stating that the people of this nation will bring "a gift of homage" to the Lord when He returns to reign from Mt. Zion.

Because these verses speak of a powerful nation whose land is divided by a great river, some have jumped to the conclusion that the nation is the United States since it is divided by the Mississippi River. They further argue that we are a people who are tall and clean-shaven, and that our military might is feared throughout the world. Finally, they argue that since we are a Christian nation, we would certainly bring gifts to the Lord when He returns.

But the opening verses of this chapter indicate it is speaking of "Cush," the ancient name of Ethiopia. At the time Isaiah wrote this passage, Ethiopia was the seat of the powerful 25th Egyptian Dynasty (730-660 BC). The river referred to is undoubtedly the Nile.

Isaiah 18 has nothing to do with the United States in prophecy, and even if it did, it would not answer the question about the role of

America in end time world politics. It is a prophecy about the millennial reign of Jesus that will be established after His return.

A "village" of Tarshish?

Probably one of the most popular passages where people claim to have found the United States is in Ezekiel 38 where the prophet describes an invasion of Israel that will be launched in the end times by a nation "from the remote parts of the north." The descriptive verses about the northern power make it clear that this nation is Russia. What is not so clear is where the U.S. fits into this invasion.

Those who find us in the passage point to Ezekiel 38:13 which says that "the merchants of Tarshish and all its villages" (or "young lions" depending on translation) will speak out against the invasion. The argument is that Tarshish is Britain and the "villages" or "young lions" are the English speaking nations like the U.S. and Australia that were founded by British immigrants.

To say the least, this is a highly imaginative interpretation. Its validity is seriously questioned by the fact that no one knows for certain the true identity of "Tarshish." Furthermore, recent archaeological developments indicate that Tarshish was most likely ancient Tartessus in modern day Spain.

Tarshish is used in Scripture as a symbol of the areas west of Israel. Therefore, the most likely meaning of Ezekiel's statement is that the nations of Western Europe will speak out against the Russian-led invasion of Israel in the end times.

One thing is certain — Ezekiel 38 does not settle the search for America in prophecy.

A "great eagle"?

Another favorite passage for applied imagination is Revelation 12:13-17. These verses state that in the middle of the Tribulation God will provide a means of escape for the Jewish remnant in Israel. They will flee into the wilderness to a hiding place on the "wings of a great eagle."

Some people have seized on this imagery to teach that the United States, whose national symbol is the eagle, will supply the end time air lift that will save the Jewish remnant.

But the Bible is its own best interpreter. And when you look up the phrase, "wings of an eagle," you will find that it is the same one that God used in Exodus 19:4 to describe how He brought the Israelites out of Egypt: "You yourselves have seen what I did to the Egyptians, and how I bore you on eagles' wings, and brought you to Myself." The same imagery is used in Deuteronomy 32:11 where it speaks of God's protection of Israel in the wilderness: "Like an eagle that stirs up its nest, that hovers over its young, He [the Lord] spread His wings and caught them, He carried them on His pinions."

God is often portrayed in the Scriptures symbolically as a protective bird. In Psalm 91 the reader is told to put his trust in God and He will "cover you with His pinions, and under His wings you may seek refuge" (Psalm 91:2, 4). In Psalm 17:8 David cries out to the Lord in a prayer, asking God to "hide me in the shadow of Your wings." (See also Psalms 36:7, 57:1, 61:4, and 63:7.)

In Revelation 12, God is the "eagle," not the United States. All the passage in Revelation 12 teaches is that God is going to supernaturally protect the Jewish people when they flee from the Antichrist into Jordan in the middle of the Tribulation.

"Babylon the great?"

This brings us to the final and most widely used passage for identifying the U.S. in Bible prophecy. It is Revelation 18 where the destruction of "Babylon the great" is described.

There is no doubt that the United States shares many similarities with the corrupt commercial empire depicted in this chapter. The empire is described as one that is in rebellion against God, to the point that it has become "a dwelling place of demons" (verse 2). It further states that the immorality of this empire has corrupted all the nations of the world (verse 3).

It is also made clear that this "Babylon the great" will completely dominate the world economy, and its destruction will result in the collapse of the economies of all nations (verses 9, 11, 17).

In the present international context, it certainly sounds like the United States. But, again, the Bible is its own best interpreter, and chapter 17 of Revelation makes it clear that "Babylon the great" is an empire whose capital is Rome, not Washington, D.C.

In Revelation 17:9 we are told that the seven heads of the beast (the Antichrist) are representative, in part, of "seven mountains." In the First Century context, this could only be a reference to Rome, for it was known as "the city of seven hills." This identification is further reinforced by verse 18 which states that the woman riding the beast "is the great city, which reigns over the kings of the earth." Again, there is only one city that could fit that description in the First Century context of the passage, and that is Rome.

The United States is not a fulfillment of Revelation 18. That chapter is describing the last Gentile world empire that will dominate the earth at the time of the Lord's Second Coming. It is the empire of the Antichrist.

Some Conclusions

So, where is the United States in Bible prophecy? A partial answer is that we are not mentioned directly and specifically. We are covered by general prophecies that relate to all nations, but beyond that, our end time destiny is not specifically mentioned.

General prophecies that apply to the United States include those that say all nations will be judged (Isaiah 34:2-3) and all nations will cease to exist except the nation of Israel (Jeremiah 30:11 and 46:28).

But how could God overlook the world's most important and powerful nation? I don't think He has. I believe America can be found in Bible prophecy, not specifically, but in prophetic type. In other words, I believe there is a nation in Scripture that is a forerunner of America in its origin, its purpose, and its destiny.

America's Prophetic Type

I believe the biblical prophetic type of the United States is the nation of Judah. This was the southern nation that was formed when the united kingdom of David and Solomon broke up after Solomon's death.

The northern nation of Israel, consisting of ten tribes, was born in rebellion, and it was never blessed by God. Throughout its 208 year history it never had one king who was considered to be righteous in the eyes of God.

In stark contrast, the southern kingdom of Judah, which contained both the city of Jerusalem and the Jewish temple, was blessed like no other nation that had ever existed. The nation was given eight righteous kings during its 344 years of existence. The combined rule of those kings constituted 224 years of the nation's history. These included great men of God like Jehoshaphat, Hezekiah, and Josiah. This godly leadership produced a nation blessed with freedom, prosperity, justice and peace.

But the nation's greatest blessing was the presence of God Himself in the form of His Shekinah Glory which resided in the Jewish Temple's Holy of Holies.

The American Parallel

No other nation has since been so richly blessed except the United States of America. God gave us a great expanse of territory filled with every conceivable natural resource. Additionally, He gave us the ingenuity to harness our natural resources and talents to produce the greatest wealth the world has ever known.

Like ancient Judah, God blessed us with godly political leaders who loved Him and who cherished freedom. He also gave us great spiritual leaders who preached the gospel with zeal and developed a citizenry grounded in Christian principles of justice and brotherhood.

And working through our wealth and churches, the Lord sent forth missionaries all over the world to establish churches and translate the Bible into many languages.

It would be great if we could conclude our comparison of Judah and America at this point. But unfortunately, the parallels in the histories of the two nations do not end here.

Pride and Rebellion

When Judah reached the height of her glory as a nation, the people began to wallow in pride, and this led to rebellion against God and His Word.

Often when I am asked, "Where is the United States in Bible Prophecy?" I respond by saying, "Look in Isaiah chapter 5. Or consider Jeremiah 5 and 6." I say that because these chapters contain an inventory of the national sins of Judah as catalogued by Isaiah and Jeremiah, and they are the same sins that characterize American society today.

Destruction

Judah refused to repent, and God finally responded by sending the Babylonians to destroy the nation. One of the saddest passages in the Bible is found in 2 Chronicles 36:15-16 where the writer describes God's painful decision to destroy His beloved nation of Judah. It reads as follows:

15 And the Lord, the God of their fathers, sent word to them again and again by His messengers, because He had compassion on His people and on His dwelling place;

16 but they continually mocked the messengers of God, despised His words and scoffed at His prophets, until the wrath of the Lord arose against His people, until there was no remedy.

Judah was destroyed for committing the same sins that characterize the United States today. Why should our fate be any different?

- We have been blessed like Judah.

- We have sinned like Judah.

- We are now being warned like Judah.

- We are responding like Judah.

- The conclusion seems inescapable: We are heading for the same fate as Judah.

What is that fate likely to be? What form will it take? We can only guess, because the Bible is silent.

Economic Collapse

The first thing that comes to mind is an economic catastrophe that will result from our out of control debt situation. The official outstanding debt of the U.S. government is currently 6.2 trillion dollars. That amounts to $21,540 per person. This debt is increasing at the rate of 1.1 billion per day! Private debt is even more horrendous. At the beginning of the 21st Century, there was a staggering $25.6 trillion of credit market debt outstanding in the U.S. America's total debt, public and private (including state and local government) stands at around $32 trillion dollars! That's $115,322 per man, woman, and child.

There is no way to escape the conclusion that America has become a debt junkie. We are living on money we do not have and will never have, and sooner or later the weight of this debt is going to collapse our economy.

I believe an unprecedented economic collapse is highly likely because money is the real god of America, and the true God of this universe is a jealous One who does not tolerate idolatry. God, by His very nature, is going to be compelled to destroy our false god.

External Attack

Another possible fate for the United States is destruction from a Russian nuclear attack. This, of course, could happen in conjunction with an economic collapse, or it could be the cause of that collapse.

The reason a Russian attack is so likely is because the Bible says that the Russians will lead an end time invasion of Israel (Ezekiel 38 and 39). Since we are Israel's only ally, it seems inconceivable to me that the Russians would attack Israel without unleashing a preemptive nuclear attack on us in order to prevent us from coming to Israel's defense.

This attack may be hinted at in Ezekiel 39:6 where it says that at the time of the Russian invasion, fire will fall on "those who inhabit the coastlands in safety." The Russian attack would come most probably from submarines deployed off our East and West coasts. Each Russian submarine carries more fire power than all the bombs dropped in World War II. Such an attack would give us only seven minutes, not even enough time to launch a counter attack.

Some argue that since the collapse of the Soviet government, Russia is now too weak to launch any attack against Israel or the United States. It is true that the economy of Russia is in shambles, but the military power is intact, including thousands of nuclear warheads. The truth of the matter is that Russia is far more dangerous today than before the Soviet collapse. The increased danger is due to the instability of the government and the chaos in the economy.

Internal Attack

Another way in which American power could be rapidly dissipated is through internal terrorist attacks. Just stop and think for a moment about the overwhelming impact that the 9/11 attack had upon our society and economy. In the months that followed, the stock markets lost over 7 trillion dollars in value. The travel industry (airlines and hotels) was devastated. Civil liberties were severely curtailed. And don't forget that our national government was brought to a standstill by the subsequent anthrax scare.

Multiply such terrorist attacks, including the poisoning of water supplies and the explosion of "dirty bombs" containing nuclear waste materials, and you can readily see how our nation could be brought to its knees. In fact, it is not beyond the realm of possibility that terrorists could detonate an atomic bomb that has been smuggled into one of our major ports aboard a cargo ship. No matter how vigilant we may be, in the final analysis, there is no way to protect against terrorists who have no regard for their own lives, much less those who believe that dying for their cause will guarantee their entry into paradise.

Internal Rot

Internal collapse could also result from the moral rot that has our nation by its throat. This is what ultimately destroyed the Roman Empire, and it is what led to the sudden collapse of Soviet Russia.

As we have abandoned our Judeo-Christian heritage, we have evolved into an amoral society that has lost its respect for the sanctity of life. Individualism has been carried to the brink of anarchy as everyone does what is right in his own eyes. Greed is fracturing our society between young and old, rich and poor, black and white. Class warfare could easily deteriorate into civil warfare with outbreaks of uncontrollable violence in our major cities.

Another Alternative

There is another scenario that could explain the silence about America in the Scriptures. It is the possibility that the United States might be suddenly destroyed by the Rapture of the Church.

There is no doubt that the Rapture would devastate contemporary America. We have more born again Christians than any other nation in the world — more than all of Western Europe and England combined.

Furthermore, we have many evangelical Christians in high positions of leadership, in both government and business. The sudden removal of these people would throw our whole society into chaos.

Our Ultimate National Destiny

Regardless of how we are removed from the international scene as a world power, we are most likely to end up absorbed into the European Union as one of its members states. This seems only natural in view of all the historic and cultural ties we have with that part of the world.

Will it be the headquarters of the Antichrist?

Whenever a war breaks out in the Middle East, prophetic speculation always shifts into high gear, and that is understandable since end time Bible prophecy focuses on the Middle East and mentions several wars that will take place there.

Common Speculations

The first question seems always to be whether or not the war is the War of Armageddon. I guess this question is a natural one because this is the prophetic war that people have heard the most about. But that war is one that will occur at the end of the Tribulation, following a seven year period of unparalleled destruction on the earth.

Those who are more familiar with Bible prophecy often speculate as to whether any new war in the Middle East might be the War of Gog and Magog. Actually, Bible prophecy talks about two wars of Gog and Magog. One occurs either at the beginning of the Tribulation or in the middle, depending on how you interpret the relevant verses which are found in Ezekiel 38 and 39. This war consists of a Russian coalition of Islamic nations that invade Israel and are supernaturally destroyed by God (Ezekiel 38:18-22 and 39:1-6).

The other War of Gog and Magog occurs at the end of the Millennium when once again the peoples of Russia rally the whole world to attack the throne of Jesus in Jerusalem. The nations that join this revolt are also supernaturally destroyed (Revelation 20:7-10).

New Speculations

I was astonished to hear one of the best known teachers of Bible prophecy propose a new theory when the United States attacked Iraq. He speculated that the war was a fulfillment of a prophecy in Jeremiah 50:9-10 which reads as follows:

> For behold, I am going to arouse and bring up against Babylon a horde of great nations from the land of the north, and they will draw up their battle lines against her; from there she will be taken captive. Their arrows will be like an expert warrior . . and Chaldea will become plunder . . .

The first problem with this interpretation is that it violates the context in which the passage is found. That context is the destruction of the Antichrist's kingdom that will take place at the end of the Tribulation. The second problem is that the U.S. led coalition was anything but a 'horde of great nations." We had three allies who supplied combat troops: England, Australia, and Poland. And the invasion certainly did not come from the north. It came out of Kuwait, from the southeast.

Incredibly, this prophecy teacher, who was determined to force this passage on the War in Iraq, tried to argue that the invasion really came from the north because, as he put it, "If you will check the latitude line that runs through Baghdad, you will find that it is the same one that runs through Savannah, Georgia, and thus the majority of the United States lies north of Baghdad." To say the least, I was dumbfounded by this lame attempt to twist the Scriptures to fit this teacher's preconceived idea.

The most popular new speculation that I found all over the Internet was one that argued the United States is Babylon and would therefore experience an overwhelming defeat in Iraq in accordance with the prophecies contained in Isaiah 13 and 14 and Jeremiah 50 and 51. The outcome of the war put an end to this speculation.

A more credible speculation that many outstanding Bible prophecy teachers proposed was that the War in Iraq would lead to the destruction of Baghdad and the subsequent rise of Babylon as the new capital of Iraq. This speculation also failed to materialize because of the precision bombing that was aimed almost exclusively at military targets.

A Biblical Speculation

The speculation about the rise of Babylon in the end times is biblically based. This is the reason that Tim LaHaye, in his "Left Behind" series of books, presents Babylon as the capital city of the Antichrist's world kingdom.

Let's take a look at the biblical basis of this assumption. It begins in the Hebrew Scriptures in Isaiah 13 where the prophet says that Babylon will be destroyed in "The day of the Lord" (Isaiah 13:6, 9). This terminology is a clear reference to the end times and, of course, Babylon cannot be destroyed unless it is rebuilt.

Isaiah 14:1-17 says that the king of Babylon at the time of its end time destruction will be an oppressor of unparalleled ruthlessness. This is an image that certainly brings to mind the Antichrist.

The book of Revelation in the New Testament confirms these Old Testament prophecies. Revelation 17 associates the end time apostate world religion with Babylon. And in a similar manner, Revelation 18 associates the political empire of the Antichrist with Babylon.

Consider Revelation 18:1-10. This passage clearly teaches that Babylon will be the capital city of the Antichrist and that at the end of the Tribulation, the city will be destroyed in one hour of one day (Revelation 18:8, 10).

Now, in view of these biblical passages from both the Old and New Testaments, you might wonder how anyone who takes Bible prophecy seriously could doubt that Babylon will be rebuilt and serve as the seat of power of the Antichrist. Yet, there are many outstanding Bible prophecy teachers, like Dave Hunt and Ed Hindson, who argue that Babylon will never be rebuilt and that the world headquarters of the Antichrist will be Rome.

The Argument for Rome

Let's take a look at the other side of the argument — that the Babylon of the end times will really be modern day Rome.

There are two reasons that are usually given as to why the end time Babylon may not be the Babylon of Iraq;

1) The Bible indicates that after Babylon is conquered by the Medes, it will become a heap of ruins and will never be rebuilt again.

2) There is strong evidence that Babylon is used symbolically in the book of Revelation to refer to Rome.

The Fate of Babylon

With regard to Babylon being destroyed and never being rebuilt again, let's take a look at Isaiah 13:17-20 —

17 Behold, I am going to stir up the Medes against them [the Chaldeans] . . .

19 And Babylon, the beauty of kingdoms, the glory of the Chaldean's pride, will be as when God overthrew Sodom and Gomorrah.

20 It will never be inhabited or lived in from generation to generation.

Those who argue for the rebuilding of Babylon discount this passage for several reasons. First, they argue it is an end time prophecy referring to the destruction of Babylon at the end of the Tribulation.

But this simply is not true. The context is clearly speaking of the conquest of Babylon by the Medes. There certainly are end time prophecies about Babylon in Isaiah 13, but this is not one of them. End time prophecies are often mixed with contemporary prophecies. For example, in Luke 21 some of the prophecies about the destruction of Jerusalem pertain to 70 AD, whereas others refer to the end times.

The Nature of Babylon's Destruction

The second way people try to discount the clear meaning of Isaiah 13:17-20 is to argue that it could not refer to the Medes' conquest of Babylon because that victory was so surprising and swift that it did not result in the destruction of the city. "The passage says Babylon will be destroyed in the same manner as Sodom and Gomorrah, and that means sudden, total destruction."

It is true that the Medes conquered the city in a relatively bloodless and non-devastating manner. Supposedly, they dammed up the Euphrates River, which ran through the center of the city. Then, while the Babylonian rulers were in the midst of a drunken feast, the armies of the Medes simply walked down the dried-up riverbed, underneath the walls!

But the passage does not say that Babylon will be overthrown like Sodom and Gomorrah! That claim is based on an interpretation that the text does not justify. Read the passage carefully. It simply says that after the Medes conquer the city, it "will be as when God overthrew Sodom and Gomorrah."

And that is exactly what happened. The city was conquered by the Medes in 539 BC. Thereafter, it went into a sharp decline. By the time Alexander the Great arrived 200 years later, it was in ruins. He announced his intentions to rebuild it, but he died suddenly before he could do anything. His generals abandoned the city and moved the capital to the Tigris River where they built a new city called Selucia.

Babylon became like Sodom and Gomorrah — a heap of ruins — and it has been in that condition ever since, just as prophesied in Isaiah 13.

Saddam's Rebuilding

But those who believe Babylon will be rebuilt counter by asserting that its rebuilding was begun by Saddam Hussein.

It is true that Saddam built one of his many presidential palaces there, on the outskirts of the ancient city. But he did not rebuild the city for habitation. All he did was restore some of the ruins of Nebuchadnezzar's palace as a tourist attraction. Modern day satellite photos of the site still show it to be an uninhabited heap of ruins.

Of course, with modern building techniques, the Antichrist could quickly build an international headquarters on the site, but Isaiah 13:20 says that once it is conquered by the Medes, "it will never be inhabited or lived in from generation to generation."

The References in Revelation

So, what about the references in the book of Revelation which clearly indicate that Babylon will be the headquarters of the Antichrist during the Tribulation? The problem is that a qualifying term is used that makes it highly questionable that the meaning is literal Babylon.

The passage is Revelation 17:5. In the New American Standard Version, the translation introduces the reader to "a mystery, Babylon the Great." The King James and New King James Versions both render the meaning as "Mystery Babylon the Great."

Either way, the use of the qualifying word, mystery, seems to indicate that Babylon is to be taken symbolically. This conclusion is reinforced by Revelation 11:8 where Jerusalem is referred to symbolically as the city "which mystically is called Sodom and Egypt." Notice again the use of the word mystically as a tip-off that the author is speaking symbolically.

In like manner, Peter uses Babylon as a symbol of Rome in 1 Peter 5:13. He was writing from Rome, and he closes the epistle by sending greetings from "the church which is in Babylon." This statement makes it clear that among First Century Christians, Babylon was a nick-name for Rome.

Keep in mind that when John wrote Revelation, he was a Roman prisoner. He could not, therefore, make any disparaging references to Rome in his writings, so he used the nick-name of Babylon and even emphasized that it was a code word by referring to it as "Mystery Babylon."

That John had Rome in mind is indicated later in chapter 17 of Revelation in two places. In verse 9 he refers to it as the city of "seven mountains." In the First Century context, this could only refer to Rome, which was known as "the city of the seven hills." In verse 18, John refers to the city as "the great city that reigns over the kings of the earth." Again, this could only have been Rome in a First Century setting.

A Challenge

So, there you have it — a summary of all the arguments pro and con concerning whether or not the end time capital of the Antichrist will be ancient Babylon or modern Rome. I challenge you to be a good Berean (Acts 17:10-11). Dig into the Scriptures, study diligently, and draw your own conclusions.

The important thing to keep in mind is that it doesn't really make any difference whether it will be Babylon or Rome, because either way, Almighty God is going to destroy the city, its king, and all its sinful activities in one hour of one day (Revelation 18:8, 10).

The point is, that regardless of the true identity of Babylon, Jesus is going to triumph, and we, the Redeemed, are going to win in the end.

Jerusalem in Prophecy   14

Does it have a future?

There is no other city on the face of the earth as important as the city of Jerusalem. All the other great cities of the earth — New York, London, Moscow, Paris, and even Rome — pale by comparison. What other city can claim to be "the city of God" or "the city of the Great King"? (Psalm 48)

God loves Jerusalem, and He intends to dwell in it eternally. Psalm 68:16 says that God has desired the mountain of Zion "for His abode" and that He intends to "dwell there forever." Psalm 132:13-14 contains a similar promise: "The Lord has chosen Zion; He has desired it for His habitation. 'This is my resting place forever; here I will dwell, for I have desired it.'"

When you read these kind of statements, you can understand why Jerusalem is identified in Ezekiel 5:5 as "the center of the nations" and in Ezekiel 38:12 as "the center of the earth."

Jerusalem is where the Son of God shed His precious blood. It is where Jesus ascended into Heaven. It is where Jesus will return to be crowned King of kings. It is the city from which Jesus will reign over all the nations of the world.

And Jerusalem will be the scene of history's last battle when Satan rallies the nations at the end of the Millennium and leads them in revolt against the Lord. Finally, Jerusalem is where God Himself will come to reside eternally with the Redeemed.

It is no wonder that Jerusalem has always been an important topic of Bible prophecy.

Jewish Jerusalem

The first set of prophecies relating to Jerusalem are those that pertain to it as a Jewish capital before the time of Jesus. Keep in mind that the kingdom of David split into two nations after the death of his son Solomon.

The northern nation of Israel was totally apostate from the beginning. It was given over to idolatry and did not have one righteous king in its 200 year history. In sharp contrast, the southern nation of Judah was blessed with many righteous kings. It was also blessed with Jerusalem as its capital. And it was blessed even more by having the Shekinah glory of God residing in its temple.

But despite all these blessings, the people of Judah became proud and began to drift in their relationship with God. As the nation started to turn its back on God, the Lord mercifully raised up prophets to warn them and call them to repentance. When they refused to repent, the prophets prophesied that the city of Jerusalem would be destroyed and the nation would be taken into captivity.

The first of these prophecies was delivered by Micah in the 8th century BC — about 130 years before the city was actually destroyed. Micah spoke out against both political and religious corruption, saying, "Her [Judah's] leaders pronounce judgment for a bribe, Her priests instruct for a price, and her prophets divine for money" (Micah 3:11).

He lamented the fact that every time these leaders were called to repentance lest the city be destroyed, they always responded arrogantly by observing, "Is not the Lord in our midst? [A reference to the Shekinah in the Temple.] Calamity will not come upon us." To which Micah replied: "Therefore, on account of you, Zion will be plowed as a field, Jerusalem will become a heap of ruins, And the mountain of the temple will become high places of a forest" (Micah 3:12).

One hundred years later Jeremiah also warned that Jerusalem would be destroyed (Jeremiah 7:12-15). Speaking for the Lord, Jeremiah declared, "I will make Jerusalem a heap of ruins, a haunt of jackals; and I will make the cities of Judah a desolation, without inhabitant" (Jeremiah 9:11).

When the people refused to believe his words and even sought to kill him as a traitor, Jeremiah reminded them of the previous prophecy of Micah (Jeremiah 26:18). But the people still refused to repent, and the prophecies were fulfilled in 587 BC when Nebuchadnezzar destroyed the city and its temple.

Gentile Jerusalem

After 70 years of captivity in Babylon, the Jews returned to Jerusalem and rebuilt their temple and their city. But they refused to receive their Messiah, and so they were given a second group of prophecies relating to a period of time when Jerusalem would fall under Gentile control.

Jesus Himself delivered these important prophecies during the last week of His life. As He was sitting on the Mount of Olives talking with His disciples, He pointed at Jerusalem and its temple and said: "As for these things which you are looking at, the days will come in which there will not be left one stone upon another which will not be torn down" (Luke 21:6).

Later, in the same discourse, Jesus stated that the city would be surrounded by armies which would proceed to desolate it (Luke 21:20). Referring to the Jews in the city at that time, He said, "they will fall by the edge of the sword, and will be led captive into all the nations . . ." (Luke 21:24a).

These prophecies were fulfilled 40 years later when the Romans, under Titus, completely destroyed the city, including the temple.

But notice, Jesus made another prophecy about the city in the same speech: He said, "Jerusalem will be trampled under foot by the Gentiles until the times of the Gentiles be fulfilled" (Luke 21: 24b). The Romans were followed by the Byzantines, and they were succeeded, in order, by the Muslims, the Crusaders, the Mamelukes, the Turks, the British, and the Jordanians.

Just as Jesus prophesied, the city suffered under a long period of Gentile control until June 7, 1967 when — for the first time in 1,897 years — the Jews regained sovereignty over the city. It was on that day that Rabbi Shlomo Goren went to the Western Wall and cried out: "I proclaim to you the beginning of the Messianic Age."

The third group of prophecies about the city explain why he said these words.

End Time Jerusalem

Four hundred years before Jesus, the prophet Zechariah gave a remarkable series of prophecies about the events that would affect Jerusalem in the end times, right before what we call the Second Coming of the Messiah. These prophecies are recorded in Zechariah 12:1-6. Specifically, the prophecies are as follows:

- The Jews will be back in the land of Israel.

- The Jews will be back in the city of Jerusalem.

- The Israeli army will be like a "firepot among pieces of wood."

- Jerusalem will become the focal point of world politics.

- All the nations of the world will come together against Jerusalem.

Please note that these are prophecies that have been fulfilled! The Jews are back in their land and their city. Despite the minuscule size of the nation, its military forces are considered to be among the most powerful in the world. They have truly been like a "flaming torch among sheaves" in war after war.

Israel became the focal point of world politics in 1973 during the Yom Kippur War. When the West came to the aid of Israel, the Arabs pulled an oil boycott (remember those long gas lines?), bringing the Western nations to their knees. The result was that all the nations of Western Europe withdrew their support from Israel and either took a neutral position or else lined up with the Arabs in their determination to annihilate the Jewish state.

Concerning the last prophecy cited above, in just the past few years, all the nations of the world, including the United States, have come against Israel, forcing her into a suicidal appeasement policy of trading land for peace.

Zechariah lists some other end time prophecies regarding Jerusalem that have not yet been fulfilled. These exciting prophecies are contained in Zechariah 12:8-10. They state that the Lord will defend Jerusalem against its enemies and that the result of all the end time battles will be the repentance of a great remnant of the Jews "who will look on Me whom they have pierced; and they will mourn for Him, as one mourns for an only son, and they will weep bitterly over Him, like the bitter weeping over a firstborn" (Zechariah 12:10). In response, the Lord will save this remnant by opening a fountain of salvation in Jerusalem "for sin and for impurity" (Zechariah 13:1).

In chapter 14, Zechariah describes in detail how the Lord will rescue Jerusalem at the last moment when there appears to be no hope: "Then the Lord will go forth and fight against those nations, as when He fights on a day of battle" (Zechariah 14:3). He will speak a supernatural plague that will kill all the enemy soldiers in their tracks (Zechariah 14:12). Verse 9 tells us that the outcome of this momentous day will be the coronation of Jesus as "king over all the earth."

This wonderful promise introduces us to the fourth category of prophecies that relate to Jerusalem.

Millennial Jerusalem

A glorious day is coming for Jerusalem, for when the Lord returns, He is going to reign over all the world for a thousand years, and His reign of peace, righteousness and justice will be based in Jerusalem: "For from Zion will go forth the law, even the word of the Lord from Jerusalem" (Isaiah 2:3 and Micah 4:2).

Jerusalem will be the political, economic and religious center of the world (Micah 4:1-7).

The city will be very different from the one we know today. The great worldwide earthquake that will occur when Jesus returns will radically change the earth's topography, including that of Jerusalem (Isaiah 40:4, Revelation 6:12 and Revelation 16:18). The Bible indicates that Jerusalem will be greatly expanded in area and will be lifted up higher, perhaps becoming the highest point on the earth (Zechariah 14:10).

The city will be considerably enlarged and greatly beautified, and the most magnificent temple in history will be built in the midst of it under the personal supervision of the Messiah. That temple is described in detail in chapters 40-48 of Ezekiel.

The glory of Jerusalem in those days is best summarized in Isaiah 62:1-7 where we are told that the city will be "a crown of beauty in the hand of the Lord" (verse 3). The prophet also says the city will be "a praise in the earth" (verse 7). For the first time in its long bloody history, it will be a refuge of peace (Joel 3:16-17 and Zephaniah 3:14-20).

It will also be the greatest wonder on the earth. Think about it — it will house the Prince of Peace and will contain His temple. It will also serve once more as the home of God's spectacular Shekinah glory. But that glory will not be contained within the Holy of Holies. Incredibly, Isaiah says that the Shekinah will hover over the whole city of Jerusalem as a cloud by day and a fire by night, providing a canopy to protect the city from heat and rain (Isaiah 4:5-6).

Zechariah says the nations of the world will send delegations to Jerusalem each year to celebrate the Feast of Tabernacles. And the last verse of Ezekiel says that in that day the Hebrew name of the city will be changed from Yerusaliam to Yahweh-shemmah, meaning "The Lord is there" (Ezekiel 48:35).

Eternal Jerusalem

Finally, the prophets tell us that the millennial Jerusalem will be replaced by a new Jerusalem which Jesus is preparing in Heaven now.

At the end of the Millennium, after the earth has been renovated by fire, the new Jerusalem will be lowered down to the new earth, and the Redeemed, in their new glorified bodies, will live in this new city in the presence of Almighty God, who will come down from Heaven to live forever with His children (Revelation 21:1-3).

This very clear teaching from the book of Revelation comes as a shock to a lot of Christians who have always been taught that they will live eternally in an ethereal world call Heaven.

What an amazing city this new Jerusalem will be! The apostle John devotes 24 verses to its detailed description in Revelation 21 and 22. It will be a 1,500 mile cube with 12 foundations made of precious stones — each one named for one of the 12 apostles. Likewise, there will be 12 pearly gates, one named for each tribe of Israel. The walls will be made of jasper. The city itself will be pure gold, like clear glass.

Have you ever stopped to think about the shape and size of this phenomenal city? For example, why will it be 1,500 miles high? The reason, most likely, is that in our glorified bodies, we will be immune to the laws of gravity. We will thus be able to utilize all the space of the city, and not just the ground floor.

And how much space will we have? Will there be enough for all the Redeemed? Henry Morris, founder of the Institute for Creation Research, has calculated the space that would exist for each person, assuming that at least 50% of the area would be used for common purposes (streets, parks, recreation centers, etc.) and assuming that 20 billion people have been saved in the course of human history. The result is astounding: each person would have a cube with 75 acres on each surface! That's certainly more space than most of us have now.

But the best part of this city will not be its beauty or its spaciousness. The best part will be the personal presence of Jesus our Lord and Almighty God, His Father. Revelation 22 says we will eternally serve God in this city and that we will "see His face." I think that means we will have intimate, personal fellowship with our Creator eternally. And that causes me to stand in awe.

The Message for Us

What does all this mean for you and me?

First, it means that God is faithful. Just as He has fulfilled prophecies about Jerusalem in the past and is doing so now, we can be confident that He will continue to do so in the future. There is going to be a millennial Jerusalem and there is going to be an eternal one, and we, the Redeemed, are going to be richly blessed by both beyond anything we can imagine.

Second, the record of Jerusalem in prophecy means that God is sovereign. He is in control. Even when everything seems to be out of control here on earth, we can be assured that God has the wisdom and power to orchestrate all the evil of Mankind to the triumph of His will in history.

Third, God is calling you and me to live with an eternal perspective. In Hebrews 11 we are told that Abraham lived by faith as "an alien" in this world, "looking for the city which has foundations, whose architect and builder is God" (Hebrews 11:9-10). Isn't that interesting? Abraham did not consider his arrival in the Promised Land to be the fulfillment of God's promises to him. Rather, he lived yearning for his ultimate reward, namely, life with God in an eternal city — the new Jerusalem.

In Hebrews 11:13 it says that *all* the heroes of the faith who are listed in that chapter lived their lives as "strangers and exiles on the earth" because they desired the city which God had prepared for them. The book of Hebrews concludes with a reminder to us that in this world we do not have a lasting city. Instead, we are to seek "the city which is to come" (Hebrews 13:14).

Jesus is adding rooms to that city right now to accommodate the members of His body (John 14:1-4). Let us therefore live as aliens and strangers in this world, never becoming comfortable with it. Let us live looking for the coming of the Lord (2 Timothy 4:7-8).

And let us live praying for the peace of Jerusalem (Psalm 122:6), realizing that in doing so we are really praying for the return of the Lord, for Jerusalem will never experience true peace until the Prince of Peace returns.

Is it destined for the Tribulation or Heaven?

One of the hottest debates in prophecy today revolves around the question of whether or not the Church will go through the Tribulation or be taken to Heaven before it begins in an event called the Rapture.

The concept that the Church will be taken out of the world before the Tribulation begins is called the "pre-Tribulation Rapture." It is a comforting thought, but is it biblical?

The Term

Before we consider the timing of the Rapture, let's make sure you understand the concept of the Rapture. This is essential because I happen to know that many people have gone to church all their lives and have never even heard of the Rapture. That was certainly true in my case. After my first thirty years of church attendance, if you had asked me to define the Rapture, I probably would have said, "It's a sensation you feel when your girlfriend kisses you."

I have often heard preachers assert that the Rapture is an unbiblical concept because the word cannot be found in the Bible. Well, that depends upon what Bible you are reading.

The only Bible used by Western civilization for 1,200 years was the Latin Vulgate. The term, Rapture, is derived from the Latin word, *rapiere*, which appears in this Bible. The word means to catch up, to snatch away, or to take out.

The word can be found in 1 Thessalonians 4:17. In the New American Standard Version, the English phrase, "caught up," is used. The same phrase is used in the King James and New International versions.

A Promise to the Church

The concept of the Rapture was not revealed to the Old Testament prophets because it is a promise to the New Testament Church and not to the saints of God who lived before the establishment of the Church.

The saints of Old Testament times will be resurrected at the end of the Tribulation and not at the time of the Rapture of the Church. Daniel reveals this fact in Daniel 12:1-2 where he says that the saints of that age will be resurrected at the end of the "time of distress."

Biblical References

The first clear mention of the Rapture in Scripture is found in the words of Jesus recorded in John 14:1-4. Jesus said, "I will come again, and receive you to Myself; that where I am, there you may be also." Notice that there is no mention here of Jesus coming to earth. He is not talking about His Second Coming.

The most detailed revelation of the actual events related to the Rapture is given by Paul in 1 Thessalonians 4:13-18. He says that when Jesus appears, the dead in Christ (Church age saints) will be resurrected and caught up to meet the Lord in the sky. Then, those of us who are alive in Christ will follow. We will also meet the Lord in the air and be taken back with Him to Heaven. Paul then exhorts us to "comfort one another with these words."

Paul mentions the Rapture again in 1 Corinthians 15 — his famous chapter on the resurrection of the dead:

> "Behold, I tell you a mystery; we shall not all sleep, but we shall be changed, in a moment, in the twinkling of an eye, at the last trumpet." (verses 51 and 52)

Paul's reference here to being changed is an allusion to the fact that the saints will receive glorified bodies that will be perfected, imperishable and immortal (1 Corinthians 15:42-44, 50-55). This promise applies to both the living and dead in Christ at the time of the Rapture. The dead will be resurrected; the living will be translated from mortal to immortal. That means the generation of Christians who are living at the time of the Rapture will not experience death.

The Timing

The most controversial aspect of the Rapture is its timing. Some place it at the end of the Tribulation, making it one and the same event as the Second Coming. Others place it in the middle of the Tribulation. Still others believe that it will occur before the Tribulation begins.

The reason for these differing viewpoints is that the exact time of the Rapture is not precisely revealed in Scripture. It is only implied. There is, therefore, room for honest differences of opinion, and lines of fellowship should certainly not be drawn over differences regarding this point, even though it is an important point.

Post-Tribulation Rapture

Those who place the timing at the end of the Tribulation usually base their argument on two parables in Matthew 13 and on the Lord's Olivet Discourse in Matthew 24.

In Matthew 24 the Lord portrays His gathering of the saints as an event that will take place "immediately after the tribulation of those days" (Matthew 24:29). This certainly sounds like a post-Tribulation Rapture. But it must be kept in mind that the book of Matthew was written to the Jews, and therefore the recording of Jesus' speech by Matthew has a distinctively Jewish flavor to it as compared to Luke's record of the same speech.

Note, for example, Matthew's references to Judea and to Jewish law regarding travel on the Sabbath (Matthew 24:15-20). These are omitted in Luke's account. Instead, Luke speaks of the saints looking up for deliverance "to escape all these things" when the end time signs "begin to take place" (Luke 21:28, 36). The saints in Matthew are instructed to flee from Judea and hide. The saints in Luke are told to look up for deliverance.

It appears, therefore, that Matthew and Luke are speaking of two different sets of saints. The saints in Matthew's account are Jews who receive Jesus as their Messiah during the Tribulation. The saints in Luke are those who receive Christ before the Tribulation begins. Most of those who accept the Lord during the Tribulation will be martyred (Revelation 7:9-14). Those who live to the end will be gathered by the angels of the Lord (Matthew 24:31).

The parable of the wheat and tares (Matthew 13:24-30) and the parable of the dragnet (Matthew 13:47-50) can be explained in the same way. They refer to a separation of saints and sinners that will take place at the end of the Tribulation. The saints are those who receive Jesus as their Savior during the Tribulation (Gentile and Jew) and who live to the end of that awful period.

Mid-Tribulation Rapture

There are variations of the mid-Tribulation Rapture concept. The most common is that the Church will be taken out in the exact middle of the Tribulation, at the point in time when the Antichrist is revealed.

This concept is based upon a statement in 1 Corinthians 15:52 which says that the Rapture will occur at the blowing of "the last trumpet." Mid-Tribulation supporters then identify this trumpet with the seventh trumpet of the trumpet judgments in the book of Revelation. Since the blowing of the seventh trumpet is recorded in Revelation 11, the mid-point of the Tribulation, the conclusion is that the Rapture must occur in the middle of the Tribulation.

But there are two problems with this interpretation. The first is that the last trumpet of 1 Corinthians 15 is blown for believers whereas the seven trumpets of Revelation 8, 9 and 11 are sounded for unbelievers. The Revelation trumpets have no relevance for the Church. The last trumpet of 1 Corinthians 15 is a trumpet for the righteous. The last trumpet for the unrighteous is the one described in Revelation 11.

Another problem with this interpretation is that the passage in Revelation 11 that portrays the sounding of the seventh trumpet is a "flash forward" to the end of the Tribulation. Flash forwards are very common in the book of Revelation. They occur after something terrible is described in order to assure the reader that everything is going to turn out all right when Jesus returns at the end of the Tribulation.

Thus, the eighth and ninth chapters of Revelation, which describe the horrors of the trumpet judgments, are followed immediately by a flash forward in chapter 10 that pictures the return of Jesus in victory at the end of the Tribulation. The mid-Tribulation action resumes in chapter 11 with a description of the killing of the two great prophets of God by the Antichrist. Then, to offset that terrible event, we are presented with another flash forward, beginning with verse 15. The seventh trumpet is sounded and we find ourselves propelled forward to the end of the Tribulation when "the kingdom of the world becomes the kingdom of our Lord."

The point is that the seventh trumpet of Revelation relates to the end of the Tribulation and not the middle. It is therefore no basis for an argument in behalf of a mid-Tribulation Rapture.

Pre-Wrath Rapture

A variation of the mid-Tribulation Rapture is the pre-wrath Rapture concept that places the Rapture at the beginning of the last quarter of the Tribulation, about 5½ years into the Tribulation.

The cornerstone of this concept is that the terrifying events during the first half of the Tribulation are due to the wrath of Man and Satan, and not to God. Since the Church is only promised protection from the wrath of God, the Rapture will not occur until near the end of the Tribulation when God will pour out His wrath on the world.

This concept raises a serious theological problem because it questions the sovereignty of God. It assumes that Man and Satan can act apart from God's will, when the fact of the matter is that neither can do anything God is not willing to permit. The Bible often portrays God carrying out His will through evil persons or nations. One of the classic examples is when He allowed the evil nation of Babylon to discipline Israel by destroying Jerusalem and the temple and by carrying the surviving Jews away into captivity. It was an action that prompted the prophet Habakkuk to ask why God would punish those who are evil with those who are more evil (Habakkuk 1:13).

Any carnage wrought by Man or Satan during the Tribulation will still constitute the wrath of God. They will simply be His instruments. The Bible says God sits in the heavens and laughs over the plots and deeds of evil men, not because He does not care, but because He has everything under control (Psalm 2:1-6). The point is that He has the wisdom and power to orchestrate all evil to the triumph of His will in history. That's why the psalmist wrote that "the wrath of man shall praise You [God]" (Psalm 76:10).

I think it is also important to note that when God pours out His wrath, He does not always do so directly. One of His most common ways is to simply back away from the nation or person and lower the hedge of protection around them. This is clearly spelled out in Romans 1:18-32. That passage says that when people rebel against God to the point that they begin to worship the creation rather than the Creator, God "gives them over" to the evil in their hearts. In other words, He just steps back and lets evil multiply. The passage further states that if they still refuse to repent, He steps back again and "gives them over to degrading passions." And if they persist in their rebellion and sin, He finally "gives them over to a depraved mind" at which point the society destroys itself. Such destruction could be viewed as the wrath of Man, but it is really the wrath of God working through Man.

Other Problems with Pre-Wrath

There is another serious problem with the pre-wrath Rapture concept. It relates to the fact that all the wrath of Revelation is specifically portrayed as the wrath of God. Where do the seal judgments originate? The answer is from the throne of God as Jesus opens each seal of the scroll that was in the Father's right hand (Revelation 6:1). And where do the trumpet judgments originate? The same place — from the throne of God (Revelation 8:2). When we arrive at the bowl judgments in Revelation 15:1, we are told that with them, "the wrath of God is finished."

Another problem with the pre-wrath concept is that it does violence to the chronological order of Revelation. The seal judgments are viewed as the wrath of Man and Satan, occurring during the first half of the Tribulation. The trumpet and bowl judgments are considered to be the wrath of God. They are lumped together at the end of the Tribulation. There is no justification for putting the trumpet judgments at the end of the Tribulation. They are clearly placed in the first half of the Tribulation in the chronological layout of the book of Revelation.

One final problem with the pre-wrath concept of the Rapture is that it disputes the fact that there is no purpose for the Church being in the Tribulation. The Tribulation is the 70th week of Daniel, a time devoted to God accomplishing His purposes among the Jewish people, not the Church.

The Pre-Tribulation Rapture

I believe the best inference of Scripture is that the Rapture will occur at the beginning of the Tribulation. The most important reason I believe this has to do with the issue of imminence. Over and over in Scripture we are told to watch for the appearing of the Lord. We are told to "be ready" (Matthew 24:44), to "be on the alert" (Matthew 24:42), to "be dressed in readiness" (Luke 12:35), and to "keep your lamps alight" (Luke 12:35). The clear force of these persistent warnings is that Jesus can appear at any moment.

Only the pre-Tribulation concept of the Rapture allows for the imminence of the Lord's appearing for His Church. When the Rapture is placed at any other point in time, the imminence of the Lord's appearing is destroyed because other prophetic events must happen first.

For example, if the Rapture is going to occur in mid-Tribulation, then why should I live looking for the Lord's appearing at any moment? I would be looking instead for an Israeli peace treaty, the rebuilding of the temple, and the revelation of the Antichrist. Then and only then could the Lord appear. (For further arguments in behalf of a Pre-Trib Rapture, see chapter 26.)

The Focus of Attention

This raises the issue of what we are to be looking for. Nowhere are believers told to watch for the appearance of the Antichrist. On the contrary, we are told to watch for Jesus Christ. In Titus 2:13 Paul says we are to live "looking for the blessed hope and the appearing of the glory of our great God and Savior, Christ Jesus." Likewise, Peter urges us to "fix your hope completely on the grace to be brought to you at the revelation of Jesus Christ" (1 Peter 1:13). John completes the apostolic chorus by similarly urging us to fix our hope on Jesus at His appearing (1 John 3:2-3).

Only Matthew speaks of watching for the Antichrist (Matthew 24:15), but he is speaking to the Jews living in Israel in the middle of the Tribulation when the Antichrist desecrates the rebuilt temple.

The Promise of Deliverance

Another argument in behalf of a pre-Tribulation Rapture has to do with the promises of God to protect the Church from His wrath. As has already been demonstrated, the book of Revelation shows that the wrath of God will be poured out during the entire period of the Tribulation.

The Word promises over and over that the Church will be delivered from God's wrath. Romans 5:9 says that "we shall be saved from the wrath of God through Him [Jesus]." First Thessalonians 1:10 states that we are waiting "for His Son from heaven . . . who delivers us from the wrath to come." The promise is repeated in 1 Thessalonians 5:9 — "God has not destined us for wrath, but for obtaining salvation through our Lord Jesus Christ."

Supernatural Protection?

Some argue that God could supernaturally protect the Church during the Tribulation. Yes, He could. In fact, He promises to do just that for the 144,000 Jews who will be sealed as bond-servants at the beginning of the Tribulation (Revelation 7:1-8).

But God's promise to the Church during the Tribulation is not one of protection but one of deliverance. Jesus said we would "escape" the horrors of the Tribulation (Luke 21:36). Paul says Jesus is coming to "deliver" us from God's wrath (1 Thessalonians 1:10). Likewise, Peter says that if God could rescue righteous Lot from Sodom and Gomorrah, then He "knows how to rescue the godly from trials" (2 Peter 2:6-9).

Escapism?

The pre-Tribulation concept of the Rapture has often been condemned as "escapism." I think this criticism is unjustified. Again, Jesus Himself, told us to pray that we might escape the Tribulation (Luke 21:36).

The Bible itself says that Christians are to "comfort one another" with the concept of the Rapture (1 Thessalonians 4:18). Is it a comfort to think of the Rapture occurring at the end of the world's worst period of war instead of at the beginning?

Regardless of when the Rapture actually occurs, we need to keep in mind that the Bible teaches that societal conditions are going to grow increasingly worse the closer we get to the Lord's return. That means Christians will suffer tribulation whether or not they go into the Great Tribulation. And that means all of us had better be preparing ourselves for unprecedented suffering and spiritual warfare.

If you are a Christian, you can do that on a daily basis by putting on "the full armor of God" (Ephesians 6:13), praying at all times in the Spirit that you will be able to stand firm against the attacks of Satan (Ephesians 6:14-18).

If you are not a Christian, your only hope is to reach out in faith and receive the free gift of God's salvation which He has provided through His Son, Jesus (John 3:16).

Will it be destroyed or is it eternal?

Did you know we are living on earth number three? Did you know the Bible reveals that there are two earths yet to come? Did you know the Bible teaches that the earth is eternal?

Earth I

The first earth was the one created in the beginning (Genesis 1:1). It was perfect in every respect (Genesis 1:31). But because of Man's sin, God placed a curse upon the earth (Genesis 3:17-19).

The Bible indicates that this curse radically altered the nature of God's original creation. Instead of Man exercising dominion over nature, as originally planned (Genesis 1:26, 28), nature rose up in conflict with Man, as poisonous plants, carnivorous animals and climatic cataclysms (like tornados) suddenly appeared.

Earth II

The curse radically altered the original earth, but Earth II was still quite different from the one we live on today. There is much biblical evidence in both Genesis and Job that the second earth had a thick vapor canopy which shielded life from the ultraviolet radiation of the sun, producing the long life spans recorded in Genesis (see Genesis 2:5-6 and Job 38:8-11).

The whole earth was like a greenhouse with thick vegetation growing everywhere, even at the poles. There was also probably only one large land mass.

Once again the sinful rebellion of Mankind motivated God to change the nature of the earth (Genesis 6:11-13). The change agent this time was water. It appears that God caused the vapor canopy to collapse (Genesis 7:11). He also caused "fountains of the great deep" to break forth upon the surface of the earth (Genesis 7:11).

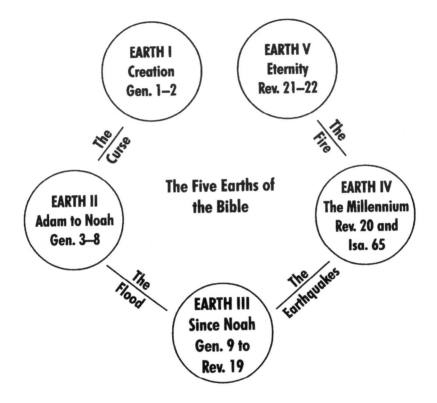

Earth III

Like the curse, the flood radically altered the nature of the earth. It produced Earth III, the earth we now live on.

The earth tilted on its axis, forming the polar caps. The unified land mass was split apart, forming the continents as we now know them (which is why they fit together like a jigsaw puzzle — see Genesis 10:25). And the vapor canopy was so completely depleted that ultraviolet radiation began to reach the earth in unprecedented levels, resulting in greatly reduced life spans, first to 120 years and then to 70 years.

The Bible reveals that the current earth, Earth III, will be radically changed again at the Second Advent of Jesus. The change agents will be earthquakes on the earth and supernatural phenomena in the heavens.

The changes produced will so totally alter the earth and its atmosphere that Isaiah refers to "the new heavens and the new earth" which will exist during the reign of the Lord (Isaiah 65:17).

Earth IV

Earth IV — The millennial earth — will be very different from the present earth. The earthquakes that will produce it will be the most severe in history.

Every valley will be lifted, every mountain will be lowered, and every island will be moved (Revelation 6:12-14 and 16:17-21). Jerusalem will be lifted up, and Mt. Zion will become the highest of all the mountains (Zechariah 14:10 and Micah 4:1).

The vapor canopy will likely be restored because life spans will be expanded to what they were at the beginning of time (Isaiah 65:20, 22).

Further evidence that the vapor canopy will be restored is to be found in the fact that all the earth will become abundant once again with lush vegetation (Isaiah 30:23-26 and Amos 9:13-14). The Dead Sea will also become alive (Ezekiel 47:1-9).

Most important, the curse will be partially lifted, making it possible for Man to be reconciled to nature and for nature to be reconciled to itself. The wolf will dwell with the lamb because the wolf will no longer be carnivorous. The nursing child will play with the cobra because the cobra will no longer be poisonous (Isaiah 11:8).

Earth V

But Satan's last revolt at the end of the Millennium will leave the earth polluted and devastated (Revelation 20:7-9). Thus, at the end of the Lord's reign, God will take the Redeemed off the earth, place them in the New Jerusalem, and then cleanse the earth with fire (2 Peter 3:10-13).

In other words, God will superheat this earth in a fiery inferno and then reshape it like a hot ball of wax. The result will be the "new heavens and new earth" prophesied in Isaiah 66 and Revelation 21.

This will be Earth V, the perfected, eternal earth where the Redeemed will spend eternity in the new Jerusalem in the presence of God (Revelation 21:1-4). The curse will be completely lifted from this earth (Revelation 22:3).

Some argue that the new earth will be totally new, and not a renovation of the current earth. But the Bible teaches that the present earth is eternal: "Generations come and generations go, but the earth remains forever" (Ecclesiastes 1:4; see also Psalm 78:69 and Psalm 148:6).

It is true that 2 Peter 3:10 says the current earth will be "destroyed with intense heat," but the same context says that the earth of Noah's time was "destroyed" by water (2 Peter 3:5-6). Noah's earth did not cease to exist, rather, it was "destroyed" in the sense that it was radically changed.

Restoration in the Old Testament

God loves His creation, and He is determined to restore it to its original perfection.

This purpose of God was reflected in the rites of the Tabernacle of Moses. Each year when the High Priest entered the Holy of Holies to make atonement for the sins of the nation, he would sprinkle blood on the Mercy Seat of the Ark — and also on the ground in front of the Ark (Leviticus 16:15).

The blood on the Mercy Seat pointed to the promise of God that one day He would send a Messiah who would shed His blood so that the mercy of God could cover the Law and make it possible for us to be reconciled to our Creator. The blood on the ground pointed to the promise of God that the sacrifice of the Messiah would also make it possible for the creation to be redeemed.

In the Old Testament, Isaiah 11 gives us a beautiful picture of the redeemed creation during the Millennium. We are told that the meat eating animals will cease to prey on each other and "will eat straw like the ox." The poisonous animals will also be transformed.

They will cease to be dangerous (Isaiah 11:6-9; 35:9).

The plant kingdom will similarly be transformed back to its original perfection before the curse. The result will be incredible agricultural abundance (Amos 9:13):

> "Behold, days are coming," declares the Lord,
> "When the plowman will overtake the reaper
>   And the treader of grapes him who sows seed;
>   When the mountains will drip sweet wine . . ."

The prophet Joel adds that "the threshing floors will be full of grain, and the vats will overflow with the new wine and oil" (Joel 2:24).

The implication of these passages is that Man will no longer have to strive against nature because weeds and poisonous plants will cease to exist and rainfall will be abundant.

In fact, Isaiah tells us that areas of wilderness will be transformed into glorious forests (Isaiah 35:2) and deserts will become "springs of water" (Isaiah 35:7).

Restoration in the New Testament

The promise of a redeemed and restored creation is reaffirmed in the New Testament.

Peter referred to the promise in his second sermon at the temple in Jerusalem. He told his audience that Jesus would remain in Heaven until the time comes for the "restoration of all things" (Acts 3:21).

Paul elaborates the theme in Romans 8:8-18. He declares that the whole creation is in "slavery to corruption" (verse 21). This is a reference to what physicists call the Second Law of Thermodynamics; namely, that all of creation is running down, moving from order to disorder — that all of creation is in bondage to decay.

Paul then pictures the creation as a pregnant woman waiting anxiously for the moment of delivery when the curse will be lifted and the creation will be redeemed. He says that will occur at "the revealing of the sons of God" (verse 19).

That is a reference to the resurrection of the saints, a point he makes clear in verse 23 when he says that the saints should yearn with nature for that same event because that is when we will receive "the redemption of our body."

The Eternal Earth

The Old Testament has little to say about the eternal earth which God will create at the end of the Millennium. Isaiah simply asserts that such an earth will be provided (Isaiah 66:22). Isaiah's only other reference to a "new earth," in Isaiah 65:17, is a reference to the renovated earth of the Millennium.

In Revelation 21 the apostle John gives us the most detailed look at what the new, eternal earth will be like. And yet, his description is tantalizingly vague. He makes a cryptic reference to the fact that there will no longer be any sea (Revelation 21:1). Beyond that, all he tells us is that God will make "all things new" (Revelation 21:5).

Some believe the reference to the sea is symbolic since that word is often used in prophecy to refer to the Gentile nations (see Luke 21:25 and Revelation 13:1). They thus interpret this statement about the sea to mean that the nations will no longer be divided between and against each other.

Others interpret the reference literally and argue that it is a clue that there will be one land mass on the new earth and that the seas will no longer separate peoples of the world as they do today.

The description of the New Jerusalem in Revelation 21 infers that the eternal earth will be much larger than the current earth. This inference is drawn from the fact that the New Jerusalem will be shaped as a fifteen hundred mile cube. Such a structure would be completely out of proportion to the size of the current earth.

A Glorious Blessing

I think the reason the passages about the eternal earth tell us so little about the features of that earth is because they focus on one glorious fact that overshadows any concern with what the new earth will be like. That fact is that the Redeemed will live in the presence of Almighty God (Revelation 21 and 22). We will "serve Him" and we will "see His face" (Revelation 22:3-4). What the earth will be like pales in comparison to this revelation.

Are you an heir of this wonderful promise? The Bible says that "he who overcomes shall inherit these things" (Revelation 21:7).

Are you an overcomer? The Bible defines an overcomer in 1 John 5:1-5 as any person "who believes that Jesus is the Son of God." Such a person is portrayed as being "born of God."

A Warning

As we await the Lord's return, we are to be good caretakers of the earth God has given us. We are to be concerned about all aspects of ecology — both plant and animal life.

But we are to keep that concern in check. We are not to become worshipers of the creation rather than the Creator (Romans 1:25). "Mother Earth" is not God.

Our focus must be on the Creator, our Father God. His creation has been polluted by our sins (Isaiah 24:5). Let us yearn for that day when His Son will return and the creation will be restored to its original perfection (Acts 3:21).

The Wrath of God 17

Is it a myth or a reality?

Several years ago, a popular radio talk show host on an Oklahoma City secular station interviewed me live on the air via telephone. He had seen some articles I had written, and he had liked them.

He began the interview by graciously giving me the opportunity to talk non-stop for about ten minutes about the way God had transformed my life and called me into the ministry. He then asked me to summarize the purpose of my ministry.

The Unmentionable Word

I responded by saying that the purpose of Lamb & Lion Ministries was to proclaim the soon return of Jesus. I then pointed out that this message cuts two ways. For the believer, it is a call to holiness. For unbelievers, it is a call to flee from the wrath that is to come by fleeing into the loving arms of Jesus.

At that point, the radio host cut me short. "What do you mean, 'wrath'?" he asked.

"I mean that Jesus is going to return very soon to pour out the wrath of God upon those who have rejected God's love and grace and mercy."

"Your God is a monster God!" he snapped. He then added, "I happen to be a Christian, and I can tell you that my God wouldn't hurt a flea!"

That was the end of the interview. He hung up on me. I was not given an opportunity to respond to his misrepresentation of God.

Satan's Grand Deception

The radio host's vehement response to the wrath of God did not surprise me. It is characteristic of both Christians and non-Christians, and I have encountered it many times.

Satan has sold the world a bill of goods concerning the nature of God. Most people, both Christian and non-Christian, tend to view God as being a sort of cosmic teddy bear.

They see Him as big and warm and soft, full of infinite love and forgiveness. He couldn't hurt a fly, and He certainly wouldn't be so cruel as to condemn or harm any beings created in His own image. On the Day of Judgment, God will simply give everyone a big hug and wink at their sins.

The only problem with this wonderfully comforting image is that it is a lie straight from the pit of Hell.

The True God

Yes, the Bible teaches that God is loving, patient, caring, and forgiving (Psalms 86:15 and John 3:16). As the apostle John put it, "God is love" (1 John 4:8).

Two of my favorite passages in the Bible emphasize the personal loving nature of God. One was penned by the apostle Peter. In 1 Peter 5:6-7 he says that we are to cast all our anxieties upon God "because He cares for you." That is a very comforting thought.

The other passage that I love to read over and over consists of words spoken by the prophet Jeremiah in Lamentations 3:22-24 (RSV):

22) The steadfast love of the Lord never ceases,
His mercies never come to an end;

23) They are new every morning;
Great is Thy faithfulness.

24) "The Lord is my portion," says my soul,
"Therefore I will hope in Him."

Yes, our Creator is a God of love, but the Bible also clearly teaches that there is another aspect of God's character that is equally important. It is the aspect that Satan wants us to ignore, and he has been very successful in prompting ministers to overlook it. After all, it doesn't produce popular sermons! I'm speaking, of course, of the holiness of God (Leviticus 11:44; Isaiah 6:3; and 1 Peter 1:16).

Grace or Wrath?

The Bible teaches that God is perfectly holy. Because of this attribute of His character, He cannot tolerate sin (Numbers 14:18). The Bible says God must deal with sin, and He does so in one of two ways — either grace or wrath.

Every person on the face of this earth is at this moment under either the grace of God or the wrath of God. John the Baptist made this point in one of his sermons when he said: "He who believes in the Son has eternal life; but he who does not obey the Son shall not see life, but the wrath of God abides on him" (John 3:36).

It's amazing how all Christians seem to know John 3:16. But almost none seem to be aware of John 3:36. It shows how little preaching has been done on the wrath of God.

Like John the Baptist, the apostle Paul emphasized God's wrath in his preaching and teaching. In Ephesians 5 he warned against immorality, covetousness, and idolatry, and then he added this observation: "Let no one deceive you with empty words, for because of these things, the wrath of God comes upon the sons of disobedience" (Ephesians 5:6).

We come under God's grace by placing our faith in Jesus and appropriating His atoning sacrifice for our lives (1 John 1:7). There is no salvation apart from Jesus (Acts 4:10-12). Those who have rejected God's free gift of grace in Jesus are under God's wrath (John 3:36), and they have no one to blame but themselves.

The Coming Wrath

God's wrath will fall when Jesus returns (Jude 14-15). The passage in Revelation which pictures the return of Jesus says that He will return in righteousness to "judge and wage war" (Revelation

19:11).

The first time Jesus came, He came in loving compassion with eyes filled with tears. But when He returns, He will come in vengeance (Revelation 6:12-17), with eyes like a flame of fire (Revelation 19:12). He will come to destroy the enemies of God (Revelation 19:11).

The presidents and kings and prime ministers of the world will crawl into holes in the ground and cry out for the rocks and mountains to fall upon them, so great will be the terror of the Lord (Revelation 6:15-17). The unrighteous will stumble about like blind men, and their blood will be poured out like dust (Zephaniah 1:17).

The Meaning of Wrath

Does this make God a "monster"? No! On the contrary, it proves His goodness, for how could a good God ignore the evil of sin and allow it to go unpunished? His wrath against evil will demonstrate His righteousness.

The prophet Nahum summed it up best. Writing of the love of God, he said, "The Lord is good, a stronghold in the day of trouble, and He knows those who take refuge in Him" (Nahum 1:7). But a few verses earlier Nahum had also spoken of the holiness of God (Nahum 1:2-3):

> 2) The Lord is avenging and wrathful.
> The Lord takes vengeance on His adversaries,
> And He reserves wrath for His enemies.

> 3) The Lord is slow to anger and great in power,
> And the Lord will by no means leave
> the guilty unpunished.

God's wrath is never motivated primarily by a desire to punish. Rather, it is designed to bring people to repentance so that they might be saved. Isaiah put it this way: "When the earth experiences Your judgments, the inhabitants of the world learn righteousness" (Isaiah 26:9). Even in His wrath, God remembers mercy.

God demonstrates His mercy in wrath by never pouring out His wrath without warning. He tried to warn Sodom and Gomorrah through Abraham. He warned Noah's world through the preaching of Noah for 120 years. He sent both Jonah and Nahum to warn the pagan city of Ninevah.

Consider too how He sent prophet after prophet to call the nations of Israel and Judah to repentance (2 Chronicles 36:15-16):

> 15) And the Lord, the God of their fathers, sent word to them again and again by His messengers, because He had compassion on His people and on His dwelling place;

> 16) but they continually mocked the messengers of God, despised His words and scoffed at His prophets, until the wrath of the Lord arose against His people, until there was no remedy.

God's mercy in wrath is also manifested in the fact that He always leads up to His final outpouring of wrath through a series of progressive judgments. These judgments are outlined in detail in Deuteronomy 28:15-57.

Wrath During the Tribulation

This characteristic of God's wrath is demonstrated in the prophecies concerning the Tribulation. Rather than simply pouring out His wrath on the rebellious nations of the world, destroying them in one instant of overwhelming catastrophe, He subjects the world to a series of judgments that sequentially increase in scope and intensity (Revelation, chapters 6, 8-9, and 16).

Although most people will refuse to repent in response to these judgments (Revelation 9:20-21), there will be "a great multitude, which no one could count, from every nation and all tribes and peoples and tongues" who will repent and respond to Jesus in faith (Revelation 7:9).

These radically different responses to the wrath of God illustrate the point that is often made by Billy Graham: "The same sun that melts the butter also hardens the clay." The wrath of God melts some hearts in repentance, but it has the effect of hardening the hearts of many others.

Wrath and the Redeemed

Many Christians respond negatively to Bible prophecy. It's not at all unusual to hear a Christian say something like this: "I don't want to hear anything about prophecy because it's too full of gloom and doom."

Well, there is a lot of gloom and doom for those who refuse to respond to God's gift of love in Jesus. But there is only good news for the Redeemed.

The Old Testament ends with a passage that presents both the gloom and the joy of end time prophecy. Malachi says that when the Lord returns, the day will be "like a furnace; and all the arrogant and every evildoer will be chaff" (Malachi 4:1). That's the bad news.

But consider the good news: "But for you who fear My name, the sun of righteousness will rise with healing in its wings; and you will go forth and skip about like calves from the stall" (Malachi 4:2).

There is no reason for any child of God to fear the wrath of God. Paul wrote that since we have been justified by the blood of Christ, "we shall be saved from the wrath of God through Him" (Romans 5:9). And in a most comforting verse, Paul told the Thessalonians that Jesus will "deliver" the Redeemed "from the wrath to come" (1 Thessalonians 1:10). The reason, Paul explained, is that "God has not destined us for wrath, but for obtaining salvation through our Lord Jesus Christ" (1 Thessalonians 5:9).

A Plea

Are you under grace or wrath? The choice is yours. Jesus is coming soon. When He appears, will He be your Blessed Hope or your Holy Terror? Will you cry for the mountains to fall upon you? Or, will you go forth leaping with joy like a calf released from a stall?

God loves you and He wants you to accept His Son as your Savior so that you will come under grace and can participate in an event described in Isaiah 35:10 —

And the ransomed of the Lord will return,
And come with joyful shouting to Zion,
With everlasting joy upon their heads.
They will find gladness and joy,
And sorrow and sighing will flee away.

This passage will be fulfilled during the millennial reign of Jesus when the earth will be flooded with peace, righteousness, and justice. Will you be there to experience it? The choice is yours.

What will be his origin and fate?

The Bible teaches that in the end times, right before the return of Jesus, the greatest political leader in the history of Mankind will emerge from Europe. After taking over that area by diplomatic cunning and deceit, he will launch a military campaign that will result in his acquiring "authority over every tribe and people and tongue and nation" (Revelation 13:7). His empire will be the most extensive in all of history, encompassing the entire world, and his rule will be the most demonic the world has ever experienced.

He will begin his rise to power as a dynamic, charismatic, insightful, visionary leader who will astound the world with the cleverness of his solutions to world problems. He will appear to be the savior of the world. But as he consolidates his power, his true nature will be revealed. He will emerge as a Satan-possessed and empowered person who hates God and is determined to annihilate both Christianity and Judaism. For this reason, he is identified in Scripture as the Antichrist (1 John 2:18), for he will stand against God and His anointed one, Jesus Christ.

His Origin

Where will this sinister person come from? Some have speculated that he will come out of Syria since one of his prophetic types in history — Antiochus Epiphanes (215-164 BC) — was a Syrian tyrant. But Antiochus was actually of Greek heritage.

It is much more likely that he will rise out of the heartland of the old Roman Empire and that he will be of Italian descent. This conclusion is based upon a statement in Daniel 9:26. In that passage the

Antichrist is referred to as "the prince who is to come," and he is identified as being from the people who "will destroy the city and the sanctuary."

We know from history that both Jerusalem and the Jewish Temple were destroyed by the Romans in 70 AD. Therefore, according to Daniel, the Antichrist must be of Roman heritage.

Jew or Gentile?

Will he be a Jew? Many assume he will be because Jesus said, "I have come in My Father's name, and you do not receive Me; if another shall come in his own name, you will receive him" (John 5: 43). Based on this statement, people ask, "How could the Jews possibly receive a Gentile as their Messiah?"

But the Bible does not teach that the Jews will receive the Antichrist as their Messiah. It teaches they will accept him as a great political leader and diplomat and that they will put their trust in him as the guarantor of peace in the Middle East.

But the moment he reveals himself as the Antichrist by desecrating the Jew's rebuilt temple and blaspheming God, the Jewish people will revolt. They will reject him as Messiah, and he will respond in fury by attempting to annihilate them.

The Antichrist does not have to be a Jew. And, in fact, the Bible makes it clear that he will be a Gentile. In Revelation 13:1 he is portrayed as a "beast coming up out of the sea." The sea is used consistently throughout the prophetic scriptures as a symbol of the Gentile nations (Daniel 7:3; Luke 21:25; and Revelation 17:1).

By contrast, the Antichrist's right hand man, the False Prophet, who will serve as his religious leader, will be a Jew. This is revealed in Revelation 13:11 where it says that John saw "another beast coming up out of the earth [literally, the land]." Just as the sea is used symbolically in prophecy to refer to the Gentile nations, the land (or earth) is used to refer to Israel. This does not mean the False Prophet will be an Orthodox Jew. It only means that he will be of Jewish heritage. Religiously, he will be an apostate Jew who will head up the One World Religion of the Antichrist.

Resurrected from the Dead?

There is one other issue concerning the origin of the Antichrist that we need to consider. Many argue that he will be a person resurrected from the dead — most likely Nero or Judas Iscariot. This assumption is based on a statement in Revelation 13:1-3 where John describes the Antichrist as a beast with seven heads. He then makes the observation that one of his heads appeared "as if it had been slain, and his fatal wound was healed." He comments that "the whole earth was amazed" by this and therefore "followed after the beast" (Revelation 13:3).

The problem with this interpretation is that "the fatal wound" referred to in the passage has nothing to do with the person of the Antichrist. The seven heads represent seven Gentile empires — namely, Egypt, Assyria, Babylon, Medo-Persia, Greece, Rome, and the final empire of the Antichrist. The head with the fatal wound that has been healed is the Roman Empire. We know this from the book of Daniel where it is prophesied that the Roman Empire will be the last of the Gentile empires until the end times when the empire of the Antichrist will emerge from a reunited Europe — that is, from a revival of the old Roman Empire (Daniel 2:31-45 and 7:1-8, 24-28).

Another passage that is used to justify the idea of the Antichrist being a resurrected person is Zechariah 11:17 —

> Woe to the worthless shepherd
> Who leaves the flock!
> A sword will be on his arm
> And on his right eye!
> His arm will be totally withered,
> And his right eye will be blind.

It is argued that this passage indicates that the Antichrist will be a person who has suffered a fatal wound. Now, there is no doubt this passage refers to the Antichrist, but I believe it is talking about his fate rather than his origin. Using symbolic language, it seems to me the prophet is saying that divine judgment (the sword) will fall upon the Antichrist's power (his arm) and his intelligence (his eye), and that he will suffer complete defeat (the withering of his arm and the blinding of his eye).

The idea that the Antichrist will be a resurrected person raises a serious theological problem concerning the power of Satan. The Scriptures make it clear that the Antichrist will be Satan's man, empowered by him and possessed by him. But there is no indication in Scripture that Satan has the power to give life to anyone. Satan is not omnipotent. Jesus is the one who has "the keys to death and Hades" (Revelation 1:18).

Living Now?

One of the most commonly asked questions is whether or not the Antichrist is alive today. I believe he is, and I believe so for two reasons.

First, I believe the Scriptures teach that the generation that sees the re-establishment of Israel (May 14, 1948) will live to see all the end time prophecies fulfilled (Matthew 24:32-34). Second, I believe the signs of the times clearly indicate that we are standing on the threshold of the Tribulation, the most important of those signs being the regathering of the Jews to their land (Isaiah 11:10-12) and their re-occupation of the city of Jerusalem (Luke 21:24).

If the Antichrist is alive today, does he know who he is? I think not. I don't think he has the foggiest idea of the role that Satan has in mind for him. He will not become the Antichrist until Satan possesses him and empowers him to deceive Europe and the Jews. His full revelation will not occur until he enters the rebuilt temple in Jerusalem in the middle of the Tribulation and declares himself to be god.

But we are getting ahead of our story. Let's consider his character before we take a look at his career.

His Character

The Bible is very specific about the character of the Antichrist, and the picture it paints is a disgusting one. The most detailed information can be found in the book of Daniel.

Over and over emphasis is given to the Antichrist's mouth. He will boast non-stop about himself (Daniel 7:8). He will "speak monstrous things against the God of gods" (Daniel 11:36). He will be "given a mouth speaking arrogant words and blasphemies" (Revelation 13:5). First and foremost, he is going to be a braggart and a blasphemer.

He will be strong willed and reckless in his determination to have his way. He will show contempt for human traditions and will, of course, change even the calendar so that it will no longer be related to the birth of Jesus (Daniel 7:25).

Another point that is emphasized repeatedly is that the Antichrist will be possessed by Satan, just as Judas was (Luke 22:3). Daniel says his power will be mighty, *"but not by his own power"* (Daniel 8:24). Paul says his coming will be "in accord with the activity of Satan, with all power and signs and false wonders" (2 Thessalonians 2:9). John says that Satan will give his power and authority to the Antichrist (Revelation 13:2).

Because he will be demonized, he will be a man who cannot be trusted. Psalm 52:2 says he will be a "worker of deceit." Psalm 55:21 says his speech will be "smoother than butter" but his heart will be filled with war. Psalm 5:6 calls him "a man of bloodshed and deceit." In Psalm 43:1 he is referred to as a "deceitful and unjust man."

Daniel indicates that he will be a sexual pervert, most likely a homosexual. As Daniel puts it, the Antichrist will show no regard "for the desire of women" (Daniel 11:37).

The overall picture is that of an ego-maniac who abhors God and exploits people for his own purposes. He is deceptive and ruthless. He is a man devoid of integrity. This is probably the reason that when Jesus returns, John characterizes Him as the "Faithful and True" One (Revelation 19:11), in contrast to the Antichrist who has been both unfaithful and untrue.

His Rise to Power

The Rapture of the Church is the event that will launch the career of the Antichrist. This is revealed in 2 Thessalonians 2 where Paul states that the Antichrist cannot be revealed until "he who now restrains" him is "taken out of the way" (verse 7). The restrainer of evil in the world today is obviously the Holy Spirit, and the Spirit performs that task by working through the Church.

It is the Church that will be "taken out of the way," not the Holy Spirit. We know this for certain because the book of Revelation teaches that a great multitude will be saved during the Tribulation (Revelation 7:9-14), and no one can be saved apart from the witness of the Spirit (John 6:44, John 15:26, and 1 John 5:7). The Spirit will remain in the world, but the agency the Spirit currently works through to restrain evil, the Church, will be removed.

The Rapture itself is likely to be the event that will catapult the Antichrist to power. This is because the Rapture will produce international chaos and panic. The Antichrist, energized by Satan (Daniel 8:24), will seem to have all the answers to the world's problems. He will take over the European Union through skillful intrigue (Daniel 8:23) and will establish his headquarters in Rome (Revelation 17:3, 9, 18).

The seven year time period of the Tribulation will actually begin when the Antichrist negotiates a treaty that will bring true peace to the Middle East, enabling the Jews to rebuild their temple (Daniel 9:27). With his European base consolidated and peace achieved in the Middle East, he will set forth to subdue the whole world.

His Consolidation of Power

One of the myths about the Antichrist that has developed in modern day interpretation is that the whole world will become so enamored with him that all the nations will surrender their sovereignty to him voluntarily. The Bible does not teach this. It is also contrary to common sense. Africa and Asia and Latin America have not spent a century casting off European colonialism in order to suddenly turn around and receive a European dictator with open arms.

The world will resist him, and the result will be a Third World War in which he "will destroy to an extraordinary degree" (Daniel 8:24). This war will initially result in the death of one-fourth of humanity, or 1.5 billion people in today's terms (Revelation 6:2-8). As the Tribulation approaches its mid-point, this war will escalate into a nuclear holocaust that will result in the deaths of an additional one-third of those still alive — another 1.5 billion (Revelation 8 and 9).

It will be a empty victory because in the process of his conquest, one-third of the earth will be destroyed and half its population will be killed. He will then consolidate his "victory" by instituting a one-world economy and a one-world religion.

His Totalitarian Control

The key to his economic control will be a mark that each person will have to bear on their right hand or on their forehead (Revelation 13:16-18). No one will be able to buy or sell unless they have this mark. The mark will consist of "either the name of the beast or the number of his name" (Revelation 13:18).

His religious control will be exercised by a false prophet who will head up his pagan religious system (Revelation 13:11-15). The False Prophet will force all of humanity to worship the Antichrist. He will be a deceiver who will astound people with "great signs" that appear miraculous in nature.

In order to consolidate this Satanic religious system, the Antichrist will launch a great persecution of all those who have placed their faith in the true God since the Rapture of the Church (Revelation 12:13-17). The result will be a mass slaughter of believers (Revelation 7:9-14).

His Obsession With The Jews

Nor will all this slaughter satisfy his blood thirst. About the time that the Antichrist has consolidated his world empire, Satan will be cast from Heaven and will come to earth in "great wrath, knowing that he has only a short time" (Revelation 12:12). At that point he will possess the Antichrist, even as he possessed Judas (Luke 22:3).

When the Antichrist becomes Satan incarnate, he will be transformed into a megalomaniacal tyrant obsessed with two things: himself and the Jewish people.

He will suddenly march into the rebuilt temple in Jerusalem, stop the sacrifices, blaspheme God, and declare himself to be the one and only true god (Daniel 9:27 and 2 Thessalonians 2:4). And when the Jews reject this horrible blasphemy, he will turn on them and seek to annihilate them. This will be his all-consuming passion during the second half of the Tribulation. That's why Jesus told the Jews that this period of time would be the "great tribulation" (Matthew 24:21) — not because it would be worse than the first half, but because the wrath would be focused upon them as a nation and a people.

Satan has an insane hatred for the Jews. He hates them because they gave the world the Scriptures. He hates them because God sent the Messiah through them. And he hates them because God has promised that He will bring a great remnant of them to salvation in their Messiah. He wants to destroy them so that God cannot keep that promise.

During the second half of the Tribulation, he will almost succeed in accomplishing this goal. We are told in Zechariah 13:8-9 that two-thirds of the Jewish people will die during this holocaust (another 8.5 million people).

His Fate

The Bible indicates that as the Antichrist becomes obsessed with the Jews, he will lose interest in his worldwide empire, and segments of that empire will begin to revolt. The core of the revolt will be centered in the Asian nations who raise an army of 200 million and send it marching across Asia toward Israel where they hope to engage the Antichrist in a decisive battle for their freedom.

Daniel says that while the Antichrist and his armies are rampaging around the Middle East, looting the nations and killing the Jews, the Antichrist will suddenly hear "rumors" that "disturb him" (Daniel 11:40-44). He evidently hears about the great Asian army coming to challenge him. He responds by consolidating his forces "between the seas and the beautiful Holy Mountain" (Daniel 11:45). This is the same area that is referred to in Revelation as the Valley of Armageddon.

We are told that the Euphrates River dries up at this time and the great Asian army crosses to engage the Antichrist and his armies in battle (Revelation 16:12). As they fight, the Lord Jesus Christ breaks from the heavens, returns to the Mount of Olives in Jerusalem, and speaks a supernatural word that causes all the armies to drop dead in their tracks. "Their eyes rot in their sockets and their tongues rot in their mouths" (Zechariah 14:12), and the valley is filled with blood up to the horses' bridles for a distance of two hundred miles (Revelation 14:20).

Paul says the Antichrist will be slain by "the breath of the Lord" (2 Thessalonians 2:8). John says the Lord will make war against the Antichrist "with the sword of His mouth" (Revelation 2:16). Daniel says the Antichrist's "dominion will be taken away, annihilated and destroyed forever" (Daniel 17:26). Daniel also says that the Antichrist will be thrown into "the burning fire" (Daniel 7:11).

John confirms the fate of the Antichrist in Revelation when he says that both the Antichrist and the False Prophet will be thrown into "the lake of fire which burns with brimstone" (Revelation 19:20) where "they will be tormented day and night forever and ever" (Revelation 20:10). This means that the Antichrist and the False Prophet will be the first occupants of Hell. (Satan will not be confined there until the end of the Millennium — Revelation 20:10.)

Our Hope

The good news for believers is that we will not have to experience the horror of the Antichrist.

We are never told to watch for the Antichrist; rather, we are told to look for Jesus Christ. In 1 Thessalonians 1:10 we are assured that we who are believers are waiting for Jesus to return to "deliver us from the wrath to come." That is a glorious promise. That's why Paul calls the Rapture our "blessed hope" (Titus 2:13), and its also the reason that he tells us to "comfort one another" with the promise of the Rapture (1 Thessalonians 4:18).

Is it an ethereal or tangible place?

For many years I had little desire to go to Heaven. My only interest in Heaven was prompted by a desire to avoid Hell.

My apathy was also rooted in what I had been taught about Heaven. Basically, I had been led to believe that going to Heaven meant being a disembodied spirit residing in an ethereal world, floating around on a cloud playing a harp. I just couldn't get excited about that picture!

My interest in Heaven developed slowly over a long period of time. It became a passion, not as a result of my study of prophecy, but because of my growing relationship with the Lord.

The more I came to know Him, the more I desired to be with Him.

The New Earth

The reason my study of prophecy did not play the key role in developing my interest in Heaven is because the Bible is strangely silent about the subject. The Bible tells us in great detail what the Millennium will be like, but it gives us almost no detailed information about the Eternal State.

What it does tell us often comes as a great surprise to most Christians because the scriptures about Heaven have been so terribly spiritualized. For example, the Bible plainly says the Redeemed will spend eternity on a new earth, not in an ethereal place called Heaven.

Isaiah was the first to speak of this truth when he spoke of "the new heavens and the new earth" which will endure forever before the Lord (Isaiah 66:22). This truth is repeated in the book of Revelation where the apostle John says he was shown a new earth, "for the first heaven and the first earth passed away" (Revelation 21:1).

John goes on to describe the new Jerusalem descending to the new earth, "coming down out of heaven from God" (Revelation 21:2). And then he states that God Himself will come to live on the new earth (Revelation 21:3):

> Behold, the tabernacle of God is among men, and
> He shall dwell among them, and they shall be His
> people, and God Himself shall be among them.

This truth had already been revealed to the Old Testament prophets. While being taken on a prophetic tour of the millennial temple, Ezekiel was told by his guide (the Lord Jesus in a pre-incarnate appearance): "Son of man, this is the place of My throne and the place of the soles of My feet, where I will dwell among the sons of Israel forever" (Ezekiel 43:7).

The Redeemed are going to dwell forever in new bodies on a new earth in a new Jerusalem in the presence of Almighty God and His Son, Jesus. Heaven will come to earth!

The New Jerusalem

The most detailed information which the Scriptures give about Heaven pertains to our eternal abode — the new Jerusalem. Twenty verses in Chapter 21 of Revelation are devoted to a description of it.

The information contained in Revelation 21 is not the first reference in the Bible to the new Jerusalem. It is mentioned in Hebrews 11:10 as a city "whose architect and builder is God." Jesus made a reference to it that is recorded in John 14:1-4. He called it His "Father's house," and He said He would prepare a place in it for His Church.

Jesus is currently expanding, embellishing, and beautifying this house which God the Father designed and built. Jesus is preparing it for His bride, just as in Old Testament times a bridegroom would add a room onto his father's house to accommodate himself and his bride.

The city is described in Revelation as beautifully decorated, like "a bride adorned for her husband" (Revelation 21:2). Later, John actually refers to the city as the bride of the Lamb (Revelation 21:9), because the city contains the bride of Christ, His Church.

I believe this implies that at the end of the Millennium all the Redeemed will be taken off the earth and placed in the new Jerusalem which will most likely be suspended in the heavens. From that vantage point we will watch as God burns up this earth and reshapes it like a hot ball of wax into a new earth, a perfected earth like the one which God created in the beginning. Then, we will be lowered down to that new earth inside the new Jerusalem.

The city will be spectacular in both size and appearance. It will be in the form of a cube that is 1,500 miles in every direction! And it will reflect "the glory of God" (Revelation 21:11, 16).

The Size of the City

The incredible size means the city would stretch from Canada to the Gulf of Mexico and from the Atlantic coast of America to Colorado. It would also extend 1,500 miles into the atmosphere.

This tremendous extension of the city vertically into the air is a clue that the new earth may be considerably larger than the current earth. Otherwise, the city would not be proportional to its surroundings.

Would such a city be able to adequately accommodate all the Redeemed? That's a good question. The best answer I have ever run across is the one provided by Dr. Henry Morris in his book *The Revelation Record* (Tyndale House, 1983).

Dr. Morris postulates the total number of Redeemed might be as many as 20 billion. He further guesses that approximately 50 percent of the new Jerusalem might be devoted to streets, parks and public buildings. Can 20 billion people be squeezed into only half the space of this city?

The answer is yes! In fact, it can be done easily. Each person would have a cubical block with about 75 acres of surface on each face. We are talking about an immense city!

This assumes, of course, that our new glorified bodies will be immune to the current law of gravity, as are the bodies of angels. This is a safe assumption, for Philippians 3:2 says that our glorified bodies will be like the body of Jesus after His resurrection, and His body was not subject to gravity, as evidenced by His ascension into Heaven.

This is the reason the city will be so tall. We will be able to utilize and enjoy all levels of it. There will most likely be vertical streets as well as horizontal ones.

The Beauty of the City

And what streets they will be! The Bible says they will be "pure gold, like transparent glass" (Revelation 21:21). In fact, the whole city will be made of pure gold with the appearance of clear glass (Revelation 21:18).

The city will sit on a foundation made of 12 layers of precious stones (Revelation 21:19-20). Each layer will feature the name of one of the 12 apostles (Revelation 21:14). The city will be surrounded by a jasper wall over 200 feet high (Revelation 21:17). There will be 12 gates, three on each side, and each one will be named for one of the tribes of Israel (Revelation 21:12).

And yes, the gates will be "pearly gates," each one consisting of one huge pearl (Revelation 21:21).

Best of all, God the Father and Jesus will both reside in the city with us (Revelation 21:22). The Shekinah glory of God will illuminate the city constantly, and thus there will be no night nor will there ever be any need for any type of artificial light or the light of the sun (Revelation 22:5).

The throne of God and His Son will be in the city, and "a river of the water of life, clear as crystal" will flow down the middle of the city's main street with the tree of life growing on both sides of the river, yielding 12 kinds of fruit — a different fruit each month (Revelation 22:1-2).

That's it. God's Word only gives us a glimpse of Heaven. But what a tantalizing glimpse it is! It's a glimpse of perfect peace and joy and beauty.

The Activities of Heaven

What will we do for eternity? Again, the Word is strangely silent. All it says is that we "shall serve Him" (Revelation 22:3).

I have fantasized a lot about our Heavenly activities. I can imagine us spending a great deal of our time in worship, singing the psalms of King David, with him directing us. I think it is likely that our talents will be magnified, and we will be able to sing or paint or write with a majesty and scope we never imagined possible — and all to the glory of God!

Surely we will spend considerable time in the study of God's Word. Think of studying the gospel of John with the apostle John as the teacher! I thrill to the thought of Jesus teaching the Old Testament, even as He did to His disciples following His resurrection (Luke 24:44-45). The Word of God is infinite in its depth, and I believe we will continue learning from it forever.

As we study the Word, I believe we will grow in spiritual maturity in the likeness of Jesus. And since God is infinite, no matter how much we grow in His likeness, there will just be that much more growing ahead of us. In this regard, I suspect that our spiritual growth will pick up where it left off in this life.

Sometimes, I really get far out in my thinking about Heaven. For example, I can imagine the Lord giving us the opportunity to see "instant video replays" of great events in Bible history. I hope so. I would like to see the dividing of the Red Sea, the destruction of Jericho, and the resurrection of Lazarus.

And what about tours of the universe? Surely we will be able to travel through space in our glorified bodies and see the miracles of God's creation up close. Imagine visiting all the planets in our galaxy as well as touring thousands of other galaxies!

Reigning with Jesus

But what does it mean in Revelation 22:3 where it says we will serve God as His "bond-servants"? I'm not sure. I suppose it means we will be given productive work to do. What that work will be I can't say for sure. But there is a hint in Revelation 22:5 where it says we will reign with the Lord "forever and ever."

To reign implies, of necessity, that we must reign over someone. Who will that be? Again, there is a intriguing clue. Revelation 21:24-27 refers to "nations" that will live on the new earth outside the new Jerusalem. Revelation 22:2 indicates that the people composing these nations will be in fleshly bodies, for it says that the leaves of the tree of life will be used for "the healing of the nations."

A Prophetic Mystery

Who are these "nations"? This is one of the greatest mysteries of Bible prophecy. There are as many different guesses as there are commentaries on the book of Revelation.

Could they be the Redeemed who accept Jesus during the Millennium? Nothing is said about the ultimate destiny of those who are saved during the Millennium. No promises are made to them of glorified bodies.

I don't know the answer. It is one of those areas where we look into a dimly lit mirror and will not understand fully until we stand "face to face" with the Lord (1 Corinthians 13:12).

Heavenly Fellowship

This brings me to the greatest blessing of Heaven. Revelation 22:4 says we shall see the face of God!

The Word says in Exodus 33:20 that no man has ever seen the face of God. But we will be given that privilege when we fellowship with Him in Heaven.

And that is really what Heaven is all about. We will experience an intimacy with the Lord that transcends anything possible in this life. We were created for fellowship with God (John 4:23), and that purpose will reach its zenith in the eternal state as we live in God's presence.

That is why Paul wrote, "to live is Christ, and to die is gain" (Philippians 1:21). He went on to explain that to continue living in the flesh meant the opportunity for fruitful labor in the Lord's kingdom. But he still had a desire to depart this life, for that departure would open the door for sweet, intimate, personal fellowship with the Lord (Philippians 1:22-23).

What about you? Are you clinging to this world, or do you yearn for Heaven?

The more you come to know the Lord, the more you will love Him. And the more you love Him, the more You will desire to be with Him.

That's only natural. We always desire to be with those whom we love.

Longing for Heaven

I love my wife dearly. We have been married for more than forty years. I have to travel a lot. I call her every night I'm on the road to tell her that I love her. I send her mushy love cards. And when I have to be gone for an extended period, I send her gifts like bouquets of flowers.

I love to talk with my wife by phone. I love to send her love notes. I love to surprise her with gifts. But none of these are substitutes for being with her! When you love someone you want to be with them.

In like manner, I love to fellowship with the Lord in worship, in Bible study, and in prayer. But these spiritual activities are no substitute for actually being with the Lord.

Because I love Him, I want to be with Him. Personal, intimate fellowship with the Lord — that is the essence of Heaven. May it become a reality very soon!

Eternal punishing or an eternal punishment?

The Bible presents Hell, like Heaven, as a real place. The Bible says that God created this terrible place to serve as the ultimate destiny of the Devil and his angels (Matthew 25:41). The Bible also teaches that Hell will be the destiny of all people who reject the grace and mercy God has provided through Jesus and who chose, instead, to follow Satan (Matthew 25:46).

Hell is described in the Scriptures as a place of darkness and sadness (Matthew 22:13), a place of fire (Matthew 5:22), a place of torment (Revelation 14:10), a place of destruction (Matthew 7:13), and a place of disgrace and everlasting contempt (Daniel 12:2).

Its Distinction from Hades

Hell is not Hades. A careful study of the Scriptures will reveal that Hades in the New Testament is the same place as Sheol in the Old Testament (Psalms 49:15).

Before the Cross, Hades (or Sheol) was the holding place for the spirits of the dead who awaited their resurrection, judgment, and ultimate consignment to Heaven or Hell. According to Jesus' story of the rich man and Lazarus (Luke 16:19-31), Hades was composed of two compartments — Paradise and Torments. At death, the spirits of the righteous (those who had put their faith in God) went to a compartment in Hades called Paradise. The unrighteous went to a compartment called Torments. The two compartments were separated by a wide gulf that could not be crossed.

The Bible indicates that the nature of Hades was radically changed at the time of the Cross. After His death on the Cross, Jesus descended into Hades and declared to all the spirits there His triumph over Satan through the shedding of His blood for the sins of Mankind (1 Peter 3:18-19; 4:6).

The Bible also indicates that after His resurrection, when He ascended to Heaven, Jesus took Paradise with Him, transferring the spirits of the righteous dead from Hades to Heaven (Ephesians 4:8-9 and 2 Corinthians 12:1-4). The spirits of the righteous dead are thereafter pictured as being in Heaven before the throne of God (Revelation 6:9 and 7:9).

Thus, since the time of the Cross, the spirits of dead saints no longer go to Hades. They are taken, instead, directly to Heaven. The spirits of Old Testament saints could not go directly to Heaven because their sins had not been forgiven. Their sins had only been covered, so to speak, by their faith. Their sins could not be forgiven until Jesus shed His blood for them on the Cross.

The souls of the unrighteous dead will remain in Hades until the end of the millennial reign of Jesus. At that time they will be resurrected and judged at the Great White Throne judgment portrayed in Revelation 20:11-15. They will be judged by their works, and since no person can be justified before God by works (Ephesians 2:8-10), all the unrighteous will be cast into Hell, which the passage in Revelation refers to as "the lake of fire" (Revelation 20:14).

The Duration of Hell

How long will the unrighteous be tormented in Hell? The traditional view holds that Hell is a place of eternal, conscious torment. According to this view, a person who ends up in Hell is doomed to a never-ending existence of excruciating pain and suffering. Hell is a place of no escape and no hope.

Another point of view — the one I hold — takes the position that immortality is conditional, depending upon one's acceptance of Christ. I believe the Bible teaches the unrighteous will be resurrected, judged, punished in Hell for a period of time proportional to their sins, and then suffer destruction (the death of body and soul).

In a moment we will take a brief look at both views, but before we do, I would like to remind us all of a sobering truth: Hell is a reality, and it is a dreadful destiny. Hell exists because God cannot be mocked (Galatians 6:7). He is going to deal with sin, and He deals with sin in one of two ways — either grace or wrath. John 3:36 says, "He who believes in the Son has eternal life; but he who does not obey the son shall not see life, but the wrath of God abides on him."

Whatever we conclude from the Scriptures about the duration of Hell, we must remember that Hell is to be avoided at all costs. Whether the wicked suffer there eternally or are destroyed after enduring God's terrible punishment, Hell is an unimaginably terrifying place.

We must also remember that our beliefs about the duration of Hell are not on the plane of cardinal doctrine. Sincere, godly Christians may study the same scripture passages about Hell and end up with differing conclusions about the issue of its duration. Our varied viewpoints, arrived at through earnest and godly study, should not be allowed to cause division or rancor in the body of Christ.

The Traditional Viewpoint

Few traditionalists are happy about the doctrine of the eternal torment of the wicked, but they accept it anyway because they believe it to be biblical. In this they are to be commended.

Most point to scriptures such as Matthew 25:46 for support: "Then these [the wicked] will go away into eternal punishment, but the righteous into eternal life." Since the word "eternal" is used of both the wicked and the righteous, they conclude that the punishment must be eternal in the same way that the life is.

Many traditionalists also cite Revelation 20:10 — a verse specifically about the Devil, the Antichrist and the False Prophet — to prove that a God of love can indeed sentence at least some of His creatures to eternal torment: "And the devil who deceived them was thrown into the lake of fire and brimstone, where the beast and the false prophet are also; and they will be tormented day and night forever and ever." If it is possible for God to treat one set of His creatures in this way, they reason, why should it be impossible for Him to do the same thing with another set?

Still another Revelation passage also figures in the traditionalist argument. Revelation 14:9-11 reads:

> 9 And another angel, a third one, followed them, saying with a loud voice, "If anyone worships the beast and his image, and receives a mark on his forehead or upon his hand,
>
> 10 he also will drink of the wine of the wrath of God, which is mixed in full strength in the cup of His anger; and he will be tormented with fire and brimstone in the presence of the holy angels and in the presence of the Lamb.
>
> 11 And the smoke of their torment goes up forever and ever; and they have no rest day and night, those who worship the beast and his image, and whoever receives the mark of his name."

Traditionalists notice that not only are these unbelievers tossed into the lake of fire where "the smoke of their torment goes up forever and ever," but they have no rest "day or night." This is in stark contrast to the saved, who will enjoy rest eternally (Revelation 14:13). To traditionalists, both the "rest" of believers and the "unrest" of unbelievers seem to imply a conscious state.

Other Traditionalist Arguments

In other parts of the Bible, several passages which talk about Hell use the word "destroy" or "destruction" to describe what happens to the unrighteous. Traditionalists claim that the picture in these passages is not of obliteration but of a ruin of human life out of God's presence forever. In this way they are able to conceive of a "destruction" which lasts forever.

A more philosophical traditionalist argument concerns Mankind's creation in the image of God. Some traditionalists believe that the torments of Hell must be eternal, since humankind was made in the image of God and that image cannot be "uncreated."

Thus they believe that immortality was bestowed on Mankind when God created male and female in His image.

Last, many traditionalists believe that Hell must be eternal because of the nature of sin itself. All sin is an offense against God, goes this argument, and since God is infinite, all sin is infinitely odious. Jonathan Edwards (1703-1758), the great Puritan theologian, took this line of argument in his famous sermon, "The Justice of God in the Damnation of Sinners."

As you can see, these arguments seem both biblical and substantial. And yet they are not without significant problems. Allow me to explain why I believe the conditionalist approach is a better solution to the difficulty.

The Conditionalist Viewpoint

The doctrine of the duration of Hell has been so strongly held throughout the history of Christianity that few have dared to challenge it. Adding to the reluctance has been the fact that most modern challenges have come from the cults. Thus, a person who dares to question the traditional viewpoint runs the risk of being labeled a cultist.

A classic characteristic of modern-day "Christian" cults is their denial of the reality of Hell. Some argue that everyone will be saved. Most take the position that the unrighteous are annihilated at physical death.

The views of the cults regarding Hell have always been repulsive to me because they deny the clear teaching Scripture that the unrighteous will be sent to a place of suffering called Hell. Yet, I have never been able to fully embrace the traditional viewpoint of conscious, eternal punishment.

Traditionalist Difficulties

My first difficulty with the traditional view is that it seems to impugn the character of God. I kept asking myself, "How could a God of grace, mercy and love torment the vast majority of humanity eternally?" It did not seem to me to be either loving or just. I realize He is a God or righteousness, holiness and justice, but is eternal suffering justice? The concept of eternal torment seems to convert the true God of justice into a cosmic sadist.

Second, the concept of eternal torment seems to run contrary to biblical examples. God destroyed Sodom and Gomorrah with fire — suddenly and quickly. He destroyed Noah's evil world with water — suddenly and quickly. He ordered the Canaanites to be killed swiftly. In the Law of Moses there was no provision for incarceration or torture. Punishments for violation of the Law consisted either of restitution or death. Even sacrificial animals were spared suffering through precise prescriptions for their killing that guaranteed a death that would be as quick and painless as possible.

As a student of God's Prophetic Word, I found a third problem with the traditional view. It seems to contradict a descriptive phrase that is used in prophecy to describe Hell. That term is "the second death." It is a term peculiar to the book of Revelation (Revelation 2:11; 20:6, 14; 21:8). How can Hell be a "second death" if it consists of eternal, conscious torment?

The Problem of Destruction

A fourth reason the traditional view has always troubled me is that it seems to ignore an important biblical teaching about Hell; namely, that Hell is a place of destruction. Jesus Himself spoke of Hell as a place of "destruction" (Matthew 7:13). Further, in Matthew 10:28 Jesus said: "Do not fear those who kill the body, but are unable to kill the soul; but rather fear Him who is able to destroy both soul and body in Hell."

Likewise, in 2 Thessalonians 1:9 Paul says that those who do not obey the gospel "will pay the penalty of eternal destruction." The writer of Hebrews says that the unrighteous will experience a terrifying judgment that will result in their consumption by fire (Hebrews 10:27). Even one of the most comforting verses in the Bible speaks of the destruction of the unrighteous: "For God so loved the world, that He gave His only begotten Son, that whoever believes in Him should not *perish*, but have eternal life" (John 3:16, emphasis added).

The traditionalist argument that the word "destroy" or "destruction" should be interpreted as "irreparable loss" seems a stretch to me. It seems much more likely that "destroy" should be taken to mean exactly that.

The Meaning of Punishment

Fifth, there is a difference between eternal punishment and eternal punishing. It is one thing to experience a punishment that is eternal in its consequences; it is another thing to experience eternal punishing.

The Bible also speaks of eternal judgment (Hebrews 6:2). Is that a judgment that continues eternally, or is it a judgment with eternal consequences? Likewise, the Bible speaks of eternal redemption (Hebrews 9:12). But this does not mean that Christ will continue the act of redemption eternally. That act took place at the Cross, once and for all. It was an eternal redemption because the result of the redemption had eternal consequences.

Symbolism

Sixth, I noted earlier that traditionalists often cite Revelation 14:9-11 to demonstrate that the suffering of the wicked will be eternal. They most often highlight two phrases. The first refers to those who take the mark of the beast during the Tribulation, who will be "tormented with fire and brimstone in the presence of the holy angels." The second is that "the smoke of their torment goes up forever and ever." Notice that this passage does not speak of eternal torment. Rather, it speaks of "the smoke of their torment" ascending forever.

The Bible is its own best interpreter, and when you look up statements similar to this you will find that they are symbolic for a punishment that has eternal consequences, not a punishment that continues eternally. For example, consider Isaiah 34:10 which speaks of the destruction of Edom. It says the smoke of Edom's destruction will "go up forever."

I have been to Edom (the southern portion of modern day Jordan in the area around Petra). I have seen its destruction. But there was no smoke ascending heaven. The reference to eternal smoke is obviously symbolic, indicating that Edom's destruction will give eternal testimony to how God deals with a sinful society.

The same is true of Jude 7 when it says that Sodom and Gomorrah experienced "the punishment of eternal fire." Again, I have been to the area at the southern tip of the Dead Sea where these twin cities existed. The area is one of utter devastation, but there is no smoke going up to heaven. They are not burning eternally. They simply suffered a fiery destruction that had eternal consequences.

Immortality

Last, many traditionalists believe that the soul is immortal. But is it? I believe the Bible denies the immortality of the soul point blank.

In 1 Timothy 6:15-16 Paul says that God alone possesses immortality. And 1 Corinthians 15:53 teaches that the Redeemed will not become immortal until the time of their resurrection.

In other words, immortality is a gift of God which He gives in His grace to the Redeemed at the time of their resurrection. There is no need to believe in an eternal Hell if the soul is not intrinsically immortal. And it isn't.

Can History Decide the Question?

You should see by now that both the traditional and the conditional positions on Hell can muster good, biblical support for their point of view. Can church history help us decide which is right?

Unfortunately, it cannot, for both viewpoints can be found in very early writings. The idea of a Hell where the impenitent are eternally tormented can be traced to a time even before Jesus. The intertestamental *Book of Enoch*, as well as the *Fourth Book of the Sibylline Oracles*, both speak of the eternal suffering of the wicked. The great Rabbi Hillel, who lived at about the same time as Jesus, taught that one class of sinner would be punished "to ages of ages" — even though he maintained that most of the damned would be annihilated.

These are all non-Christian sources. But Cyprian, a Christian from the Third Century, wrote that "the damned will burn forever in hell." If we ask who was responsible for systematizing and popularizing the traditional viewpoint, we find that it was Augustine around the year 400 AD. But the position certainly was taught before his time.

The conditionalist viewpoint can also be traced back to Bible times. For example, it can be found in the writings of Justin Martyr (114-165 AD). In his *Dialogue with Trypho the Jew,* Martyr states that the soul is mortal, that the souls of the unrighteous will suffer only as long as God wills, and that finally their souls will pass out of existence. The concept is also affirmed in the *Didache,* a Second Century Christian handbook. That book speaks of "two ways" — the way of life and the way of death. It says the unrighteous will perish.

A Summary

In defining any doctrine, everything the Bible has to say about the issue must be considered. Concerning the issue of Hell, the only way I have been able to incorporate all that the Bible has to say is to conclude:

1) Those who die outside a faith relationship with Jesus are initially confined to a compartment in Hades called Torments.

2) At the end of the Millennium, they will be resurrected and judged of their works by Jesus at the Great White Throne Judgement.

3) All of them will be condemned to Hell because no one can be justified before God by their works.

4) They will be cast into the lake of fire (Hell) where they will suffer a time of torment in proportion to their sins.

5) They will then experience the "second death" (death of body, soul and spirit).

The Reality of Hell

Which viewpoint is right— the traditional one or the conditionalist concept? I have cast my vote for the conditionalist understanding. You may decide that the evidence points in the other direction.

But whatever you conclude, based on our study of Scripture, we can agree that Hell is a terrifying, horrendous, ghastly place that should be avoided at all costs. You certainly do not want your friends or your family to go there, and you should make certain that it is not your final destination. Those who think they are going to party in Hell are sadly mistaken.

The truth is — as I have stressed repeatedly — your eternal destiny is in your hands. You can choose eternal life by receiving Jesus as your Lord and Savior. Or, you can choose eternal destruction by refusing to accept God's gift of love and grace. I urge you to choose life by accepting Jesus (Deuteronomy 30:15-19).

Midnight Cry

Alvin Slaughter

I hear the sound
Of a mighty rushing wind,
And it's closer now
Than its ever been.
I can almost hear the trumpet
As Gabriel sounds the chord.
At the midnight cry,
We'll be going home.

(Chorus)

When Jesus steps out
On a cloud to call His children,
The dead in Christ shall rise
To meet Him in the air.
And then those that remain
Will be quickly changed
At the midnight cry,
When Jesus comes again.

I look around me,
I see prophecies fulfilling.
And the signs of the times,
They're appearing everywhere.
I can almost hear the Father
As He says, "Son go get my children."
At the midnight cry,
We'll be going home.

Part Three

Prophetic Views

"Surely the Lord God does nothing
unless He reveals His counsel
to His servants the prophets."
Amos 3:7

Why are there so many different concepts?

I almost gave up studying Bible prophecy the very first week I started. I was turned off by the vocabulary.

I kept running across terms like premillennial, amillennial, post-millennial, chiliast, and anti-chiliast. It sounded to me like much of prophecy was written in tongues!

Thankfully, the Holy Spirit encouraged me to stick with the task, and before long I began to realize that the terms really were not all that difficult to understand.

Basically, there are four major end time viewpoints. Or, to put it another way, there are four different interpretations about what the Bible says concerning end time events.

Historic Premillennialism

The oldest viewpoint is called historic premillennialism. It is termed "historic" for two reasons: to differentiate it from modern premillennialism and to indicate that it was the historic position of the early Church.

It is called "premillennial" because it envisions a return of Jesus to earth before (pre) the beginning of the Millennium. The word, millennium, is a combination of two latin words — *mille annum* — which simply mean one thousand years.

A diagram of this viewpoint which prevailed among the early Church Fathers is presented in Figure 1 on the next page. It divides the future of the world into four periods:

1) The current Church Age.

2) A seven year period called the Tribulation.

3) A reign of Christ on earth lasting one thousand years (the Millennium).

4) The Eternal State when the redeemed will dwell forever with God on a new earth.

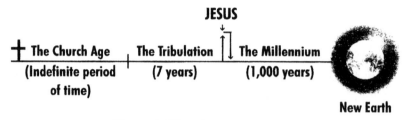

Figure 1: Historic Premillennialism

This view is based on a literal interpretation of what the Bible says will happen in the end times. One of its distinctive features is that it places the Rapture of the Church at the end of the Tribulation.

According to this view, the Church will remain on earth during the Tribulation. At the end of that period, Jesus will appear in the heavens and the Church will be caught up to meet Him in the sky. The saints will be instantly glorified, and then they will immediately return to the earth to reign with Jesus for a thousand years.

The Church Fathers

This is the only systematic view of end time events that existed during the first 300 years of the Church. With only a couple of exceptions, all the Church Fathers who expressed themselves on the topic of prophecy were premillennial until 400 AD. Justin Martyr, who was born in 100 AD, went so far in his writings on the subject as to suggest that anyone with a different viewpoint was heretical!

Those today who disagree with this view respond to the near unanimity of the early Church Fathers by saying they were simply wrong in their interpretation of the prophetic Scriptures.

It certainly should be noted that these early church leaders were not prophetic scholars. They wrote very little on prophecy, and what they wrote was sketchy. Their main concern was not prophecy, but the deity of Jesus, the oneness of God, the practical problems of church organization, and survival amidst persecution.

Yet their concept of end time events should not be dismissed out of hand as crude and primitive, for anyone who has studied the prophetic Scriptures will have to admit that the Church Fathers' viewpoint presents a plain sense summary of the Bible's teachings about the end times.

The Challenge

The person who laid the groundwork that produced a major challenge to the premillennial view was Origen (185-254 AD). His approach to all of Scripture was either to spiritualize it or allegorize it. He therefore denied the literal meaning of prophecy. He looked upon its language as highly symbolic and expressive of deep spiritual truths rather than of future historical events.

Origen's allegorical approach was specifically applied to prophecy by a man named Tyconius (died about 400 BC). He argued that the prophecies concerning the Millennium were being fulfilled in the Church Age and that the thousand year period of time was not literal. He also argued that the first resurrection mentioned in Revelation 20:4 was a spiritual resurrection — namely, the new birth.

The greatest of the Church Fathers, Augustine (354-430 AD) popularized the views of Tyconius. In the process, he developed a whole new scheme of end time events. This new view was presented in his book, *The City of God*, published in 427 AD.

Amillennialism

The concept formulated by Augustine is illustrated in Figure 2. It is called amillennialism. This strange name derives from the fact that in the Greek language a word is negated by putting the letter "a" in front of it. Thus, amillennial literally means "no thousand years."

The term is misleading, however, because most amillennialists do believe in a millennium, but not a literal, earthly one. They argue that the Millennium is the current spiritual reign of Christ over the Church and that it will continue until He returns for His saints. They thus interpret the thousand years as a symbolic period of time.

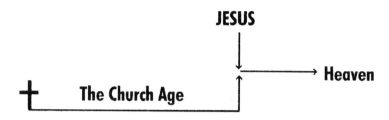

Figure 2: Amillennialism

One appealing aspect of the amillennial view is its simplicity. The Church Age comes to a screaming halt as a result of the Rapture of the Church. There is no Tribulation, no literal earthly Millennium, and no eternity on a new earth. Augustine spiritualized everything, arguing that the kingdom is the Church, the Millennium is the current Church Age, and the new earth is symbolic language for Heaven.

Augustine's view of end time events was endorsed by the Council of Ephesus in 431 AD when the Council condemned the premillennial view as "superstitious." The view became Catholic dogma and remains so to this day. It is also the current majority viewpoint among mainline Protestant denominations. In other words, the amillennial viewpoint is the one that is held today by the vast majority of all those who profess to be Christians.

Postmillennialism

The third view of end time events, called post-millennialism, did not develop until the mid-seventeenth century, long after the Reformation. The Reformation had little impact on prophetic views because the Reformation leaders had their attention riveted on the questions of biblical authority and justification by faith.

The postmillennial view was a product of the rationalistic revolution in thinking. It was developed in the mid-1600's by a Unitarian minister named Daniel Whitby. It was immediately dubbed "post-millennialism" because it envisioned a return of Jesus after (post) a literal thousand year reign of the Church over all the earth.

Figure 3: Postmillennialism

Postmillennialism spread quickly within the Protestant world, probably for two reasons. First, it gave Protestants an opportunity to differ from the Catholic position. More importantly, it was a theological expression of the prevailing rationalistic philosophy of the age, a philosophy that boldly proclaimed the ability of Mankind to build the kingdom of heaven on earth.

The postmillennial view holds that the Church Age will gradually evolve into a "golden age" when the Church will rule over all the world. This will be accomplished through the Christianization of the nations.

To its credit, it can be said that this viewpoint served as a mighty stimulus to missionary efforts during the eighteenth and nineteenth centuries. Missionaries were seized with the vision of speeding up the return of the Lord by preaching the gospel to all the world.

A Sudden Death

By 1900 nearly all segments of Protestant Christianity had adopted the postmillennial viewpoint. But the view was to be quickly dropped.

Postmillennialism died almost overnight with the outbreak of the First World War. The reason, of course, is that this great war undermined one of the fundamental assumptions of the postmillennial viewpoint — the assumption of the inevitability of progress. This had always been a fatal flaw in the postmillennial concept, due mainly to its birth in rationalistic humanism. Its visions of the perfectibility of man and the redemption of society were destroyed by the atrocities of the war.

Another fatal flaw of the postmillennial viewpoint was its lack of a consistent Biblical base. To expound the view, it was necessary to literalize some prophecies (those concerning the Millennium) while at the same time spiritualizing other prophecies (the personal presence of the Lord during the Millennium). Also, it was necessary to ignore or explain away the many prophecies in the Bible that clearly state that society is going to get worse rather than better as the time approaches for the Lord's return (Matthew 24:4-24 and 2 Timothy 3:1-5).

The sudden death of postmillennialism left a prophetic vacuum among Protestant groups. Since the postmillennial view was based to a large extent upon a spiritualizing approach to Scripture, most Protestant groups returned to the spiritualized amillennial viewpoint they had abandoned in the 1700's.

However, the more fundamentalist Protestant groups turned to a new prophetic viewpoint that had been developed in England. This view was technically called "dispensational premillennialism" because it originated with a group who had been nicknamed "Dispensationalists." I call it the modern premillennial viewpoint.

Modern Premillennialism

The modern premillennial viewpoint crystallized in the early 1800's among a group in England known as the Plymouth Brethren.

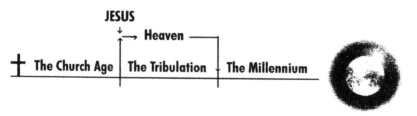

Figure 4: Modern Premillennialism   **New Earth**

As can be readily seen, this viewpoint revives the historic premillennial view except for its concept of the Rapture of the Church. The Plymouth Brethren envisioned two future comings of Jesus, one *for* His Church and one *with* His Church. Their concept of the Rapture has since come to be known as the "pre-Tribulation Rapture."

This viewpoint has been attacked as being "too new to be true." But its advocates are quick to point out that the Bible teaches the principle of "progressive illumination" regarding prophecy (Daniel 12:4 and Jeremiah 30:24). What they mean by this is that the Bible itself indicates that end time prophecy will be better understood as the time nears for its fulfillment.

Comparisons

Looking back over these four views of the end times, we can see some significant differences. But let's not overlook the similarities.

- All agree that Jesus is coming back for His saints.

- All agree that the redeemed will spend eternity in the presence of God.

These two points of agreement are far more important than the many points of disagreement.

Still, the areas of disagreement are significant. Two of the views (the amillennial and postmillennial) deny that Jesus will ever manifest His glory before the nations in a world wide reign of peace, justice and righteousness. The postmillennial view also denies the soon coming of the Lord, for according to this view, the Lord cannot return until His Church has ruled over the world for a thousand years.

The key to the differences is the approach to Scripture. If you tend to spiritualize Scripture, you will end up with an amillennial or postmillennial viewpoint. If you tend to accept Scripture for its plain sense meaning, you will have a premillennial viewpoint.

A Plea

I urge you to accept the plain sense meaning of Scripture. Don't play games with God's Word by spiritualizing it. When you do so, you can make it mean whatever you want it to mean, but in the process you will lose the true meaning that God intended.

Remember, the First Coming prophecies meant what they said. That should be our guide for interpreting the prophecies of the Second Coming.

When you accept the plain sense meaning of Bible prophecy, you will clearly see that there is going to be a time of great tribulation lasting seven years which will be followed by a one thousand year reign of Jesus over all the nations of the earth. You will also understand that the Redeemed are destined to live eternally on a new earth. The only question you will have to struggle with is the timing of the Rapture. (This issue is dealt with in chapters 15 and 26.)

Are we really in the Millennium now?

A friend of mine enrolled in a prominent seminary where the amillennial viewpoint was taught. When he attended his first class in Bible prophecy, the teacher began the class by saying, "There is one fact you must keep in mind about prophetic literature and that is that it never means what it says. So, for example, if you are reading a prophetic verse and it mentions a cow, the only thing you can know for certain about that verse is that the cow is not a cow!"

Such an interpretive approach makes a mockery of the Word of God. It allows individuals to play god by giving a verse any interpretation they desire. The only limit is one's imagination. Yet, this is the interpretive principle that serves as the foundation for the amillennial viewpoint.

Augustine's Spiritualizing

The culprit behind this travesty is St. Augustine, the man who formulated the amillennial viewpoint around 400 AD. Augustine "platonized" the prophetic Scriptures, reading and interpreting the words of the Bible's Hebrew writers as if they had been written by Greek philosophers.

Keep in mind that the Greeks had a creation-negating viewpoint. They viewed the material world as essentially evil. In contrast, the Hebrew view contained in the Scriptures is a creation-affirming one. To the Hebrew mind, the creation is basically good, even though it has been corrupted by the curse. Thus, the psalmist writes: "The heavens are telling of the glory of God; and their expanse is declaring the work of His hands" (Psalms 19:1).

Whereas the Greeks looked toward the dissolution of the universe, the Hebrews yearned for the redemption of the creation. Isaiah dreamed of "the new heavens and the new earth" (Isaiah 66:22), and Paul wrote that the whole creation is longing for its redemption so that it will "be set free from its slavery to corruption" (Romans 8:18-21).

Augustine's Greek world view would not allow him to accept at face value what the Bible said about end time events. What the Bible prophesied was too much tied to this world — a future kingdom of Christ on this earth and eternity with God on a new earth.

Using the spiritualizing approach, Augustine tried to explain away the Tribulation, the Millennium and the new earth. The result was the amillennial viewpoint of end time events which holds that the current Church Age will end abruptly with the Rapture of the Church. At that point the Redeemed will be resurrected in spiritual bodies, the unrighteous will be consigned to Hell, the material universe will cease to exist, and the Redeemed will take up residence with God in an ethereal Heaven.

The Impact of the New View

This view caused a considerable stir when it was originally presented by St. Augustine because it differed so drastically from the premillennial view of the early Church. The premillennial viewpoint envisioned that the Church Age would end with a seven year period of Tribulation which would be followed by a thousand year reign of Christ upon the earth. Eternity would be spent in glorified bodies on a new earth, not in an ethereal Heaven. (The two views are illustrated on the next page for comparison.)

Augustine's view was adopted quickly by the Catholic Church at the Council of Ephesus in 431 AD because it gave enhanced importance to the Church. Based on this new view, the Church could claim that it was the fulfillment of all the kingdom promises in the Bible and that it had a right to rule over the nations.

But Augustine's view raised some serious problems of biblical interpretation.

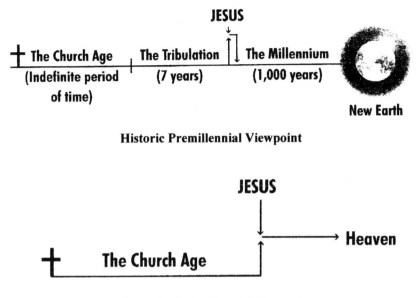

Historic Premillennial Viewpoint

Augustine's Amillennial Concept

Where is the Millennium?

Augustine argued that we are currently in the Millennium! He said the Millennium began at the Cross and would end a thousand years later with the return of Jesus. To him, the establishment of the Church constituted the founding of the Millennial Kingdom. There would be no future kingdom of Jesus on this earth.

When people asked how they could be in the Millennium when there was so much evil in the world, Augustine responded that the level of evil is relative. He said we are in the Millennium because the Holy Spirit is in the world restraining evil. If the Holy Spirit were not here, things would be much worse. Thus, relatively speaking, we are in the Millennium.

For Augustine, the thousand year length of the Millennium was no problem because he lived in 400 AD. When the year 1000 passed and the Lord did not return, amillennialists simply spiritualized the number. Since that time they have argued that the number is symbolic and thus represents the period from the Cross to the Second Coming, regardless of how long that may be!

Where is the Tribulation?

Augustine responded to this question by arguing that we are simultaneously in both the Millennium and the Tribulation!

We are in the Millennium because the Holy Spirit is in the world restraining evil, but we are also in the Tribulation because the Church will suffer persecution until the Lord returns.

When it was pointed out that the Bible says the Tribulation will last only seven years, Augustine dismissed the number as symbolic. He argued that the number seven represents a complete period of time, and therefore it (like the number one thousand) represents the period from the Cross to the Second Coming.

Is Satan Bound?

Revelation 20:1-3 reveals that when the Millennium begins, Satan will be bound. This fact forced Augustine to argue that Satan was bound at the Cross. But was he?

Satan was certainly defeated at the Cross due to the power of the resurrection. But that victory at the Cross has not yet been manifested in history in all its aspects. The curse continues. Death stalks the earth. Satan still retains his dominion over the world (1 John 5:19).

The ultimate destruction of Satan is yet future. That's why the Bible speaks of the "crushing" of Satan as a future event that will take place at the Second Coming of Jesus (Romans 16:20). At that time, Satan will be stripped of his authority and bound for a thousand years. At the end of the Millennium, he will be cast into the lake of fire where he will be tormented forever (Revelation 20:7-10).

Amillennialists often respond to these points by quoting Matthew 28:18 where Jesus said, "All authority has been given to Me in heaven and on earth." But what they overlook is that although Jesus has been given all authority, He is not yet exercising it. That's why the world is still in such a wretched state.

Jesus is now serving as our High Priest before the throne of God (Hebrews 8:1). When He returns, He will come as the King of kings, and He will begin to exercise in full the authority He won at the

Cross (Revelation 19:16). Thus, the writer of Hebrews says that although everything has been put in subjection under the feet of Jesus, "we do not yet see all things subjected to Him" (Hebrews 2:5-8). In fact, 1 Corinthians 15:23-26 teaches that everything will not be put under the authority of Jesus until the end of His millennial reign when Satan is crushed and death is destroyed.

If Satan is bound now, then he is bound on a very long chain, because he is always nipping at my heels, chewing on my leg, and lunging for my throat! He is portrayed in 1 Peter 5:8 as an "adversary" who "prowls around like a roaring lion seeking someone to devour." He sure doesn't sound very "bound" in that passage!

There is certainly a sense in which Satan was limited by the Cross, because since that time believers in Jesus have received the indwelling power of the Spirit, enabling them to be overcomers in their combat with Satan (1 John 5:1-5). But the limitations which the Cross placed on Satan do not constitute the binding of Satan that the Scriptures say will take place at the beginning of the Millennium.

Revelation says Satan will be bound so that he can no longer "deceive the nations" (Revelation 20:3). How can anyone argue that the nations of the world are not deceived today?

Where are the Resurrections?

Another problem with the amillennial viewpoint is that it does not provide for the two resurrections which the Bible says will occur in the future. These are the resurrections of the just and the unjust (Acts 24:15).

As will be pointed out in this book's chapter on resurrections (chapter 38), the premillennial view provides for two resurrections. The first, the resurrection of the righteous, takes place in three stages — the resurrection of Jesus; the resurrection of the Church at the time of the Rapture; and the resurrection of Tribulation martyrs and Old Testament saints at the time of the Lord's Second Coming. The second resurrection, the resurrection of the unrighteous, takes place all at once at the end of the Millennium.

But in the amillennial view, there is only one resurrection. It takes place at the end of the Church Age when history comes to an end. Both the just and the unjust are resurrected at the same time. Where are the two resurrections?

Augustine "solved" this problem by spiritualizing the first resurrection. He said it is a spiritual resurrection that occurs when a person accepts Jesus as Lord and is born again! The second resurrection is a literal one that occurs when everyone is raised from the dead at the Lord's return.

The two resurrections are spoken of specifically in Revelation 20:4-6. The passage says the resurrections are separated by a thousand years. When a person chooses to interpret one of these spiritually and the other literally, he is playing games with words that render them meaningless.

Where is the New Earth?

Augustine completely spiritualized the concept of a new earth. His Greek mindset kept him from accepting the truth that the redeemed will live eternally on a new earth. He equated the new earth with Heaven.

From his Greek perspective, it was impossible to mix perfected, holy beings with an evil, material creation. The creation had to cease to exist. Eternity would be spent in an ethereal spirit world.

A Liberal View

To summarize, the amillennial view is based on a spiritualizing approach to Scripture which contends that the Bible does not mean what it says.

This is a consistent view for theological liberals who also spiritualize the creation, the miracles, the virgin birth, and the resurrection of Jesus. But what is astounding is the number of Evangelicals who endorse the amillennial view. In effect, they take the position that the Bible always means what it says unless it is talking about the Second Coming of Jesus!

The Church and the Kingdom

One final point. There is no doubt that the Church is the current manifestation of God's kingdom in the world today. But to say that the kingdom is the Church is not the same as saying that the kingdom is *only* the Church.

The Scriptures clearly teach that the Church is the kingdom. They do not teach that the kingdom is only the Church. Consider these references to the kingdom in scripture:

1) The kingdom is identified with the creation itself, for God is sovereign over the creation. See Psalm 93:1-2 and 1 Chronicles 29:11.

2) The kingdom is expressed in the nation of Israel. See Exodus 19:6 and 1 Samuel 8:7.

3) The kingdom is equated with the Church. See Colossians 1:13 and Revelation 1:9.

4) The kingdom is viewed as something more than the Church, yet to come in the future. See Matthew 8:11, Luke 22:28-30; Acts 14:22; 1 Corinthians 6:9; and 2 Peter 1:11.

5) The kingdom is yet future, to take the form of a reign of Christ and His saints upon the earth. See Daniel 7:18, 27; 2 Timothy 2:12; Revelation 3:21; and Revelation 20:6.

6) The kingdom is yet future, to take the form ultimately of a reign of God over the redeemed upon a new earth. See 1 Corinthians 15:24-28 and Revelation 21:1-4.

The Unity of the Kingdom Concept

I believe these scriptures teach that God has always had a kingdom upon this earth, but it has been manifested in different ways. The kingdom was originally expressed in the creation itself, in its perfect obedience to God's will. With the corruption of the creation through the sin of man, the kingdom was expressed in the lives of the patriarchs who, like Job, responded obediently in faith to God's will. The kingdom became focused in a more tangible manner after the call of Abraham and the emergence of the nation of Israel.

Since Pentecost, the kingdom has been expressed in the institution of the Church. But the Bible promises different expressions of the kingdom in the future — first, in the form of a thousand year rule of Jesus upon this earth, and second, in the form of an eternal rule of God upon a new earth.

Notice that the progression here is both circular and expansive. It is circular in that it begins and ends with the reign of God over a creation that is in perfect submission. It is expansive in that after the Fall it constantly expands in scope from a few patriarchs and their families, to the nation of Israel, to the Church, and finally to all nations of the world.

The kingdom is thus past, present, and future. It is currently expressed in the Church, but it is like a rose in the bud, yet to bloom in its full glory. The kingdom has always been coming, and it will continue to come until God's will is done perfectly. Even during the Millennial reign of Jesus the kingdom will be coming, for the Bible teaches that rebellion will be lurking in the hearts of men.

The consummation of the kingdom will not come until all enemies of God have been subdued. That will occur at the end of the Millennial reign of Jesus (Revelation 20:7-15) at which time He will surrender the kingdom to His Father who will reign forever over a redeemed creation (1 Corinthians 15: 24-28).

The Test of Reality

The amillennial view does not stand the test of either the Scriptures or reality. How can anyone truly believe that we are currently living in the Millennium? The Bible says that during the Millennium "the earth will be full of the knowledge of the Lord as the waters cover the sea" (Isaiah 11:9). Does that sound like the world we live in?

Let's not sell God short. When He promised a world characterized by peace, righteousness and justice (Isaiah 2:2-4), He surely did not have in mind the corrupt world system we are living in now. To characterize this age as the Millennium is to render meaningless some glorious promises of God. Don't surrender your promises to a spiritualizing approach.

Will the Church convert the world?

I never thought I would live long enough to see the revival of the thoroughly discredited doctrine of postmillennialism. But it has occurred, and it has happened quickly.

The doctrine is sweeping through Christendom today, and strangely enough, it is appealing primarily to two segments at opposite ends of the spectrum — namely, the Charismatics and those with a heritage of Reformed theology.

The doctrine is being presented in new clothes. Although it appears under many different names — Restoration, Reconstruction, New Wave, Latter Rain, and Manifest Sons of God — the two most frequently used titles are Kingdom Now Theology and Dominion Theology.

Characteristics

Regardless of the name, the various groups advocating this confused doctrine hold certain beliefs in common:

1) The Church has replaced Israel, and God has no purpose left for the Jews. Accordingly, some of the proponents are virulently anti-Semitic, even to the point of arguing that the Jewish people are the Antichrist.

2) The Church is destined to take over the world by itself and reign over all the nations for at least one thousand years.

3) Jesus cannot return for the Church until the Church has completed its reign and is ready to present the kingdom to Him.

The Birth and Death

Postmillennialism was born in the middle of the 17th Century as a product of the rationalistic revolution in thinking that produced Humanism with its belief in the goodness of Man. If Man is capable of perfection through education, as the Humanists believed, then surely Mankind is capable of building the kingdom of God on earth.

Such was the reasoning of a Unitarian minister by the name of Daniel Whitby (1638-1726). He envisioned the Church converting the world and then reigning over a kingdom of Christianized nations for a thousand years, at which time the kingdom would be presented to the Lord. Since his scheme of end time events had Jesus returning at the end of the Millennium, it came to be known as postmillennialism, meaning "after the millennium."

This viewpoint was adopted quickly by the mainline Protestant denominations, and it served to fuel their zeal to send forth missionaries to covert the world to Christ. By the end of the 19th Century, most Protestant Christians were expecting the 20th Century to be the "Christian Century" when the Christianization of the world would be completed and the Church's reign of worldwide peace would begin.

World War I quickly shattered the hopes and dreams of postmillennialists. This horrific war made it very difficult, if not impossible, to believe in the inevitable progress of Mankind. When the War was followed quickly by the Great Depression and then the Second World War, the Humanistic foundation of postmillennialism was revealed to be a delusion.

The Resurrection

From the First World War until the 1980's, only one major popular book was written which advocated the postmillennial view. Published in 1957, it was entitled *The Millennium*. The author was a Reformed theologian by the name of Loraine Boettner (1901-1990).

When I read this book, I concluded the author probably lived on an isolated island cut off from all news sources. The reason is that he spent a good portion of the book trying to convince the reader that the world really was getting better!

Boettner's book had little impact. The real resurrection of post-millennialism took place in the decade of the 1980's when the market was suddenly flooded with postmillennial books. The two most prolific and influential authors were Earl Paulk (born in 1927) and David Chilton (1955-1997).

Two Flavors

Although Paulk and Chilton both came to the same erroneous conclusion that the Church will take over the world without the presence of Jesus, their reasoning and methods differed rather drastically.

Paulk's approach was a natural outgrowth of the confused hyper-faith doctrines that had come to characterize much of the Charismatic movement at that time. Paulk asserted that Christians are "little gods" with the authority of Christ. We can therefore confess dominion over the earth and, through faith, what we confess will come to pass. Paulk's theology is the one referred to as Kingdom Now.

The other major flavor of the postmillennial revival is called Dominion Theology. Its roots are very different. It is advocated by non-Charismatic, Calvinist theologians.

The philosophical father of Dominion Theology was Rousas John Rushdoony (1916-2001). Although he was on the scene for a long time, his writings were obtuse and were therefore popular among only a handful of intellectuals. But in the 1980's his theories were popularized by his son-in-law, Gary North of Tyler, Texas and by David Chilton, a Presbyterian preacher in California.

Dominion Theology differs from Kingdom Now not only in its roots but also in its methods. Kingdom Now supposedly relies on supernatural methods. Believers, as "little gods," assert their godhood by speaking dominion over the nations.

Dominion Theology, in contrast, relies on more traditional methods. The world is to be claimed for Christ through missionary effort and political activism.

Scriptural Arguments

There are three cornerstone scriptures that are often used to justify the Kingdom Now/Dominion doctrines. The first and foremost is Acts 3:21.

This verse is usually quoted to say, "Jesus must remain in heaven until all things have been restored." Therefore, the argument goes, Jesus cannot return until the Church has emerged triumphant over the world and has restored God's creation through a reign of peace, righteousness and justice.

The problem with this very neat argument is that the verse does not say what the Dominionists quote it to say. Instead, the verse says, "Jesus will remain in heaven until the time for the restoration of all things." What the verse actually says is therefore drastically different from the subtle Dominionist paraphrase of it.

The verse means exactly what it says: Jesus must remain in Heaven until it is time for the restoration of all things. He will then return and restore the creation and restore God's dominion over the creation, just as prophesied by the Hebrew prophets (see, for example, Isaiah 11:3b-9).

The second scripture text which Dominionists often point to is Matthew 24:14 which says that the gospel of the kingdom must be preached in the whole world before the end will come. This verse, they say, requires that the world be converted to Christ before He returns.

But this verse does not say that the world must be converted. It says only that the gospel must be preached to all the world.

The Church is preaching the gospel all over the world today, but even so, not every person will hear it until the end of the Tribulation period when an angel of God will be sent forth to proclaim the gospel "to every nation and tribe and tongue and people" (Revelation 14:6). Then Jesus will return in triumph to establish His kingdom from Mt. Zion in Jerusalem (Revelation 19 and 20).

A third text sometimes used by the Dominionists is Romans 8:19 which says that "the anxious longing of the creation waits eagerly for the revealing of the sons of God." This is interpreted to mean that the creation will be redeemed as the Church matures, purifies, and spreads its influence over the earth.

But the context of this passage makes it very clear that the verse is talking about the resurrection of the saints, not the maturing of the saints. The resurrection will reveal those who are truly the sons of God (verse 23). It is at that time that the curse will be lifted from the creation, not before (verse 21).

Unscriptural Conclusions

The lack of scriptural foundation has led the Kingdom Now/Dominion theologians to conclusions that are completely unbiblical. Let's consider these conclusions one by one:

1) **The Jews** — Has God washed His hands of them? The Dominionists claim He has, but Romans 9-11 clearly teaches that the Jews are still the Chosen People of God and that God intends to bring a remnant of them to salvation in Jesus Christ. The disobedience of the Jews has not annulled God's promises to Israel because "the gifts and the calling of God are irrevocable" (Romans 11:29).

2) **The World** — Will the world be converted to Jesus as these revived postmillennialists claim? The Bible teaches that the vast majority of people will always reject the gospel. This is one of the points of the parable of the sower (Matthew 13). Jesus said, "The gate is small, and the way is narrow that leads to life, and few are those who find it" (Matthew 7:14).

3) **The Church** — Is the mission of the Church to convert all nations? Again, that's what the Dominionists claim. But the Bible teaches that it is the responsibility of the Church to preach the gospel, not to convert the world (Mark 16:15).

4) **The Kingdom** — Does the Church establish a kingdom without a king? This is the view of the Dominionists. The Bible teaches that Jesus will present the kingdom to the Church (Daniel 7:13-14, 18, 27). The Church is never pictured as presenting the kingdom to Jesus. Furthermore, the Church is always portrayed as reigning with Jesus and not as reigning alone (Revelation 3:21).

5) **Imminency** — The Bible teaches we are to be alert and sober, watching for the imminent return of the Lord for His Church (Matthew 24 and 25). The new postmillennialists deny that the return of Jesus is imminent. In fact, they say He cannot return until the Church has reigned for at least one thousand years.

6) **Jesus** — The Kingdom Now advocates of the revived post-millennialism not only replace Israel with the Church, they also replace Jesus with the Church. Paulk goes so far as to say that the Church is "the ongoing incarnation of Christ." This is blasphemy. There is only one Christ and that is Jesus of Nazareth. The focus of God's plan of redemption for all of His creation is not the Church; it is Jesus (Hebrews 1). And any doctrine that causes us to take our eyes off the Lord is profoundly false.

Compounding the Errors

Postmillennialism was originally founded upon an assumption that was fatally flawed — namely, the essential goodness of Man. The Bible teaches exactly the opposite. The Scriptures assert that Man is born with a sin nature that renders him a naturally evil being (Romans 3:9-18). In fact, the Bible states that there is nothing as "deceitful" and "desperately sick" as the heart of Man.

The errors of the viewpoint began to compound when the proponents of postmillennialism started asserting that it is possible for the Church to Christianize the world. Again, this is a very un-biblical concept. Bible prophecy never predicts the existence of such a world apart from the physical presence of Jesus ruling from Mt. Zion as King of kings and Lord of lords.

End Time Deception

The Bible prophesies that the end times leading up to the return of Jesus will be an era of wide-spread deception and apostasy (1 Timothy 4:1 and 2 Timothy 3:13). I believe that postmillennialism is a part of that end time deception.

We have been in the end times ever since the re-establishment of the state of Israel in 1948. We are currently on the threshold of the Tribulation, as all the nations of the world come against Israel over the issue of Jerusalem (Zechariah 12:2-3). As we shall see in later chapters, everywhere one looks today, there are signs of the Lord's soon return.

In a time when we should be preparing earnestly for the Rapture of the Church at any moment, the postmillennialists are telling us that there is no possibility that the Lord can return for at least a thousand years! Satan must love that message.

A Warning

Postmillennialists dream of the Church ruling over the world in its own power. They seem to forget that every time the Church has sought political power, it has ended up being corrupted by the political system. This happened when the Church was wed with the Roman Empire, leading to the spiritual darkness of the Middle Ages.

The deadest churches in the world today are the political, state churches of Europe. They have the form of religion, but they have denied its power (2 Timothy 3:5). They have political power, but they do not have the power of God's Spirit.

Do not be deceived by those who urge the Church to change the world through the pursuit of political power. It is true that a day will come when the Church will reign over all the world, but that reign will be conducted in person by Jesus through His glorified saints. A perfect kingdom requires a perfect king ruling through perfected subjects.

Preterism   24

Has the Second Coming already occurred?

Preterism is a system of interpretation for the book of Revelation. Its strange name comes from a Latin word meaning past tense. The word is appropriate because this view holds that either all or most of the book of Revelation was fulfilled in the First Century!

The Origin of the Viewpoint

The view was developed in the 17th Century by a Jesuit priest named Luis de Alcazar (1554-1613). His purpose was to defend the Catholic Church against the attacks of the Reformers. He denied the Reformers' charge that the book of Revelation was a prophecy about the apostasy of the Roman Church. Instead, he argued that the book was a prophecy about the Church's struggles during its early years.

According to Alcazar, chapters 4 through 11 of Revelation depict the Church's fight against Judaism, culminating in the fall of Jerusalem in 70 AD. Chapters 12 through 19 were viewed as the Church's struggle against paganism, ending with the fall of Rome in 476. Chapters 20 through 22 were interpreted to be a symbolic description of the glories of papal Rome. Using this clever approach, Alcazar was able to limit the range of Revelation's prophecies to the first 500 years of the Christian Era.

Forms of Preterism

Alcazar was a mild Preterist. A more radical form of Preterism gained popularity in the latter part of the 20th Century and is today the most widely held version of this interpretive approach. It sees nearly all the prophecies of Revelation as fulfilled in the 70 AD destruction of Jerusalem, except for the resurrection of believers and the Second Coming of Jesus.

Mild Preterism assigns the Tribulation to the fall of Israel, the great apostasy to the First Century Church, and the last days to the period between Jesus' ascension and the destruction of Jerusalem. The beast is viewed as a symbol of Nero in particular and the Roman Empire in general. The False Prophet is equated with the leadership of apostate Israel. Needless to say, many of the spokesmen for this viewpoint are anti-Semitic.

There is a more extreme form of Preterism whose advocates consider themselves to be "consistent Preterists." They take the position that all so-called "end time prophecy" was fulfilled in the destruction of Jerusalem in 70 AD — including the Second Coming and the resurrection of believers! They do not look forward to any future resurrection or any end of history. They believe we are currently living in the eternal state.

The Cornerstone of the Viewpoint

The cornerstone of the Preterist position is a belief that the book of Revelation was written before the destruction of Jerusalem in 70 AD. This belief flies in the face of strong evidence to the contrary.

The internal evidence of the book regarding the Roman Empire and the external testimony of the Church Fathers both point to a date of authorship around 95 AD, 25 years after the destruction of Jerusalem in 70 AD.

The type of widespread Roman persecution of the Church that is pictured in Revelation did not occur until the reign of Domitian (81-96 AD). The persecutions of Nero were limited to the area of Rome. One of the Church Fathers, Irenaeus (c.130-c.202), wrote that the book of Revelation was authored by the apostle John "toward the end of Domitian's reign." Irenaeus was discipled by Polycarp (c.70-c.155 AD) who, in turn, had been discipled directly by John himself.

References to the Temple

One of the arguments for an earlier date is based on a reference to the temple in Revelation 11:1-2. John is told to measure the temple, which in this case seems to be a command to assess the temple's spiritual condition. This reference to the temple, it is argued, must mean that the book was written before the temple was destroyed in 70 AD.

But this argument ignores the fact that the Scriptures teach there are going to be two future temples, one during the Tribulation which the Antichrist will desecrate (Daniel 9:27 and 2 Thessalonians 2:3-4), and another during the Millennium which Jesus Christ will consecrate (Ezekiel 40-46).

The temple mentioned in Revelation 11 must be the Tribulation temple since the passage says it will be trampled down by the Gentiles for 42 months (the last half of the Tribulation). It also says this will be immediately preceded by the testimony of the two witnesses for 1,260 days (the first half of the Tribulation).

The Issue of Matthew 24

Another cornerstone of Preterism is its belief that the prophecies contained in Jesus' Olivet Discourse, as recorded in Matthew 24, were all fulfilled in 70 AD.

Is Matthew 24 history or prophecy? It is a crucial prophetic question. The passage clearly portrays a period of intense tribulation that will precede the Second Coming of Jesus. Has this terrible period of tribulation already occurred or is it yet to occur? Is it past or future? History or prophecy?

I believe Matthew 24 was prefilled in symbolic type in the destruction of Jerusalem in 70 AD and is therefore yet to be fulfilled in history. And I think I can prove that from the passage itself.

Daniel's Prophecy

To begin with, consider verse 15. It says the period of intense persecution of Jews will begin when "the abomination of desolation," spoken of by Daniel, is seen "standing in the holy place."

We have no historical record of such an event taking place in 70 AD. Unlike the Greek tyrant, Antiochus Epiphanes, who desecrated the temple's holy place in 168 BC by erecting within it an altar to Zeus, Titus took no such action in 70 AD before his troops destroyed the city and the temple.

The Intensity of the Tribulation

The second point to note is found in verse 21. It says that the period of Jewish persecution that will follow the desecration of the temple will be the most intense in all of history, "since the beginning of the world until now, nor ever shall [be]."

These words were not fulfilled in 70 AD. The persecution which the Jews experienced under Titus was severe, but it pales in comparison to what the Jews suffered during the Nazi Holocaust of World War II.

Josephus says the Romans killed a million Jews in the 70 AD siege of Jerusalem. Historians are convinced that this number is greatly exaggerated. But even if it is true, it is nothing compared to the six million Jews who perished at the hands of the Nazis.

Furthermore, the prophet Zechariah tells us that during the end times a total of two-thirds of the Jewish people will die during a period of unparalleled calamity (Zechariah 13:8-9). In other words, there is a period of Jewish persecution yet to occur that will even exceed the horrors of the Nazi Holocaust.

Consider verse 21 again: "for then there will be a great tribulation such as has not occurred since the beginning of the world until now, nor ever shall." Did Jesus mean what He said or not? Surely this is not an example of hyperbole, of exaggeration to make a point. Everything in the passage seems to demand that we are to take Jesus' words literally.

The conclusion is inescapable. The tribulation experienced by the Jews in 70 AD was not the greatest "since the beginning of the world until now, nor ever shall be."

The Severity of the Tribulation

The third piece of evidence is found in verse 22. Jesus says that the period of "great tribulation" (verse 21) that He is talking about will be so severe that all life will cease unless the period is cut short.

You and I live in the only generation in history when these words could be literally fulfilled. There was no possibility in 70 AD that the siege of Jerusalem would lead to the extinction of all life.

But that is a very real threat today due to the development and deployment of nuclear weapons.

The best selling book of 1982, *The Fate of the Earth*, proved that if there is ever an all out nuclear exchange between the United States and Russia, all life on earth will cease to exist.

The Proximity of the Tribulation

The fourth clue that Matthew 24 is yet to be fulfilled is found in verse 29. It says the Lord will return "immediately after the tribulation of those days." How can we escape the impact of the word "immediately"? I don't think we can. It clearly ties the preceding events to the immediate time of Jesus' return.

Radical Preterists deal with this problem in a fanciful way by claiming that the Second Coming of Jesus actually occurred in 70 AD! That, of course, is ludicrous, but it shows the extent to which some people will go to try to make Scripture conform to a particular doctrine.

The Context of the Tribulation

The final evidence that Matthew 24 was not fulfilled in 70 AD is to be found in verses 32-35, where Jesus says that all the things He has spoken of concerning the Tribulation will be fulfilled during the generation that sees the "fig tree" reblossom. Here is the key to the timing of the prophecy's fulfillment.

What is the "fig tree"? Think back for a moment to what had happened the day before. Jesus had put a curse on a barren fig tree (Matthew 21:18-19), causing it to wither. It was a prophetic sign that God would set the Jewish nation aside because of their spiritual barrenness — that is, their refusal to accept Jesus as their Messiah. The fig tree is a symbol of the nation of Israel (Hosea 9:10; Jeremiah 24:1-10; Joel 1:7; and Luke 13:6-9).

Now, the next day, Jesus calls the fig tree to mind and says, "Watch it. When it reblossoms, all these things will happen."

The setting aside of Israel occurred in 70 AD. The reblossoming took place in 1948 when the nation of Israel was re-established.

A Fact to Ponder

Matthew 24 is not history. The terrible events of 70 AD were a classic prefillment in type of the ultimate fulfillment that will occur immediately before the Lord returns.

Matthew 24 is prophecy yet to be fulfilled. It is going to be fulfilled soon, for Israel has been regathered, the nation has been reestablished, and the nations of the world are coming together against the Jewish state. The wrath of God is about to fall. We are on the threshold of the Great Tribulation.

Unfulfilled Prophecies

The basic problem with the Preterist viewpoint is that it requires a spiritualization of prophecy. This is necessitated by the fact that the prophecies contained in the book of Revelation were not fulfilled in any literal sense in the First Century.

Think about it for a moment. There is no historical record of the two witnesses of Revelation 11 appearing in Jerusalem and preaching for three and one-half years. There was no worldwide time of tribulation. Nero did not rule the world, as Revelation 13:8 says the Antichrist will. Nor was Nero served by any individual equivalent to the false prophet described in Revelation 13:11-15.

There is also no record of any implementation of the "mark of the beast" to control buying and selling (Revelation 13:16-18). And the headquarters of the Antichrist (which in the Preterist view would be Rome) was not destroyed in one hour of one day as prophesied in Revelation 18:8-10.

When the radical Preterists argue that even the Second Coming occurred in the First Century, they deny the promise that was made to the apostles at the time of Jesus' ascension. They were told by supernatural agents of God that Jesus would one day return in just the same manner as He had ascended — that is, bodily and visibly (Acts 1:10-11).

The Preterist claim that the Second Coming of Christ occurred in 70 AD is preposterous. It is reminiscent of two fellows in the time of Paul — Hymenaeus and Philetus — who argued that the resurrection had already taken place (2 Timothy 2:17-18). Paul dismissed their claim as "worldly and empty chatter" that will "lead to further ungodliness" (2 Timothy 2:16).

An Eclectic Observation

Nonetheless, I can agree with the **Preterists** when they insist that the book of Revelation contained a message of encouragement to First Century Christians, assuring them that the Church would ultimately triumph over the Roman Empire. I can also relate to the Reformation **Historicists** when they argue that the prophecies of Revelation relate to the corruption of the Roman Church and its persecution of true believers.

In other words, I believe the book of Revelation has always had a continuing relevance as a source of encouragement to suffering Christians throughout the history of the Church. It has always served as a reminder that the Church will ultimately triumph over all its oppressors.

That's why I can even agree with the liberal, **Idealist** viewpoint when it argues that the ultimate message of the book is that good will triumph over evil. How can anyone argue with that conclusion when the book clearly teaches that Satan will be crushed and Jesus will emerge totally triumphant?

But I also believe in the **Futurist** view that most of the book of Revelation is yet to be fulfilled and is to be fulfilled in its plain sense meaning. In other words, I believe there's going to be a real Antichrist and not just a symbolic Antichrist. Yes, there have been symbolic antichrists in the past, but there is going to be a fulfillment in a literal Antichrist in the future. I also believe the Tribulation, Millennium and Eternal State are all yet future.

Relating the Views to Each Other

As I look at these four systems of interpretation (Preterist, Historicist, Idealist, and Futurist) and consider their relationship to each other, I am reminded of how an overhead projector works. You can put a transparency on the projector that shows the land of Israel in the time of Joshua. Then you can lay on top of that transparency another one that shows the boundaries of the land at the time of Jesus. Another overlay could show the land's boundaries during the time of the Crusaders. A final overlay could outline the boundaries as they exist today. Each transparency contains an element of truth about the land. The light shines through all the transparencies to give you the full picture, showing you how the boundaries have changed over the years.

I think that's the way these schools of interpretation relate to each other. Each one of the four contains an element of truth. The problem comes when you accept only one and reject all the others. We must never forget that the book of Revelation contained a very relevant message to First Century Christians. It assured them of their ultimate victory over the Roman Empire. We must also remember that the book has been given relevant application to the struggles of the Church throughout history.

Looking to the Future

But we must also keep in mind that the Futurist view is correct when it says that the ultimate fulfillment of the book's prophecies is yet future.

There really is going to be a seven year period of Tribulation. A Jewish temple is going to be rebuilt in Jerusalem. A real person empowered by Satan will march into that temple, blaspheme God, and declare himself to be a god. This Antichrist will become the scourge of the earth. He will attempt to exterminate the Jewish people. Just as he appears to be on the verge of victory in accomplishing this satanic goal, the Lord Jesus will break from the heavens with all His holy ones, returning to the Mount of Olives in Jerusalem from which He ascended into Heaven. The Lord will crush the Antichrist and inaugurate the greatest kingdom the world has ever known. And the earth will be flooded with peace, righteousness and justice — as the waters cover the sea.

Our hope is future, not past, and that is why the apostle Paul urged us to live "looking for the blessed hope and the appearing of the glory of our great God and Savior, Christ Jesus" (Titus 2:13).

Will it be one event, or will it occur in stages?

When you think of the coming of the Lord, what do you think of? What is your image? Is it positive or negative? Is it a return in love or in wrath? And what do you feel? Fear or joy? Comfort or anxiety?

How would you characterize your overall attitude about the Lord's return? Desire or apathy? Do you pray for it? Or, do you try not to think about it? Are you enthusiastic or passive?

Finally, how would you describe the Lord's coming? How would you explain it to someone who knows nothing about it?

The Scriptural Images

There are two detailed descriptions of the Lord's return in the New Testament, one written by the apostle Paul and the other by the apostle John. These descriptions are reproduced on the next page, side by side. Stop for a moment and read them carefully.

Now, let me ask you another question. How can these two descriptions be reconciled? I ask that because they are as different as night and day. Did you notice that?

Look again and make a careful comparison. Notice that they have absolutely nothing in common except that they both focus on Jesus. Beyond that common fact, they are totally incompatible.

1 Thessalonians 4:13-18

In First Thessalonians Jesus appears in the heavens, bringing with Him the spirits of those who have died in Him. There is the

The New Testament Descriptions
of the Lord's Return

1 Thessalonians 4:13-18	Revelation 19:11-16
13) But we do not want you to be uninformed, brethren, about those who are asleep, that you may not grieve, as do the rest who have no hope.	11) And I saw heaven opened; and behold, a white horse, and He who sat upon it is called Faithful and True; and in righteousness He judges and wages war.
14) For if we believe that Jesus died and rose again, even so God will bring with Him those who have fallen asleep in Jesus.	12) And His eyes are a flame of fire, and upon His head are many diadems; and He has a name written upon Him which no one knows except Himself.
15) For this we say to you by the word of the Lord, that we who are alive, and remain until the coming of the Lord, shall not precede those who have fallen asleep.	13) And He is clothed with a robe dipped in blood; and His name is called The Word of God.
16) For the Lord Himself will descend from heaven with a shout, with the voice of the archangel, and with the trumpet of God; and the dead in Christ shall rise first.	14) And the armies which are in heaven, clothed in fine linen, white and clean, were following Him on white horses.
17) Then we who are alive and remain shall be caught up together with them in the clouds to meet the Lord in the air, and thus we shall always be with the Lord.	15) And from His mouth comes a sharp sword, so that with it He may smite the nations; and He will rule them with a rod of iron; and He treads the wine press of the fierce wrath of God, the Almighty.
18) Therefore comfort one another with these words.	16) And on His robe and on His thigh He has a name written, "KING OF KINGS, AND LORD OF LORDS."

blowing of a trumpet and the shout of an archangel. The dead in Christ are resurrected. Their supernaturally reconstructed bodies ascend to meet the Lord in the sky, where their spirits will be re-united with their bodies and their bodies will be glorified (see 1 Corinthians 15:42-44, 51-58). The living in Christ will follow, and on the way up, they will be translated from mortal to immortal.

In Matthew 25:6 Jesus indicates that the archangel will shout, "Behold, the Bridegroom!" That would be appropriate, for the image in First Thessalonians is that of a bridegroom coming for his bride.

What an exciting passage! It is no wonder that it ends with the statement, "Comfort one another with these words." The dead in Christ will be resurrected and glorified (made immortal). The living in Christ will be instantly translated (changed from mortal to immortal). That means there is a whole generation of Christians who will never die — the generation that is alive at the time the Lord appears in the heavens.

Revelation 19:11-16

The image of the Lord's return contained in Revelation 19 presents a startling contrast to the one in First Thessalonians.

As Revelation 19 opens, we have come to the end of the seven years of the Great Tribulation. All the angels and saints in Heaven are shouting "Hallelujah!" because the kingdom of the Antichrist has been destroyed and the time has come for Jesus to return to the earth (Revelation 19:1-6).

But first, Jesus celebrates His union with His bride, the Church (Revelation 19:7-10). He does this by treating His bride to a great wedding feast.

At the end of the this meal, the heavens open, and Jesus and His bride return to earth in glory, riding white horses (Revelation 19:11-14). He returns as a warrior to "judge and wage war" against the enemies of God. He returns as an avenger to pour out the wrath of God on those who have rejected God's love and grace. And He returns as a king to "strike down the nations" and "rule them with a rod of iron" (Revelation 19:15-16).

A Summary Comparison

1 Thessalonians 4:13-18	Revelation 19:11-16
1) Jesus appears in the heavens.	1) Jesus returns to earth.
2) Jesus comes for His Church.	2) Jesus returns with His Church.
3) Jesus is a Deliverer.	3) Jesus is a Warrior.
4) Jesus appears in grace.	4) Jesus returns in wrath.
5) Jesus appears as a bridegroom.	5) Jesus returns as a king.

Comparison and Contrast

The passage in First Thessalonians presents a scene of love, mercy, and grace. The picture that is painted in Revelation is one of vengeance and wrath. In the Thessalonian passage, the Lord appears in the sky, but does not descend to the earth. In the Revelation account, he comes to the earth, in accordance with Zechariah 14 which says He will return to the Mount of Olives from which He ascended into Heaven.

One of the most significant differences between the two passages relates to the Church. In the Thessalonian account, the Lord appears for the purpose of taking His Church, both the dead and living members, out of this world. In Revelation, by stark contrast, He returns with His Church. This is indicated in Revelation 19:14 where it says that "the armies which are in heaven, clothed in fine linen, white and clean were following Him on white horses." We know these people constitute the Church, because the same group is described a few verses earlier (verses 7 and 8) as being the "bride" of Christ.

In Paul's description of the Lord's return, Jesus is portrayed as coming *for* His Church, to deliver believers from the "wrath that is to come" (1 Thessalonians 1:10). But in John's description, Jesus is portrayed as returning *with* His Church in great wrath. In Thessalonians Jesus appears as a Deliverer. In Revelation He comes back as a Warrior. In one scene He is coming to claim the righteous; in the other, He returns to condemn the unrighteous.

A Problem in Reconciliation

What is going on here? How could these two passages be talking about the same event? How can they be reconciled?

I believe there is only one way to reconcile them and that is to conclude that *they are describing two separate events.* That, in turn, implies rather clearly that there are going to be *two* future comings of the Lord.

One of those — the one described in 1 Thessalonians 4 — will be more of an appearing than a coming, for the Lord will not actually return to the earth. He will, instead, appear in the heavens and supernaturally draw the Church, living and dead, to Him.

The second future appearance of the Lord — the one described in Revelation 19 — will be the true "Second Coming," for the Lord will actually descend to the earth to pour out the wrath of God and establish His reign over all the world.

This means the "Second Coming" of the Lord is going to be in two stages. The first stage will be what has come to be known as the Rapture — the snatching of the Church out of the world. The second stage, which will occur later, will be the return of the Lord to the earth.

The Issue of Imminence

This method of reconciling these passages solves a serious problem that emerges when you think of only one future coming of the Lord. That problem relates to the emphasis that the Scriptures give to *imminence.*

What I am referring to, of course, is the constant warning of the Scriptures that the Lord may appear any moment and, therefore, we are to always be ready for the Lord's return (Matthew 24:36, 42, 44, 50 and 25:13).

If there is only one future coming of the Lord, then these warnings are a waste of time and there is no imminence because there are many prophecies that are yet to be fulfilled before the Lord can return. For example:

1) A peace treaty must be signed that will guarantee Israel's peace with all of its Arab neighbors (Daniel 9:27).

2) The Jewish temple must be rebuilt in Jerusalem (Matthew 24:15, 2 Thessalonians 2:3-4, and Revelation 11:1-2).

3) The Great Tribulation must begin and run its seven year course, resulting in the death of over half the world's population (Revelation 6-18).

4) The Antichrist must reveal himself and begin an unprecedented persecution of the Jews — one that will result in the death of two-thirds of all the Jews (Revelation 12:13-17 and Zechariah 13:7-9).

5) The Gospel must be preached to every person on the earth (Matthew 24:14 and Revelation 14:6-7).

6) An unprecedented system of economic control must be established that will prevent persons from buying or selling anything unless they can display on their right hands or foreheads the mark or name of the Antichrist (Revelation 13:16-18).

7) The worldwide kingdom of the Antichrist must be destroyed in "one hour of one day" (Revelation 17 and 18).

These are all events that are clearly prophesied in Scripture as occurring before Jesus returns to earth. None of them has yet been fulfilled in history. If there is only one future coming of the Lord, and it must take place after these events, then why should we be looking for Jesus Christ? We should be looking instead for the Antichrist!

Living with Expectancy

The only way that the imminence taught by the Scriptures can be maintained is to believe that Jesus can return any moment. The only way to maintain that belief is to conclude that the Lord's appearing for His Church (the Rapture) is an event that is separate and apart from the Second Coming and is an event that can occur any moment.

That is what I have concluded from my study of prophecy, and I therefore live looking for the Rapture to occur any moment. This is exactly what Paul commands us to do when he writes that we are to live "looking for the blessed hope and the appearing of the glory of our great God and Savior, Christ Jesus" (Titus 2:13).

I therefore do not believe there is one prophecy in the Bible that must be fulfilled before the Lord appears for His Church. He can appear any moment. And the imminence of His appearing becomes increasingly apparent as the signs of the time point to the events that will culminate with His Second Coming. Those signs include, among others, the re-establishment of the state of Israel, the Jewish reoccupation of the city of Jerusalem, the reunification of Europe, and the rise of Arab militancy in the Middle East.

Keep in mind that the Rapture is not the event that will kick-off the Tribulation. That event is the signing of a peace treaty that will guarantee the peace of Israel with all its Arab neighbors and will also authorize the Jews to rebuild their temple (Daniel 9:27). The Rapture could occur years before the Tribulation begins, although it is most likely to occur near the beginning because the Tribulation is the time for the pouring out of God's wrath, and 1 Thessalonians 1:10 says that Jesus will "deliver" His Church "from the wrath to come."

A Signless Event

Since the Rapture is imminent, and always has been, there are no signs that point to it. The signs of the times that the Bible gives us to watch for relate to the Tribulation and the Second Coming. But when those signs start accumulating, as they are doing so today, we can be assured that the Rapture is going to occur any moment.

I once heard Tim LaHaye describe the relationship between the Rapture and the signs of the times in a very unique way. He said he and his wife were walking through a shopping mall when she suddenly stopped him and said, "Look around and tell me what you see."

Tim surveyed the mall, and responded, "The only thing I see that is different from normal is people putting up Christmas decorations."

"That's right," she said, "and what is that a sign of?"

"Well," Tim responded, "it's a sign that Christmas is coming soon."

"Yes," she replied, "but it is also a sign that Thanksgiving is right around the corner!"

In like manner, we see increasing signs today which indicate the Tribulation is about to begin. And that means the Rapture is "right around the corner."

Hope or Terror?

To summarize, we should be looking for two future comings of the Lord — one at the beginning of the Tribulation, the other at the end. The first, the Rapture, will be the appearing of the Lord for His Church. The second, the Second Coming, will be the return of the Lord to the earth to "judge and wage war" against the enemies of God (Revelation 19:11).

The signs of the times point to the fact that we are on the threshold of the Tribulation. The Jews are back in their land and their sacred city, and the whole world is coming against them over the issue of the control of Jerusalem. Jesus must be at the very gates of Heaven, waiting for His Father's command to appear for His Church. The Rapture is imminent.

Are you ready? Will Jesus appear (the Rapture) as your Blessed Hope? Or, will He return (the Second Coming) as your Holy Terror? The choice is yours.

When is it most likely to occur?

I have already discussed the nature and meaning of the Rapture in chapters 15 and 25. Our focus here is on the timing of this important event.

This is a very controversial issue because the timing of the Rapture is not specifically revealed in the Scriptures. We are simply told repeatedly that it is imminent, meaning it can happen at any moment.

Specific concepts of timing — whether it will happen before, during, or at the end of the Tribulation — must be based upon inferences of Scripture, and thus there is room for honest differences of opinion.

I believe the best inference of Scripture is that the Rapture will occur **before** the Tribulation begins. Let's consider the evidence.

Scriptural Evidence

The Olivet Discourse, as recorded in Matthew 24, is for the Jews who will experience the horrors of the Tribulation. The same speech is recorded in Luke 21 for the Church, and it contains clues about the timing of the Rapture. For example, after mentioning a bunch of end time signs that we are to watch for, Jesus says, "When these things *begin* to take place, straighten up and lift up your heads, because your redemption is drawing near" (Luke 21: 28 — emphasis added).

In the same passage, Jesus proceeds to urge us to pray that we might "escape all these things that are about to take place, and to stand before the Son of Man" (Luke 21:36).

The Word promises over and over that the Church will be delivered from God's wrath. Romans 5:9 says that "we shall be saved from the wrath of God through Him [Jesus]." 1 Thessalonians 1:10 states that we are waiting "for His Son from heaven . . . who will deliver us from the wrath to come." The promise is repeated in 1 Thessalonians 5:9 — "God has not destined us for wrath, but for obtaining salvation through our Lord Jesus Christ." Keep in mind that the Tribulation is the period of time for the pouring out of God's wrath.

In Revelation 3:10 the church at Philadelphia, which is representative of faithful Christians, is told that those who persevere in the Lord will be kept "from the hour of testing," that hour which will "come upon the whole world."

Paul's Assurance

An interesting argument in behalf of the pre-Tribulation timing of the Rapture can be found in 2 Thessalonians. The church at Thessalonica was in a turmoil because someone had written them a letter under Paul's name stating that they had missed the "gathering to the Lord" and were, in fact, living in "the day of the Lord" (2 Thessalonians 2:1-2).

Paul attempted to calm them down by reminding them of his teaching that the day of the Lord would not come until after the Antichrist is revealed. He then stated that the Antichrist would not be revealed until a restraining force "is taken out of the way" (2 Thessalonians 2:3-7).

There has been much speculation as to the identity of this restraining force that Paul refers to. Some have identified it as the Holy Spirit. But it cannot be the Holy Spirit because there will be people saved during the Tribulation, and no one can be saved apart from the testimony of the Spirit (John 16:8-11 and 1 John 5:7).

Others have identified the restrainer as human government. It is true that government was ordained by God to restrain evil (Romans 13:1-4). But the governments of the world are in rebellion against God and His Son (Psalm 2), and they are therefore a contributor to the evil that characterizes the world. Furthermore, the Tribulation will not be characterized by a lack of government. Rather, it will feature the first true worldwide government (Revelation 13:7).

In my opinion that leaves only one other candidate for Paul's restrainer — and that is the Church. It is the Church that serves as the primary restrainer of evil in the world today as it proclaims the Gospel and stands for righteousness. When the Church fails in this mission, evil multiplies, as Paul graphically points out in 2 Timothy 3:1-5. Paul says that society in the end times will be characterized by chaos and despair because "men will hold to a form of religion but will deny its power." When the Church is removed from the world, all hell will literally break loose.

Symbolic Evidence

There are several prophetic types that seem to affirm the concept of deliverance from Tribulation. Take Enoch for example. He was a prophet to the Gentiles who was raptured out of the world before God poured out His wrath in the great flood of Noah's time. Enoch appears to be a type of the Gentile Church that will be taken out of the world before God pours out His wrath again. If so, then Noah and his family are a type of the Jewish remnant that will be protected through the Tribulation.

Another Old Testament symbolic type which points toward a pre-Tribulation Rapture is the experience of Lot and his family. They were delivered out of Sodom and Gomorrah before those cities were destroyed.

The apostle Peter alludes to both of these examples in his second epistle. He states that if God spared Noah and Lot, then He surely "knows how to rescue the godly from trial and to keep the unrighteous under punishment for the day of judgment" (2 Peter 4-9).

Another beautiful prophetic type is to be found in the Jewish wedding traditions of Jesus's time. After the betrothal, the groom would return to his father's house to prepare a wedding chamber for his bride. He would return for his bride at an unexpected moment, so the bride had to be ready constantly. When he returned, he would take his bride back to his father's house to the chamber he had prepared. He and his bride would then be sealed in the chamber for seven days. When they emerged, a great wedding feast would be celebrated.

Likewise, Jesus has returned to Heaven to prepare a place for His bride, the Church. When He returns for His bride, He will take her to His Father's heavenly home. There He will remain with His bride for seven years (the duration of the Tribulation). The period will end with "the marriage supper of the Lamb" described in Revelation 19. Thus the seven days in the wedding chamber point prophetically to the seven years that Jesus and His bride will remain in Heaven during the Tribulation.

The Structure of Revelation

The structure of the book of Revelation also implies a pre-Tribulation Rapture in a symbolic sense. The first three chapters focus on the Church. Chapter 4 begins with the door of Heaven opening and John being raptured from the isle of Patmos to the throne of God in Heaven. The Church is not mentioned thereafter until Revelation 19:7-9 when it is portrayed as the "bride of Christ" in Heaven with Jesus celebrating the "marriage supper of the Lamb." At Revelation 19:11 the door of Heaven opens again, and Jesus emerges riding a white horse on His way to earth, followed by His Church (Revelation 19:14).

The rapture of the apostle John in Revelation 4 appears to be a symbolic type of the Rapture of the Church. Note that it is initiated by the cry of a voice that sounds like the blowing of a trumpet (Revelation. 4:1). Since the Tribulation does not begin until Revelation 6, the rapture of John in Revelation 4 appears to be a symbolic type that points to a pre-Tribulation Rapture of the Church.

Some counter this argument by pointing out that although the Church is not mentioned in Revelation during that book's description of the Tribulation, there is constant mention of "saints" (for example, Revelation 13:7). But that term is not used in the Bible exclusively to refer to members of the Church. Daniel uses it to refer to Old Testament believers who lived long before the Church was established (Dan. 7:18). The saints referred to in the book of Revelation are most likely those people who will be saved during the Tribulation, after the Church has been taken out of the world.

Logical Evidence

The Bible teaches that when Jesus returns, He is going to judge all people on earth and consign unbelievers to death. The judgment of the Gentiles is portrayed in Matthew 25:31-46; the judgment of the Jews, in Ezekiel 20:33-38. In Luke 17:33 we are told that the bodies of unbelievers will be fed to the vultures. Revelation 19:17 calls this "the supper of God." It is presented in contrast to the marriage feast of the Lamb to which believers will be invited (Revelation 19:6-10).

Once these judgments are completed, all believers left alive at the end of the Tribulation — both Jews and Gentiles — will be allowed to enter the Millennium in the flesh. This group will then begin to propagate, and through them, the earth will be re-populated. These are the people that the glorified saints will reign over for a thousand years. Since death will be curtailed and life spans will be extended during the Millennium, the population of the earth will grow exponentially.

Now, if the Rapture is combined with the Second Coming as all one event at the end of the Tribulation, then all believers will be glorified and there will be no one left in the flesh to enter the Millennium! The only way to come up with a Millennial population is to place the Rapture before the Tribulation. Those saved during the Tribulation, and who live to the end of it, would then go into the Millennium in the flesh and serve as the nucleus group to repopulate the world.

The Purpose of the Tribulation

Another argument based upon logic is the fact that there is no purpose for the Church to be on the earth during the Tribulation. The purpose of the Tribulation is to provide a period of time for the pouring out of God's wrath. The Church is immune to the wrath of God (1 Thessalonians 1:10). There will be people saved during the Tribulation, but they will be saved by the witness of the Holy Spirit through reading the Bible, experiencing the Tribulation judgments, and hearing the messages of the God's two witnesses in Jerusalem.

Some have argued that the Church must go through the Tribulation in order to purify it for its presentation to the Lord. True

Christians need no such purification, for their sins have been purged by the blood of Jesus. Asserting that this is a purpose of the Tribulation has the effect of converting that time period into a Protestant Purgatory!

Furthermore, it makes no sense to say that Jesus is going to beat up His bride for seven years during the Tribulation before coming to fetch her for the wedding! What kind of bridegroom would do such a thing? What bride wold look forward lovingly to being united to such a bridegroom?

The Logic of Imminence

Perhaps the strongest argument in behalf of a pre-Tribulation Rapture is one based on logic. It is the argument of imminence.

We are told repeatedly in the Scriptures that the coming of the Lord is imminent — that it can take place any moment. We are warned "to be ready" (Matthew 24:44), "to be on the alert" (Matthew 24:42), "to be dressed in readiness" (Luke 12:35), and to "keep your lamps alight" (Luke 12:35). The clear force of these persistent warnings is that Jesus can appear at any moment.

Only the pre-Tribulation concept of the Rapture allows for the imminence of the Lord's appearing for His Church. When the Rapture is placed at any other point in time, the imminence of the Lord's appearing is destroyed because other prophetic events must happen first.

For example, if the Rapture is going to occur in mid-Tribulation, then why should I live looking for the Lord's appearing at any moment? I should be looking instead for an Israeli peace treaty, the rebuilding of the temple, and the revelation of the Antichrist. Then and only then could the Lord appear.

We are exhorted to live looking for Jesus Christ, not the Antichrist (Titus 2:13).

Counter Arguments

The first rebuttal argument that is usually presented by people who reject the Pre-Tribulation Rapture is their contention that there is no mention of the Rapture in Matthew 24 where Jesus presents a sweeping survey of end time events. The Tribulation is described by the Lord in detail in verses 9-24. Then we are told in verses 25-31 that "immediately after the Tribulation," the Lord will return and will "send forth His angels to gather together His elect." Where is the Rapture?

Again, we must keep in mind that the book of Matthew was written to the Jews, and Matthew's recording of Jesus' speech in chapter 24 focuses on the Jews in the Tribulation, not the Church. As to the Saints who will be gathered at the end of the Tribulation when Jesus returns, they would be those who were saved during the Tribulation, after the Rapture of the Church.

Keep Reading!

But Matthew 24 does not end with the description of the Lord's Second Coming. In verse 36 the writer suddenly shifts gears and starts recording the words of Jesus concerning an event that has to be something other than the Second Coming. He quotes Jesus saying, "But of that day and hour no one knows, not even the angels in heaven, nor the Son, but the Father alone."

This could not be a reference to the Second Coming because the Bible makes it crystal clear that Jesus will return to this earth exactly seven years after the Tribulation begins. It seems apparent that at this point in Jesus' discourse, He shifts His focus from the Second Coming to the Rapture.

Further evidence that this is true can be found in the next verse (verse 37). Jesus says, "For the coming of the Son of Man will be just like the days of Noah." He proceeds to explain that when the flood occurred, people were going about their daily lives with no sense of concern, "marrying and giving in marriage" (verses 38-44). This is anything but a description of the nature of society at the end of the Tribulation. By that time, the whole earth will be engulfed in chaos. People will be in a perpetual state of panic rather than going about their lives in peace and calm.

So, the Rapture can be found in Matthew 24, in verses 36-44. And two times in this section of the chapter, Jesus warns to "be on the alert for you do not know which day your Lord is coming" (verses 42 and 44). Once again, since the day of the Second Coming can be precisely determined, this passage must be speaking of the

Rapture and the fact that it is an imminent event that could occur any moment.

The Newness of the Concept

Another common rebuttal to the Pre-Tribulation Rapture is that it is "too new to be true." This argument is based on the assumption that the Pre-Tribulation concept of the timing of the Rapture was not developed until the early 1800's by a man named J. N. Darby who was a leader among the Plymouth Brethren in England.

This assumption is not correct, but even if it were true, it would not invalidate the concept. That's because the Bible makes it clear that Bible prophecy will not be fully understood until the end times. For example, when Daniel asked God the meaning of end time prophecies he had been given, the Lord told him that the prophecies were not for him to understand. "These words are concealed," said the Lord, "and sealed up until the end time" (Daniel 12:9).

Modern day historical events, like the re-establishment of Israel, and modern day technological developments, like the invention of nuclear power, are helping us to understand Bible prophecies that have never been understood before.

But the most important key has been the revival of literal interpretation. From 400 AD to about 1700, Bible prophecy was spiritualized and interpreted allegorically. Many new discoveries have been made in Bible prophecy since the 1700's, simply because people started accepting the prophecies to mean what they say. So, we are not talking about novel new truths. We are talking instead about the discovery of truths that were always in the Scriptures but which were muddled by spiritualization.

The Origin of Pre-Trib Viewpoint

But let's return to the original allegation — that the Pre-Trib Rapture originated in the early 1800's in England among a group called The Plymouth Brethren. This allegation simply is not true.

Expressions of imminency abound in the writings and sermons of Church Fathers like Clement of Rome and Ignatius of Antioch, both of whom lived in the First Century. Statements about the Lord's imminent return can also be found in early publications like

The Didache (60-100 AD), *The Epistle of Barnabas* (130-131 AD), and *The Shepherd of Hermas* (110 AD). *The Shepherd of Hermas* actually contains a pre-tribulational concept of escaping the Great Tribulation:

> If then you prepare yourselves, and repent with all your heart, and turn to the Lord, it will be possible for you to escape it [the Tribulation], if you heart be pure and spotless . . .

In a Latin manuscript dating from the 6th Century there is a sermon derived from Ephraem the Syrian (306-373 AD), who was one of the major theologians of the early Byzantine Church. The sermon speaks of the Lord's return as being "imminent or "overhanging." It then states: "All the saints and elect of God are gathered, prior to the tribulation that is to come, and are taken to the Lord lest they see the confusion that is to overwhelm the world because of our sins."

These quotations leave no doubt that there was a definite concept in the early Church of an imminent return of Jesus before the Tribulation. But with the adoption of Augustine's amillennial view by the Roman Catholic Church in 431 AD, the literal interpretation of prophecy was cast aside, and the concept of a Pre-Trib Rapture fell into obscurity.

The Development of the Pre-Trib Viewpoint

After the Reformation, when people got copies of the Bible in their own languages and started once again interpreting the Bible literally, the concept of a Pre-Trib Rapture began to be revived. The Puritan leader, Increase Mather (1639-1723), attempted to prove in his writings "that the saints would be caught up into the air beforehand, thereby escaping the final conflagration." Likewise, Peter Jurieu, in his book, *Approaching Deliverance of the Church* (1687) taught that Christ will come in the air to rapture the Saints and return to Heaven before the battle of Armageddon.

In the 1740's a Baptist pastor in England named Morgan Edwards began to espouse a Rapture 3½ years before the beginning of the Millennium. Although his concept was really a mid-Trib Rapture, it clearly shows that there were people at that time who taught a Rapture separate and apart from the Second Coming.

According to Tommy Ice, director of the Pre-Trib Study Group, J. N. Darby refined the concept of a Pre-Trib Rapture between December 1826 and January 1827 while convalescing from an injury. In addition to systematizing the concept, he and the Plymouth Brethren proceeded to popularize it. The doctrine quickly spread around the world through publications like William Blackstone's *Jesus is Coming* (1878) and *The Scofield Study Bible* (1909).

The Bottom Line

Actually, the historic development of the Pre-Tribulation Rapture doctrine is irrelevant. The only thing that is important is whether or not the doctrine is scriptural. Is it based on the Scriptures? The answer is "Yes!"

What's it all about?

I receive several phone calls each year from people — some of them ministers — asking me if I think we are in the Tribulation yet. I always respond by telling them that when the Tribulation begins, the people who are on earth will not have to call anyone to find out for sure whether or not it has begun. The Tribulation will be a living hell with a degree of violence that is unparalleled in all of history.

The Bible gives us a lot of information about this horrible period of seven years that is fast approaching. The entire book of Zephaniah is devoted to it. In addition to many other Old Testament passages, like Isaiah 24, fourteen chapters in the book of Revelation focus on it (Revelation 6-19). But despite all this information, there are many myths concerning the Great Tribulation that circulate among Christians. For example, many argue that the first half of this time period will be peaceful and that only the second half will be characterized by intense warfare. Other misconceptions relate to the Antichrist and the Church.

The Concept

Before we consider some of these myths and misconceptions, let's familiarize ourselves with the concept of the Tribulation. Where does the idea come from, and what does it mean?

The first mention of the Tribulation in the Bible is found in Deuteronomy 4:27-30. Before the Children of Israel entered the Promised Land, Moses warned them that if they were unfaithful to God, they would be scattered among the nations. He then prophesied that "in the latter days" they would come under "distress," and the result would be their "return to the Lord."

Centuries later, Jeremiah used the same terminology when he referred to the Tribulation. He called it "the time of Jacob's distress" (Jeremiah 30:7). In like manner, Daniel called it "a time of distress," and he prophesied it would be the worst period of trouble in the history of the Jewish people (Daniel 12:1). Malachi stated it would be a time of refining for the Jews, as when silver is purified by fire (Malachi 3:1-4). And Zechariah used the same imagery when he prophesied that two-thirds of the Jewish people will perish during this time. Of the remnant remaining, he wrote, "I [the Lord] will bring the third part through the fire [and] refine them as silver is refined . . ." (Zechariah 13:8-9).

The Scope

The Jews will not be the only ones to suffer during this period of unparalleled trouble. The Bible makes it clear that all the nations of the world will experience catastrophic calamities.

Isaiah says it will be "a day of reckoning" for all the nations. (Isaiah 2:10-17). Zephaniah says that "all the earth will be devoured in the fire of God's jealousy" (Zephaniah 1:18). Here's how the psalmist Asaph put it: "A cup is in the hand of the Lord, and the wine foams . . . surely, all the wicked of the earth must drain and drink down its dregs" (Psalm 75:8).

The Length

The prophet Daniel defined the length of the Tribulation. He said God would accomplish all His purposes for the Jewish people during a period of 70 weeks of years (490 years). Sixty-nine of those weeks of years (483 years) would lead up to the death of the Messiah. The final week of years would occur at the end of the age, right before the return of the Messiah (Daniel 9:24-27). This concluding week of years (7 years) corresponds to the Tribulation for, as Daniel put it, it will mark the time when "the prince who is to come" will "make desolate" — a reference to the Antichrist.

The timing established by Daniel is confirmed in the book of Revelation where the Tribulation is divided into two periods of 3½ years each (Revelation 11:3, 7 and 13:5). The dividing point between the two halves of the Tribulation will occur when the Antichrist reveals himself by entering the rebuilt temple in Jerusalem, stopping the sacrifices, and declaring himself to be god (Matthew 24:15, 2 Thessalonians 2:3-4, and Revelation 13:5-6).

The Starting Point

When will this terrible period begin? The Bible says in general terms that it will start after the Jews have been regathered and have been re-established in their homeland and in their sacred city of Jerusalem.

Specifically, the Bible says it will begin at a time when all the world comes together against Israel over the issue of who will control the city of Jerusalem (Zechariah 12:2-3). In short, we are on the very threshold of the Tribulation today as we witness the United Nations, the European Union, the Vatican, and the Arab nations demanding that the Jews surrender their sovereignty over Jerusalem.

The specific event that will mark the seven year count down of the Tribulation will be the signing of a peace treaty between Israel and her Arab enemies — a treaty that will allow the Jews to rebuild their temple (Daniel 9:27).

The Nature

The unparalleled horror of the Tribulation is spelled out in detail in both the Hebrew Scriptures and the New Testament. Isaiah wrote that it will be a day of "the terror of the Lord" when "the pride of men will be abased" (Isaiah 2:10, 17, 19). Zephaniah proclaimed that it will be a "day of wrath," "a day of trouble and distress," and "a day of destruction and desolation" (Zephaniah 1:15). Men will stumble around like they are blind and "their blood will be poured out like dust" (Zephaniah 1:17).

This dreary picture is echoed in the New Testament. Jesus said it will be a time of tribulation "such as has not occurred since the beginning of the world until now, nor ever shall" (Matthew 24:21). In fact, Jesus said it will be so terrible that if it were not stopped at the end of seven years, it would result in the destruction of all life (Matthew 24:22). The apostle John states that the chaos will be so great that the leaders of the world will crawl into caves and cry out for the rocks of the mountains to fall upon them (Revelation 6:15-16).

Misconceptions

With this biblical background, let's turn our attention now to some of the misconceptions that exist regarding the Tribulation. Five of the major ones that I would identify are listed below:

1) The Antichrist will rise to world power through cunning, flattery, and deception.

2) The whole world will flock to the Antichrist in awe and adoration.

3) The Jews will accept the Antichrist as their Messiah.

4) There will be 3½ years of peace followed by 3½ years of war.

5) The Antichrist will be the most brilliant and effective leader in world history.

6) The Church must go through the Tribulation in order to be purified.

The Antichrist's Rise to Power

The idea that the Antichrist will rise to world power through shrewdness and skilled diplomacy is based on Daniel 8:23-25a. These verses say a king will arise who is "skilled in intrigue" and who "will succeed through the practice of deceit."

But the same passage also says that he "will destroy to an extraordinary degree." He will destroy both "mighty men and the people of the saints." Many of these he will destroy "while they are at peace" (Daniel 8:24-25a).

These verses make it very clear that the Antichrist is going to use *both* diplomacy and military power to gain control of the world. The likeliest scenario is that he will initially rise to power in Europe through the use of shrewd diplomacy. But he will extend his power from his European base through war.

I believe his conquering of the world through the use of military power is what is pictured in Revelation 6:1-8. This passage pictures the Antichrist going forth at the beginning of the Tribulation with a bow "to conquer." A red horse representing war "takes peace from the earth." The result is widespread suffering and the death of one-fourth of humanity by the sword, famine, pestilence, and wild beasts.

The World's "Acceptance" of the Antichrist

I think it is a misconception to believe the non-European world will flock to the Antichrist in awe and adoration. The world outside of Europe is not going to submit willingly to the control of the Antichrist, no matter how charismatic and dynamic he may be.

Keep in mind that the nations of Asia, Africa, and Latin America have fought for the past 200 years to rid themselves of European colonial rule. They are not going to passively submit themselves to a renewal of that rule. They will fight, and the result, as Revelation 6 so clearly indicates, will be a horrible world war of unprecedented magnitude.

Acceptance of the Antichrist by the Jews

The idea that the Jews will accept the Antichrist as their Messiah during the Tribulation is based upon a statement by Jesus that is recorded in John 5:43. Jesus said, "I have come in my Father's name, and you do not receive Me; if another shall come in his own name, you will receive him."

But the relevant end time passages in Daniel and Revelation seem to make it clear that the acceptance of the Antichrist by the Jews will be as a political redeemer who miraculously works out a peace settlement that will guarantee their safety and will enable them to rebuild their temple.

There is no indication that they ever accept the Antichrist as a spiritual redeemer — as their Messiah. In fact, when the Antichrist enters the temple in the middle of the Tribulation and declares himself to be god, the Jews revolt against him (Revelation 12:13-17).

When the revolt occurs, the Antichrist becomes obsessed with annihilating the Jewish people. That is when the "great tribulation" spoken of by Jesus in Matthew 24 will begin.

The Tribulation Holocaust that will occur during the last 3½ years of that terrible period will be far worse than the Nazi Holocaust. Two-thirds of the Jews will be killed (Zechariah 13:8-9). The Antichrist will be possessed by Satan (Daniel 8:24), and Satan is determined to annihilate the Jews.

Satan's obsession with the Jews stems from the fact that he hates them with a passion. He hates them because they gave the world the Bible. He hates them because the Messiah came through them. He hates them because God loves them, and because God chose them to be a witness of what it means to have a relationship with Him. And Satan hates the Jews because God has promised over and over in His Word that at the end of the Tribulation, He is going to bring a great remnant to salvation through faith in their Messiah, Yeshua (Romans 9-11).

The First Half of the Tribulation

Another misconception relates to the nature of the first half of the Tribulation. Many believe that this period of 3½ years is going to be a time of peace that will be followed by 3½ years of war. Some feel so strongly about this that they use the word, tribulation, to apply only to the second half of the seven year period.

This view is based primarily on a statement Jesus made that is recorded in Matthew 24. According to this passage, Jesus referred to the last half of Daniel's 70th week of years as "the great tribulation" (Matthew 24:21). But it must be kept in mind that these words of Jesus were directed specifically to the Jewish people.

The second half of the Tribulation will truly be the "time of great tribulation" for the Jews. That's because they will live in peace during the first half of the Tribulation under a covenant guaranteed by the Antichrist. During that time, the Antichrist will be focused on conquering the world. Once he has accomplished that goal — as he will (Revelation 13:7-8) — he will go to Jerusalem, enter the temple, stop the sacrifices, and desecrate the temple by erecting a statue of himself (2 Thessalonians 2:3-4).

The Jewish people will be outraged and will respond in a revolt. When they do this, the Antichrist will become obsessed with destroying them. That will be his primary goal during the second half of the Tribulation.

So, to summarize, the Jews will live in peace during the first half of the Tribulation, but not the Gentile nations of the world. The wars of the Antichrist will devastate the world. One-fourth of humanity will die in the initial war (Revelation 6:8). That's 1.5 billion people in today's terms. According to Revelation 8 and 9, when the war resumes, one-third of those left alive will die (another 1.5 billion).

The first half of the Tribulation is going to be anything but a time of peace. It will, instead, be a time of unimaginable carnage, for one-half of humanity will die in the first 3½ years!

The Quality of the Antichrist's Leadership

The erroneous concept that the Antichrist will be the world's most brilliant and glorious leader is based on Revelation 13:7 where it says he will gain authority over "every tribe, people, tongue and nation" on planet earth — something no other person has ever done.

But the evidence of prophecy points to the fact that his reign will be anything but brilliant and glorious.

For example, his conquest of the world will devastate the earth. It will be like Napoleon's "victory" in Russia — he will win the battle and lose the war. The Antichrist will end up with a world that is devastated and polluted beyond imagination. Furthermore, the world's subservience to him and worship of him will be based to a large degree on force, deception, and terror — not just genuine admiration.

Also, his obsession with the Jews will undermine his kingdom and ultimately lead to its destruction. Daniel 11:40-45 indicates that when his attention is diverted to the destruction of the Jews, a worldwide revolt will break out against his kingdom. Nations will send armies against him from the North, East and South.

The Antichrist may prove to be a successful military conqueror, but he will be a miserable leader whose world wide empire will last only 3½ years — and during that time, it will be constantly ravaged by internal revolt.

A Misconception Concerning the Church

Another popular misconception about the Tribulation is that the Church will go through it and suffer mightily at the hands of the Antichrist. This concept is based upon verses like Revelation 13:7 which says that the Antichrist will "make war with the saints."

But I believe the saints referred to here are those who are saved *during* the Tribulation. There is going to be a great harvest of souls during the Tribulation. Some will be saved in response to the Rapture. Others will respond to the preaching of the Two Witnesses in Jerusalem (Revelation 11). The response of others will be stimulated by the Tribulation judgments which will motivate many to repent. Still others will respond to the special angel who will be sent by God near the end of the Tribulation to proclaim the Gospel to every living creature (Revelation 14:6-7). Many will be saved, but most of these will be martyred for their faith (Revelation 7:9-17).

There is no purpose for the Church during the Tribulation. This will be a time of God's judgment upon the unbelieving Gentiles and Jews who have rejected God's grace, love and mercy expressed in Jesus.

Some argue that the Church must go through the Tribulation to be purged or cleansed. But the true Church has already been purified by the blood of Jesus (Ephesians 5:25-27, 1 John 1:7, and Romans 8:1). The Tribulation is not a Protestant purgatory.

The Grim Purpose

What's it all about? Why is there going to be such carnage? How could a God of grace, mercy and love allow such an outbreak of unbridled terror and bloodshed?

One reason is to satisfy the justice of God. Yes, God is characterized by grace, mercy and love, but He is also a God of perfect justice, righteousness, and holiness. Therefore, He *must* deal with sin. His justice demands it. Even His love compels it. How could a God of true love simply overlook the actions of a murderer or a pedophile?

The prophet Nahum understood the true nature of God. He wrote that "The Lord is good, a stronghold in the day of trouble, and He knows those who take refuge in Him" (Nahum 1:7). That is the love and mercy of God. But the same prophet wrote these words (Nahum 1:2-3):

> A jealous and avenging God is the Lord;
> The Lord is avenging and wrathful.
> The Lord takes vengeance on His adversaries,
> And He reserves wrath for His enemies.
> The Lord is slow to anger and great in power,
> And the Lord will by no means leave the guilty
>   punished.

Truly, the Lord is "slow to anger." He allows the iniquities of Mankind to accumulate over long periods of time because He does not wish that any should perish (2 Peter 3:9). His desire, instead, is that all should come to repentance. But there is always a day of reckoning, just as there was in the days of Noah, and such a day has been set for this age. Paul referred to it in his sermon in Athens when he said, "He [God] has fixed a day in which He will judge the world in righteousness" (Acts 17:31).

A Glorious Purpose

A second reason for the Tribulation is to bring people to salvation. Amazingly, even when God pours out His wrath, His fundamental purpose is not to destroy but to save. Isaiah 26:9 explains it this way: "When the earth experiences Your judgments, the inhabitants of the world learn righteousness."

The brutal fact is that God often has to hit us over the head with a two-by-four in order to get our attention and motivate us to repentance. The equally brutal fact is that most people respond to such discipline by either cursing God or continuing to ignore Him (Revelation 9:20-21). But some people always respond in humility and are saved. As Billy Graham has put it: "The same sun that melts the butter, hardens the clay."

When God's wrath is poured out during the Tribulation, some hearts will be melted, but most will be hardened, illustrating once again that nothing is as "deceitful" and "desperately sick" as the heart of Man (Jeremiah 17:9).

Man is frivolous about sin. God is serious. The Tribulation will be a graphic expression of how serious God is about Mankind's rebellion against Him.

The Message

The signs of the times are shouting that we are standing on the threshold of the Tribulation. The message of the Holy Spirit is "Come out of Babylon" (Revelation 18:4). That message means for us to separate ourselves from the love of this world and prepare ourselves for eternity. For believers, it means a commitment to holiness. For unbelievers it means a commitment to Jesus as Lord and Savior before He returns as God's avenger.

The time remaining is short. The time for action is now.

Why must Jesus reign for a thousand years?

When I first began studying Bible prophecy, the question, "What purpose would the Millennium serve?" really bothered me. The Word clearly taught that the Lord is coming back to this earth to reign for a thousand years. But I kept asking, "Why?"

I have since discovered that most amillennialists feel that same way. "Why," they will ask, "would the Lord want to come back to this rotten world? What could possibly be His purpose in returning to this world to reign for a thousand years? Why does the Lord or the world need a Millennium?"

My study of the Word has led me to conclude that God has several vitally important purposes for the Millennium.

Promises to the Jews

The first reason there must be a Millennium is that God has made promises to the Jews which He will fulfill during that time.

God has promised that He will gather to the land of Israel the remnant of Jews who accept Jesus as their Messiah at the end of the Tribulation (Ezekiel 36:22-28 and Zechariah 10:6-9). He will pour out His Spirit upon this remnant (Isaiah 32:15 and 44:3), greatly expand their numbers and their land (Ezekiel 36:10-11 and 48:1-29), and make them the prime nation in all the world (Isaiah 60-62).

They will serve as an object lesson of the grace and mercy which God bestows upon those who turn to Him in repentance (Zechariah 8:13):

> And it will come about that just as you were a curse
> among the nations, O house of Judah and house of
> Israel, so I will save you that you may become a
> blessing.

Zechariah says the blessings of God upon the Jewish remnant
will be so great in those days that "ten men from all the nations will
grasp the garment of a Jew saying, 'Let us go with you, for we have
heard that God is with you'" (Zechariah 8:23).

Promises to the Church

A second reason for the Millennium relates to a promise which
God has made to the Church. God has promised that the Redeemed
in Christ will reign over all the nations of the world.

This promise was given through the prophet Daniel in the following words (Daniel 7:27):

> Then the sovereignty, the dominion, and the great-
> ness of all the kingdoms under the whole heaven
> will be given to the people of the saints of the High-
> est One; His kingdom will be an everlasting king-
> dom, and all the dominions will serve and obey
> Him.

In the New Testament, Paul repeated the same promise in the
simplest of terms: "If we endure, we shall also reign with Him" (2
Timothy 2:12). Jesus affirmed the promise in His letter to the church
at Thyatira when He wrote (Revelation 2:26-27): "And he who overcomes, and he who keeps My deeds until the end, to him I will give
authority over the nations; and he shall rule them with a rod of iron
. . ."

When John was taken to Heaven for a visit to the throne room of
God, he heard a heavenly host singing a song that contained the
following verse: "And You have made them [the Redeemed] to be a
kingdom and priests to our God; and they will reign upon the earth"
(Revelation 5:10).

This promise to the Church of worldwide dominion is going to
be fulfilled during the Millennium. That is what Jesus was referring
to in the Sermon on the Mount when He said, "Blessed are the gen-

tle, for they shall inherit the earth" (Matthew 5:5).

Jesus will reign as king of the world from Mt. Zion in Jerusalem (Isaiah 24:23 and Zechariah 14:9). The Redeemed, in their glorified bodies, will help Him with His reign by serving worldwide as administrators, judges, and spiritual tutors to those who enter the kingdom in the flesh — and to their children (Daniel 7:18,27; Jeremiah 3:15; and Luke 19:11-17).

Promises to the Nations

God has promised that a time will come when the nations will be provided with their greatest dream — namely, worldwide peace. This has been an international dream since the beginning of time, but it has proved to be impossibly elusive.

Peace conference after peace conference has been held. Multiple treaties have been signed. World organizations have been formed. Yet, war continues to ravage the nations.

God has promised to give Mankind and the earth a rest from its wars. But that peace will not come until the Prince of Peace returns. Only then will the nations "hammer their swords into plowshares, and their spears into pruning hooks." Only then will we realize the dream of a world where "nation will not lift up sword against nation, and never again will they learn war" (Isaiah 2:4).

God has promised that He will flood the earth with peace, righteousness, justice, and holiness: "The earth will be full of the knowledge of the Lord as the waters cover the sea" (Isaiah 11:9). Even the bells on the horses bridles and the pots in the kitchens will bear the inscription "Holy to the Lord" (Zechariah 14:20, 21).

These glorious promises of peace and righteousness will be fulfilled during the Millennium.

Promises to the Creation

God has also made promises to His creation which He will fulfill during the Millennium.

God has promised to remove the curse which He placed upon the creation due to the sin of Man. He has promised to deliver the creation from its bondage to decay and to restore it to its original beauty, balance, and peace (Romans 8:18-23).

The carnivorous animals will become herbivorous (Isaiah 11:6-7). The deadly animals will cease to be poisonous (Isaiah 11:8-9). The plant kingdom will flourish and produce bountifully (Isaiah 35 and Ezekiel 34:25-31). The land of Israel will be so radically transformed that visitors will proclaim in amazement: "This desolate land has become like the garden of Eden" (Ezekiel 36:35).

Promises to Jesus

The most important reason for the Millennium is that God is going to use it to fulfill promises which He has made to His Son.

God has promised Jesus that He will be glorified in history to compensate in part for His humiliation in history. The Bible says point blank that Jesus will return to manifest His glory (Isaiah 24:23; 66:18-19; and 2 Thessalonians 1:7-10).

God has also promised that He will give Jesus dominion over all the world and that He will reign over the nations from Mt. Zion in Jerusalem (Daniel 7:13-14; Isaiah 2:2-4; and Zechariah 14:1-9).

Psalm 2 presents a good summary of these promises. It begins by surveying the rebellion of the world's political leaders against God and His Son, referred to in the passage as "His Anointed" (verses 1-2). It describes their contempt for the Lord (verse 3).

But the psalm says that God sits in the heavens and laughs and scoffs at them because He has appointed a day of reckoning when He will "terrify them in His fury" (verse 5). That will be the day when He installs Jesus as "King upon Zion" (verse 6).

Jesus then speaks and tells of the promise that His Father has made to Him (Psalm 2:7-9):

> 7 "I will surely tell of the decree of the Lord:
>   He said to Me, 'You are My Son,
>   Today I have begotten You.
>
> 8 'Ask of Me, and I will surely give the nations
>   as Your inheritance,
>   And the very ends of the earth as Your possession.

9 'You shall break them with a rod of iron . . .'"

It must be kept in mind that Jesus is currently a "king-in-waiting." Like King David, who had to wait many years after he was anointed before he became king of Israel, Jesus has been anointed King of kings and Lord and lords, but He has not yet begun to rule.

He is currently serving as our High Priest before the throne of God (Hebrews 8:1). He is waiting for His Father's command to return and claim all the kingdoms of this world (Hebrews 2:5-9 and Revelation 19:11-16).

A Final Reason

There is one other purpose for the Millennium that should be noted. I believe God is going to use the Millennium to prove to Mankind once and for all that Satan's religion of Humanism is totally bankrupt.

All Humanists, regardless of their political or theological labels, are agreed that the source of evil in the world is external to Man. They view evil as rooted in the corruption of society. They believe that the solution to all Man's problems can be found in societal reform.

Take, as an example, their attitude toward crime. They believe society is the root cause of crime. All we have to do to eliminate crime, they argue, is to provide people with a guaranteed job that will supply them with sufficient income so that they will be able to live in a nice suburb.

But such reforms do not transform the basic nature of people. In the ghetto a man will pay 25 dollars to go to bed with a prostitute. In the suburb he will chase his neighbor's wife. In the ghetto he will throw a rock through a window and steal a TV set. In the suburb he will put on his three piece suit, go to the office, manipulate the computer and embezzle a million dollars.

You do not change people's basic nature by changing their environment. Changing their environment simply converts them into more sophisticated sinners.

The Humanist view is absolutely contrary to Scripture. The Word of God teaches that the source of evil is rooted within Man's fallen nature, and that it is Man, and not society, which needs to be changed (Genesis 8:21; Jeremiah 17:9-10; and Mark 7:20-23). The Word also teaches that the only way this change can take place is through the work of the Holy Spirit within a person who has put his faith in Jesus.

God is going to prove this point by using the Millennium like a great experimental laboratory. He is going to place Mankind in a perfect environment of peace and prosperity for a thousand years. Satan will be bound. Righteousness will abound.

Yet, at the end, when Satan is released, most people will rally to him when he calls the nations to rebellion against Jesus (Revelation 20:7-10). The Millennium will prove that what Man needs is not a new society but a new heart.

Essential to the God's Plan

The Millennium is essential for the fulfillment of all the promises that God has made to the Jews, the Church, the nations, and the creation.

It is also essential to His determination to prove that the source of all evil is the fallen nature of Man, not the corruption of society, and that the only hope for this world is Jesus, not political reform.

Most important, the Millennium is essential to God's purpose in glorifying His Son. He is going to manifest the glory of Jesus before His redeemed saints and before all the nations of the world. Here's how it is described in Psalm 22:27-31 —

> 27 All the ends of the earth will remember and
>   turn to the Lord,
>   And all the families of the nations will
>   worship before Him.
>
> 28 For the kingdom is the Lord's,
>   And He rules over the nations . . .
>
> 30 Posterity will serve Him;
>   It will be told of the Lord to the coming generation.
>
> 31 They will come and will declare His righteousness
>   To a people who will be born, that He has performed it.

God's Faithfulness

The Creator of this universe is a covenant making God who is faithful to all His promises. He cannot lie (Hebrews 6:18). He cannot forget a promise (Deuteronomy 4:31). He is faithful even when we are unfaithful (2 Timothy 2:13).

Just as He fulfilled all the promises related to the First Coming of His Son, He is going to fulfill all those that relate to His Second Coming, including the promise of a millennial reign.

Many in the Church may be ignorant of His unfulfilled promises. Others may have forgotten them. But God has not. He intends to fulfill every one of them.

We are privileged to live in a time when we can witness God orchestrating the events of this world to the fulfillment of all the promises in His master plan.

3   . . . Ascribe greatness to our God!

4   The Rock! His work is perfect.
    For all His ways are just;
    A God of faithfulness and without injustice,
    Righteous and upright is He.
                                        Deuteronomy 32:3b-4

Part Four

Prophetic Signs

"But you, brethren, are not in
darkness, that the day [of the Lord]
should overtake you like a thief."
1 Thessalonians 5:4

Can we know when Jesus will return?

The answer depends on what you mean by His "return." As I pointed out in chapter 25, I believe His return will be in two stages — first the Rapture of the Church and then the Second Coming.

The Rapture is imminent. It can happen at any moment. There are no specific signs for it. No one can know its date.

The Second Coming is a different matter. First, the Bible teaches that we can know the season of the Second Coming and the period immediately preceding it — the Tribulation. The Bible also teaches that we can know the date of the Second Coming, once the Tribulation begins. That's because the Lord will return 2,520 days after the start of the Tribulation (Revelation 11:3 and 13:5). To put it another way, the Second Coming will occur seven prophetic years (at 360 days per year) after a peace treaty is signed between the Arabs and Jews that will enable the Jews to rebuild their temple (Daniel 9:27).

Knowing the Season

The reason we can know the season of the Tribulation and the Second Coming is because the Bible is full of signs which will signal the season of the Lord's return, and we are told to watch for them. These signs are found in both the Old and New Testaments, and there are a great number of them.

For example, one out of every 25 verses in the New Testament specifically concerns the Second Coming. But what is not so well known is the fact that there are over 500 prophecies in the Old Testament which also relate to the Second Coming of Christ.

In addition to the Major and Minor Prophets, the Psalms are full of Messianic prophecies regarding the Lord's return. In fact, Psalm 2 is one of the most important Second Coming prophecies in the Bible (see Part Six).

A great variety of signs are revealed in these scriptures. There are signs of nature, spiritual signs, signs that relate to the nature of society, international political signs, signs of technology, and signs that concern the Jewish people.

An Area of Ignorance

Many, if not most, Christians have ignored the study of these signs because they believe that since "Jesus is coming like a thief in the night," it is a waste of time to try to interpret the signs to anticipate the time of His coming.

When I was growing up in the Church this phrase was used as a big put-down. If anyone got excited about the Lord's return, someone would immediately try to stifle their enthusiasm by reminding them, "He's coming like a thief." That meant "Shut up!" because we were convinced there is nothing you can really know about the Lord's return.

It is true that Jesus said He would come like a thief in the night (Matthew 24:42-43). But Paul later explained that Jesus meant this statement for non-believers, not for Christians.

Paul's Revelation

Paul makes this point in his first letter to the Thessalonians. In chapter 5 he says that although Jesus is coming back like a thief in the night, there is no reason for His return to surprise any Christian (1 Thessalonians 5:4). Why not? Because, as Paul puts it, "Brethren, you are not in darkness, that the day should overtake you like a thief; for you are all sons of light and sons of day" (1 Thessalonians 5:4-5).

What does Paul mean by this seemingly enigmatic statement? I think he was referring to the fact the when we accept Jesus as our Savior, we are given the indwelling presence of the Holy Spirit (Romans 5:5). Through the Spirit we receive the power to become spiritually enlightened. John says in 1 John 2:27 that the Holy Spirit can illuminate our minds to understand the Word of God.

In other words, Paul is saying in 1 Thessalonians 5 that we can know the season of the Lord's return because we have been given spiritual discernment through the gift of the Holy Spirit.

But the spiritual discernment Paul is talking about is not gained by praying for God to zap us with it. It comes through the guidance of the Holy Spirit as we study God's Word. And because the study of prophecy has been so sorely ignored, many, if not most, Christians are going to be surprised by the return of Christ.

Jesus' Concept

In Matthew 24, Jesus compared the signs of His return to the signs of a pregnancy. Think of it this way: You may not know the date when a pregnant woman is to deliver, but sooner or later, as you watch the development of her pregnancy, you will think to yourself, "That baby is going to be born soon!" Why? You can tell by looking.

Jesus said the signs pointing to His return would be like "birth pangs" (Matthew 24:8). Any birth mother knows what Jesus meant by this remark. As the time nears for His return, the signs will increase in frequency and intensity, just like birth pangs. For example, there will be more earthquakes and more intense ones.

This is a crucial point that is usually overlooked. Thus, people often scoff at the signs by saying, "There have always been wars and rumors of wars and earthquakes and famines." Yes, there have always been such calamities, but they are now increasing in frequency and intensity, just as Jesus prophesied.

Peter's View

Peter tells us that one of the signs of the end times will be an outbreak of scoffing at the idea of the return of Jesus (2 Peter 3:3-4). We live in such times. The tragedy is that so much of the scoffing comes from Christians who are ignorant of God's Prophetic Word.

Peter also tells us that God does not wish that any should perish but that all should be brought to repentance (2 Peter 3:9). That's why God has given us so many signs to watch for. As the prophet Amos put it: "Surely the Lord God does nothing unless He reveals His secret counsel to His servants the prophets" (Amos 3:7).

Jesus' Warning

Jesus condemned the religious leaders of His time because they refused to heed the signs of the times. On one occasion they came to Him and asked Him to perform a miracle to prove He was the Messiah. Jesus rebuked them severely. "Do you know how to discern the appearance of the sky," He said, "but cannot discern the signs of the times?" (Matthew 16: 3).

Jesus was trying to point out that although these men could predict the weather by reading the signs of nature, they could not interpret His significance by reading the signs of God's Word.

What did Jesus mean by the "signs of the times?" He was referring to the fact that the Hebrew Scriptures contain more than 300 prophecies about His First Coming.

These same scriptures contain many more signs about the Second Coming of Jesus, and those signs point to this day and age as the season of our Lord's return.

Another Warning

But as we heed the signs of the Lord's soon return, we need to keep in mind another warning that Jesus gave. With regard to the exact date of His return He said, "Of that day and hour no one knows, not even the angels of heaven, nor the Son, but the Father alone" (Matthew 24:36). This had to be a reference to the Rapture since the date of the Second Coming can be calculated, once the Tribulation begins.

As we get nearer to the era of the Second Coming, Satan is going to motivate people to set exact dates for the Rapture. Many of these will be very sincere people who will be sincerely deceived.

Satan loves date setting. It focuses people's attention on a date rather than on the Lord. It draws the ridicule of the secular press. It leads to bitter disillusionment as people put their faith in the date and then are severely disappointed when the date comes and passes without the Lord appearing.

Date setting turns people off to God's Prophetic Word. It has the same effect as a person constantly crying "Wolf!" when there is no wolf. People finally start disbelieving in wolves — and suddenly the pack is upon them.

Likewise, people who have been disappointed or embarrassed by fixing their hope on a specific date often react to the debacle by turning off to prophecy. Then, when a responsible prophecy teacher comes along teaching we can know the season, they respond with skepticism, saying, "I've heard that line before, and you're not going to make a sucker out of me again!"

Knowing the Season

Knowing the season does not mean knowing the date. A season is a general period of time.

A few years ago after I had preached a sermon trying to prove that we are living in the season of the Lord's return, an elderly man came up to me and said, "That was a pretty good sermon young man, but I've got news for you. You see, when I was a boy, my pastor preached the very same sermon during World War I."

What that man did not realize is that his boyhood pastor was right on target, for — as we shall see in the next chapter — we have been in the season of the Lord's return ever since World War I began.

Noah preached for 120 years that people were living in the season of the pouring out of God's wrath. People laughed and scoffed at him. Can you imagine what they must have been saying about him 50 years into his ministry? "That crazy old fool Noah is a one-issue-obsessionist! He's been preaching the same message for 50 years and nothing has happened yet!" Some of them laughed until they could tread water no longer.

God's Character

God is incredibly patient. David expressed it this way in Psalm 103:8 — "The Lord is compassionate and gracious, slow to anger and abounding in lovingkindness." Peter tells us why: "The Lord is

. . . patient toward you, not wishing for any to perish but for all to come to repentance" (2 Peter 3:9).

This is precisely the reason that God gives us so many signs to watch for that will mark the season of His Son's return. You see, Jesus is returning to this earth in incredible wrath (Revelation 6:12-17). He is coming to pour out the wrath of God upon those who have rejected the love, grace and mercy of God.

Because Jesus is returning in wrath, God is obligated by His character to warn us. The Bible teaches that God never pours out His wrath without warning. God is not interested in catching anyone by surprise with the return of His Son.

But tragically, most will be surprised, even shocked, because they will fail to heed the signs of the times. The Word says that the political leaders of the world will cry out for the rocks of the mountains to fall upon them (Revelation 6:15-16).

Those who are surprised will have no one to blame but themselves. God is shouting from the heavens in many different ways that the time is fast approaching when His Son will return "to judge and wage war" (Revelation 19:11).

A Challenge

Jesus is coming soon. All the signs point to it. He is "right at the door" (Matthew 24:33), and for all those who have studied God's Prophetic Word, He will return as their "Blessed Hope" (Titus 2:13) and not as a thief in the night.

Are you ready? If Jesus were to return today, would He come as your Blessed Hope or would He catch you unprepared?

The choice is yours. The time is short. God is patient, but He will not be mocked. Here's how the prophet Nahum put it: "The Lord is slow to anger and great in power, and the Lord will by no means leave the guilty unpunished" (Nahum 1:3).

What are the indicators?

In Hebrews 10:25 we are told that we are to "encourage one another; and all the more, as you see the day drawing near." The context is the Second Coming of Jesus.

This passage makes it clear that we can know the season of the Lord's return — that tangible things will be visible to alert us to the Lord's soon return. What are those things? What are the signs the Bible tells us to watch for?

There are a great number and variety of these signs. In fact, there are so many that it is difficult to get a handle on them. They tend to overwhelm you.

The best way I have found to get a grasp on them is to group them into several broad categories. Let's take a look at them in that manner.

1) The Signs of Nature

The signs pertaining to nature have gained the least respect. Often when I point to these signs, people react by saying, "You've got to be kidding!"

The problem is twofold. First, people are prone to think, "There have always been earthquakes, volcanic eruptions, hurricanes, and famine. So, what else is new?" As I pointed out in the previous chapter, they are either ignorant of or have ignored the fact that Jesus said these natural signs would be like "birth pangs" and would thus increase in frequency and intensity as the time draws near for His return.

The second problem is more philosophical. We are a very rationalistic people and, as such, we tend to be skeptical of the supernatural. If we can't see it, weigh it, and measure it, we can't accept its existence. Yet, the Bible teaches there is a whole realm of reality that is not normally perceptible to the senses — the realm of the supernatural that includes angels and demons (Ephesians 6:10-12).

Because we are so rationalistic, we tend to scoff at the idea that God would speak to us through signs of nature. But the Bible affirms this over and over. The Old Testament prophets repeatedly pointed to signs of nature and claimed that they indicated the judgment of God or His impending wrath.

The book of Joel is a classic example of this point. The book begins with the prophet pointing to a locust invasion that has stripped the land barren. He declares that this is no accident of nature or just bad luck. Rather, the locusts were sent by the Lord as a warning, calling them to repentance. And the prophet makes it clear that if they do not heed the warning, God will send something worse than the locusts — namely, a foreign army.

A Biblical Tradition

God has always spoken through signs of nature, just as He did when He put a special light in the heavens to mark the birth of Jesus. Likewise, on the day Jesus was crucified, Jerusalem experienced a great earthquake and three hours of unusual darkness. On the day Jesus returns, we are told that the greatest earthquake in history will shake the world. Every mountain will be lowered, every valley will be lifted, and every island will be moved (Revelation 16:17-21).

It is no wonder that Jesus told us to watch for "famines and earthquakes" (Matthew 24:7) and for plagues and "signs from heaven" (Luke 21:11).

Nor is it any wonder that a glance at the statistics in a world almanac will confirm that all of these natural calamities have been increasing in frequency and intensity since the start of the 20th Century. As earthquakes continue to shake our west coast, as scientists proceed to make startling new discoveries in the heavens, as famine sweeps Africa, and as AIDS stalks the world, we need to get serious about the signs of nature.

Just as He has always done, God is speaking today through signs of nature. Are you listening?

2) The Signs of Society

Jesus said He would return at a time when society would resemble "the days of Noah" (Matthew 24:37).

The Old Testament tells us that Noah's age was one of wickedness and violence because the thoughts of men's hearts were continually focused on evil (Genesis 6:5-13). The New Testament reveals even more about the degraded nature of Noah's society. Romans 1:18-32 gives a chilling description of a society wallowing in immorality.

In this passage Paul says the root cause of all the problems was man's rejection of God: "They exchanged the truth about God for a lie and worshiped and served the creature rather than the Creator" (Romans 1:25). In other words, they put their faith in Man, giving their allegiance to Humanism, the religion of Satan.

Paul says that because they turned their backs on God, He removed some of His restraints on evil and "gave them over in the lusts of their hearts to impurity" (Romans 1:24). The result was an outbreak of sexual sin in the form of fornication and adultery.

When they continued in their idolatry and immorality, God removed His remaining restraints on evil and "gave them over to degrading passions" (Romans 1:26). The result was an epidemic of homosexuality which produced woeful diseases, for men received "in their own persons the due penalty of their error" (Romans 1:27).

As the homosexual plague gained momentum, the society quickly slipped into a cesspool of wickedness. People were filled with greed, envy, deceit, hatred, arrogance, and malice. These attitudes were reflected in a growing tide of unrighteous acts. Slander, rebellion, and violence increased (Romans 1:28-31).

Paul speaks in the first chapter of Romans as an historian, telling us what the days of Noah were like. In 2 Timothy 3:1-5 he speaks as a prophet, using almost the identical language of Romans to tell us what the society of the end times will be like. In doing so, he confirms the statement of Jesus that He will return at a time when society has gone full circle, returning to the depravity of Noah's day.

Characteristics of a Collapsing Society

Paul says that the society of the end times will be characterized by great stress (2 Timothy 3:1). It will be a society in which Man will love three things: self, money, and pleasure (2 Timothy 3:2-4). What Paul identifies here is the religion, the god, and the lifestyle of the end time society.

The religion will be the same as in the times of Noah. It will be humanism, the love of self. Whenever humanism is the religion, the god is always materialism, the love of money. And when materialism is the god, the lifestyle is always hedonism, the love of pleasure.

These three Satanic loves — self, money, and pleasure — combine to produce a fourth characteristic called nihilism. It is the payoff. We reap what we sow (Galatians 6:7), and the harvest of humanism, materialism, and hedonism is nihilism — or despair.

Paul describes the resulting despair in graphic terms: "men will be . . . boastful, arrogant, revilers, disobedient to parents, ungrateful, unholy, unloving, irreconcilable, malicious gossips, without self-control, brutal, haters of good, treacherous, reckless, conceited . . ." (2 Timothy 3:2-4).

Application to America

Does this sound familiar? It sounds like the evening news to me. We call ourselves a Christian nation, but our predominant religion is really Humanism. Humanists control nearly all aspects of our government as well as our schools.

We are a nation of materialists who worship the dollar. Greed is the motivating force of big labor, big business, big government, big religion, and big sports.

And do I really need to say anything about our hedonistic lifestyle? "If it feels good, do it!" is the philosophy of our age.

What's worse is that we are exporting our pagan values and lifestyle to the rest of the world through our degrading television programs and movies. The American dream of money, sex, and power has become the world's dream.

And we are reaping what we have sown. Our society wallows in despair as people seek to fill the vacuum in their lives with drugs, alcohol, sex, and violence. Prophecy is being fulfilled before our very eyes — and Jesus is coming soon.

3) The Spiritual Signs

There are numerous spiritual signs that we are to watch for, both negative and positive ones.

The negative ones are very negative indeed. They include such things as the appearance of false Christs and their cultic groups (Matthew 24:5, 11, 24), the apostasy of the professing church (2 Timothy 3:5), the persecution of faithful Christians (Luke 21:12-19), and an outbreak of Satanism (1 Timothy 4:1).

We are in the midst of the fulfillment of all these prophecies. The cults began their major assault on the Church with the founding of the Mormon Church in the 19th Century. Since that time, the cults have multiplied profusely to the point that today they are operating all over the world, preaching a false Jesus and deceiving millions.

Meanwhile, much of mainline Christianity wallows in apostasy. Many of the old line denominations have rejected the authority of the Scriptures and are now ordaining homosexuals and preaching New Age philosophy. Some Charismatic groups have rejected the true gospel for a pollyanna gospel that promises health, wealth and power. Others have decided that preaching the Word is too offensive to the world, and so they are spooning out a positive thinking pablum that is designed to make people comfortable with their sins.

True Christians — those who live their faith, speak out against ungodliness, and stand for righteousness — are being submitted to increasing persecution. Their rights are being denied in schools. They are discriminated against in the workplace in both hiring and promotion. They are mocked by the entertainment media. Their churches are increasingly harassed by zoning codes and vandals.

Satan is on the prowl. He knows Bible prophecy, and He knows his time is short. He is attacking the Church with a vengeance. He has also gone public, and the consequent outbreak of Satanism is something to behold. It is pervasive. Satanic themes dominate books, movies, television programs and music. People are enthralled with astrology, numerology, transcendental meditation, channeling, crystal-gazing, and many other such manifestations of occultic en-trapment.

Positive Spiritual Signs

I warned you that the negative signs are very negative, pointing to a society that is spiritually sick to its core. Let's move on to the positive spiritual signs and do some rejoicing!

One is the proclamation of the gospel to all the world (Matthew 24:14). This prophecy began to be fulfilled in the 20th Century as a result of modern technology such as shortwave radio and satellite television. With the advent of computer technology, the Bible has been translated into hundreds, even thousands, of languages and dialects.

Another positive sign is the increasing understanding of Bible prophecy. Many of the prophecies concerning the end times were not even understood by the prophet who gave them. A good example is Daniel. He was mystified by many of the end time prophecies which the Lord gave him. When he complained about this, the Lord told him to stop worrying about it because "the words are concealed and sealed up until the end time" (Daniel 12:4,9).

As we get nearer to the day the Lord will return, we understand more and more of Bible prophecy. Some of the new understanding is due to the development of world events, such as the re-establishment of the nation of Israel. Other mysterious prophecies can now be understood due to modern technological developments. But some of our greater understanding is due to the illumination of the Holy Spirit — not the giving of new revelation, but the provision of enlightenment concerning the revelation that has already been given in God's Word.

One of the most glorious spiritual signs is the great outpouring of God's Spirit that the Church is receiving in these end times. The

Bible prophesies that a great Holy Spirit empowerment will come in the latter days to enable Christians who are open to the Spirit's power to stand against the assaults of Satan.

In Joel 2:23 this is put in the imagery of an "early rain and a latter rain." The early rain was at Pentecost and continued through the early history of the Church when it was young and struggling to get established. The latter rain is occurring today as the true Church stands firm against the final assaults of Satan.

4) The Signs of Technology

The explosion of scientific knowledge and its technical application to communications, transportation, data processing, and weapons of war is definitely a sign of the soon return of the Lord (Daniel 12:4).

Consider, for example, how many prophecies we can now understand for the first time due to technological developments. Revelation 11 says that two great prophets of God will preach for 3½ years during the first half of the Tribulation and then be killed by the Antichrist. Their bodies will lie in the streets of Jerusalem for 3½ days and all the people in the world will look upon them (Revelation 11:3-13).

Prior to 1957 when the first satellite was put into orbit, it was very difficult to understand how all the people of the world could look upon two bodies lying in the streets of Jerusalem. Today we don't even stop to think about it because we know the capability of satellite television.

How could all the people of the world be given the mark of the beast (Revelation 13:16-18) before the invention of lasers and computers? How could the False Prophet make an image of the Antichrist that would appear to be alive (Revelation 13:14-15) before the development of robotics?

Jesus said that in the end times one of the signs will be "men fainting from fear and the expectation of the things which are coming upon the world; for the powers of the heavens will be shaken" (Luke 21:26). It sounds like the splitting of the atom to me — and the subsequent development of nuclear weapons.

5) The Signs of World Politics

Bible prophecy forecasts the coming together of a certain international pattern of nations in the end times. We took a detailed look at this in chapter 11.

We saw that the nation of Israel will once again exist, and all the nations of the world will seek to destroy the Jewish state (Zechariah 12:1-3). Particularly menacing to Israel will be a superpower located in "the remote parts of the north" (Ezekiel 38:6). This nation is identified in Ezekiel 38 in terms that can only be interpreted to mean modern day Russia. The existence of the Jewish state will also be threatened by its Arab neighbors (Ezekiel 35).

The resurgence of China as a superpower is also prophesied (Revelation 9:12-16 and 16:12) as is the reunification of Europe (Daniel 7:7-8, 24).

The world will be characterized by wars and rumors of wars (Matthew 24:6). The nations will also be afflicted with internal political strife that will often lead to "kingdom against kingdom," or civil war (Matthew 24:7). Lawlessness will increase everywhere (Matthew 24:12), a prophecy that has been fulfilled on the international scene with the advent of modern terrorism.

It is particularly interesting that the word translated "nation" in Matthew 24:7 ("nation will rise against nation"), is the Greek word *ethnos* which refers to an "ethnic people group" rather than a political nation-state. Since the break up of the Soviet Union, we have seen great outbreaks of ethnic violence — not only in the former Soviet republics, but also in areas like Yugoslavia, the Middle East and even here in the United States, as manifested in the Los Angeles riots.

There is no doubt about the fact that we are living in a world where the end time political pattern has come together.

6) The Signs of Israel

The most important group of signs, more important than all the rest put together, is the group that pertains to the nation of Israel. These signs are outlined in detail in chapter 8.

The reason they are so important is because the Jewish people are God's prophetic time clock. By this I mean that very often when the Lord is revealing that an important event will take place in the future, He will point to the Jewish people and assert that when a certain thing happens to them, the important event will also occur.

An example of this principle is found in Luke 21:24 where Jesus told His disciples to watch Jerusalem. His point was that Jerusalem would be conquered and then "trampled under foot by the Gentiles" until it was time for Him to return. In other words, He was saying that whenever the Jews win back the city of Jerusalem from the Gentiles, it will be a sure sign that His return is near.

The Romans conquered the city about 40 years after He spoke these words. They were succeeded by the Byzantines who were, in turn, succeeded by a host of Gentile nations until June 7, 1967 when the Jews finally re-occupied the city of Jerusalem for the first time in 1,897 years.

The Gentile world may not recognize the importance of this event, but the Orthodox Jews certainly do. They know the Old Testament prophecies and they therefore know that the Messiah is coming when they are back in their land and their city. That's why you can see banners all over Israel today that read: "Prepare for the Coming of the Messiah!"

Are You Ready?

God in His grace and mercy has provided us with a host of signs to prepare us for the soon return of His Son. Prophecy is being fulfilled daily before our eyes. Jesus said in Luke 21:28 that when these signs begin to appear, "straighten up and lift up your heads, because your redemption is drawing near."

We are living on borrowed time. Are you ready? Are you yearning? Can you say with Paul in 2 Timothy 4:7-8 that you are a candidate for a "crown of righteousness" because you have lived your life in the love of His appearing?

Are there signs that are unique to our day?

Whenever I present an overview of the signs of the times that point to the soon return of Jesus, I am often confronted by someone — often a professing Christian — who will say, "Come on David, these signs you are talking about have always existed in one degree or another, so what else is new?"

They will then proceed to point out that there have always been wars and rumors of war, there have always been natural calamities, and throughout history Christians have always been persecuted. Then comes the inevitable challenge: "Show me something really new and unique that clearly points to our day and time as the season of the Lord's return."

The challenge is understandable, but it is not entirely legitimate. That's because Jesus said the end time signs would be like "birth pangs" (Matthew 24:8). In other words, the signs would increase in frequency and intensity as the time draws near for Jesus to return. There would be more earthquakes, and more intense ones. Wars would be more frequent and more horrible in their degree of devastation. And that, of course, is exactly what happened in the 20th Century. All the signs began to increase exponentially in both frequency and intensity, as I will show in the next chapter.

But still, it is legitimate to ask if there are any signs that are truly unique to our day and time — signs that have never existed before. Are there new signs that clearly point to this period of history as the time of the Lord's return? The answer is yes.

A Key Prophecy

A verse that immediately comes to mind in this regard is found in Daniel 12. Daniel was given many prophecies by the Lord. Those relating to his day and time he clearly understood. He even seemed to understand prophecies that the Lord gave him relating to distant times, such as the succession of Gentile empires that would ultimately lead to the establishment of the Roman Empire. But when it came to prophecies about the end times — the period leading up to the Lord's return as King of kings and Lord of lords — Daniel did not understand what was revealed to him.

He wrestled mightily with the prophecies and finally cried out to the Lord in despair. "I have heard," he said, "but I do not understand! What do these events mean?" (Daniel 12:8). The Lord, in effect, responded by saying, "Cool it, Daniel, because it is not for you to understand!" The Lord's actual words were: "Go your way, Daniel, for these words are concealed and sealed up until the end time" (Daniel 12:9). It was Daniel's responsibility to deliver the prophecies, not understand them.

Note that Daniel was told the prophecies would not be understood "until the end time." In fact, in the very next verse the Lord told Daniel that at the proper time "those who have insight will understand" (Daniel 12:10).

Accordingly, there are many end time prophecies that have never been understood until now, either because their understanding depended on historical events or because they were dependent upon technological developments. The fact that these prophecies have become understandable in recent years for the first time ever is proof positive that we are living in the end times. Let's look at some examples from the book of Revelation.

Revelation Examples

1) The Tribulation Slaughter — Revelation 6 says that the Tribulation will begin with a series of judgments that will result in the death of one-fourth of Mankind. The world's population is approaching six billion. That means one and a half billion people will die in the initial judgments, reducing the world's population to 4.5

billion. The next series of judgments, recorded in Revelation 8 and 9 will kill another third of Mankind. One-third of 4.5 billion is another one and a half billion. Thus, in the first 3½ years of the Tribulation, a total of 3 billion people will die. That's half the population of the world!

Is this possible apart from the use of nuclear weapons? Only if it is a supernatural intervention of God. But God normally works through natural processes.

The unparalleled carnage of the Tribulation seems to me to point to nuclear weapons. Revelation 8 speaks of one-third of the earth being burned and one-third of the seas being polluted (Revelation 8:7-8). Later in the Tribulation, near the end, we are told that people will suffer from "loathsome and malignant sores" (Revelation 16:2). That sounds like one of the effects of radiation poisoning.

The advent of nuclear weapons makes possible for the first time the overwhelming Tribulation carnage portrayed in Revelation. I think nuclear power was what Jesus referred to in His Olivet discourse when He said that the end times will be characterized by "men fainting from fear and the expectation of the things which are coming upon the world; *for the powers of the heavens will be shaken*" (Luke 21:26, emphasis added).

The prophecies concerning the Tribulation carnage have clearly depended upon a major technological breakthrough for their understanding. We are living in the time of that breakthrough.

2) The Army of 200 Million — Chapters 9 and 16 of Revelation state that an army of 200 million soldiers will march "from the east" toward Israel. Daniel 9 indicates that this will be an army representing nations in revolt against the Antichrist.

Demographers estimate that the total population of the world at the time the apostle John wrote Revelation (95 AD) was only 200 million. How could an army that size march out of the east? It made no sense. In fact, it took 1,650 years for the world's population to double to 400 million! At the beginning of the 20th Century the total world population was only 1.6 billion, still too small for an army of 200 million to march from the east.

But the 20th Century witnessed an exponential increase in population. The population count at the end of the century was 6 billion, meaning that the world's population increased 4.4 billion in 100 years! Today, just one country to the east of Israel — namely, China — could field an army of 200 million.

Here we have a clear example of a prophecy about the end times that could never be understood apart from historical developments.

3) The Two Witnesses — Revelation 11 reveals that two great witnesses of God will preach in the city of Jerusalem during the first 3½ years of the Tribulation. Then, in the middle of that terrible period, the Antichrist will kill them.

We are further told that their dead bodies will lie in the streets of Jerusalem for 3½ days and that all the people of the world will look upon them. How could that be? Prior to 1957 that prophecy was not understandable in natural terms. There was just no way that all the people of the world could look upon two dead bodies in the streets of Jerusalem.

All that changed on October 4, 1957 when the Russians sent up the first Sputnik satellite. Today, our planet has many man-made satellites circling it, making possible all sorts of instantaneous communication. When those two prophets lie dead in the streets of Jerusalem, all someone will have to do is point a TV camera at them, send the signal up to a satellite, and all the world will be able to look upon them. Once again, modern technology has made an ancient prophecy understandable for the first time.

4) The Nation of Israel — Revelation 12 focuses on the nation of Israel. It makes clear that in the middle of the Tribulation Satan will motivate and empower the Antichrist to annihilate the Jewish state and its people. A remnant of the Jews will flee into the "wilderness" where they will be supernaturally protected by the Lord (Revelation 12:14).

At the time the book of Revelation was written, Jerusalem had already been destroyed by the Romans and the worldwide distribution of the Jews had begun. Until this century, there was never any prospect that the nation of Israel would ever exist again.

There were, of course, prophetic scholars who pointed to the many promises in Scripture that say the Jews will be regathered in the end times and the nation of Israel will be reestablished once more. But people laughed at these scholars and wrote them off as "dreamers" who were out of touch with reality.

Then, on May 14, 1948 the "dream" came true. The independence of the nation of Israel was proclaimed, and the Jewish state came back into existence for the first time in almost 2,000 years.

All the end time prophecies of the Hebrew Scriptures make it clear that the Lord will return when the Jews are back in the land (Ezekiel 37) and back in their capital city of Jerusalem (Zechariah 12). Jesus emphasized these two events in His teaching. He pointed to the re-establishment of the state in his fig tree parable (Matthew 24:32-35), and He stressed the importance of the re-occupation of Jerusalem in His Olivet discourse (Luke 21:24). He stated point blank that when Jerusalem is no longer under Gentile control, all the end time events would take place. Jerusalem ceased to be under Gentile control on June 7, 1967.

The central piece of the end time world political puzzle is now in place for the first time.

5) The Image of the Beast — Revelation 13 says that the Antichrist's religious leader, the False Prophet, will make an image of the Antichrist that will appear to come alive and speak. This trickery will amaze most of the world's population and will cause many of them to give their allegiance to the Antichrist.

What is the explanation of this event? Many have concluded that Satan will empower the False Prophet to give the image life. But Satan does not have the power to create life. Satan is a liar and a deceiver.

So, again, how can the False Prophet give an image life? I don't see any way for him to do it apart from modern technology. The illusion can be created through the use of modern robotics.

Many years ago I took my family to Disneyland. We went into a theater where we saw a man who looked exactly like Abraham Lincoln get up out of his chair in stage center, walk to the edge of the stage, grab the lapels of his jacket, and proceed to quote the Gettysburg Address. When he finished, a lady behind me exclaimed, "Wasn't he a good actor!" He was not an actor. The "actor" was a robot. That was 1967. Think what could be done today with the advances in computer technology.

6) The Mark of the Beast — Another prophecy in Revelation 13 that is dependent on modern technology is the famous one that states the Antichrist will control the world's economy by requiring people to bear his mark or name on their hand or forehead in order to buy or sell anything.

Again, how could this be possible before the invention of laser and computer technology?

The Uniqueness of our Age

After reviewing the prophecies listed above, I don't think we need any handwriting on the wall to indicate to us that we are living in a unique age. Historical developments and technological inventions are making it possible for us to understand many end time prophecies for the first time.

Nor is the list above an exhaustive one. I could name many other signs unique to our day and time — such as the reunification of Europe, the exponential increase in travel and knowledge, and the preaching of the gospel to the whole world.

The Significance of Prophecy Books

Even the phenomenal success of Bible prophecy books is a unique sign of the times. Consider, for example, Hal Lindsay's book, *The Late Great Planet Earth*. This book was the number one best seller in the world, with the sole exception of the Bible, for ten consecutive years, from 1970 to 1980 (as authenticated by *Time Magazine*).

But its success pales in comparison to the *Left Behind* series of books by Tim LaHaye and Jerry Jenkins. This series of 12 books, which began publishing in 1995, has sold over 60 million copies!

What was it that the Lord told Daniel? "Seal it up to the end of time when those who have insight will understand."

The bottom line, my friends, is that we are living in the final days of the end times, when prophecies that have always mystified people are suddenly being fulfilled. We are living on borrowed time, because Jesus is coming soon!

Jesus is Coming Soon

R. E. Winsett

Troublesome times are here,
Filling men's hearts with fear.
Freedom we all hold dear
Now is at stake.
Humbling your heart to God
Saves from the chastening rod.
Seek the way pilgrims trod
Christians awake!

(Chorus)

Jesus is coming soon,
Morning or night or noon.
Many will meet their doom,
Trumpets will sound.
All of the dead shall rise,
Righteous meet in the skies,
Going where no one dies,
Heavenward bound.

Troubles will soon be o'er.
Happy forever more,
When we meet on that shore,
Free from all care.
Rising up in the sky,
Telling this world goodby,
Homeward we then will fly,
Glory to share.

What is it, and what does it mean?

Have you noticed how almost everything in life seems to be accelerating in growth? Knowledge has exploded. We are traveling faster and farther than ever before. Instant, world wide communication has become common place. And the power at our disposal is mind boggling.

A Sign of the Times

The Bible teaches that this acceleration of technology which we are experiencing will be a sign of the end times — a sign that will signal the soon return of the Lord.

Consider Daniel 12:4. In this verse the Lord tells Daniel that one of the signs of the end times will be an acceleration of travel and knowledge. Here's how the verse reads in the *Living Bible* paraphrase:

> Daniel, keep this prophecy a secret . . . Seal it up so
> that it will not be understood until the end times
> when travel and education shall be vastly increased.

The same concept of end time acceleration is found in the New Testament. Jesus spoke about it when He talked with His disciples about the signs of the end times that would herald His return (Matthew 24:5ff). He mentioned a great variety of signs — spiritual, natural, societal, and world political — and then He said these signs would be like "birth pangs" (Matthew 24:8).

As the birth of a baby approaches, the birth pangs increase two ways. They increase in frequency and intensity. Thus, Jesus was saying that the closer we get to the time of His return, the more frequent and intense the signs will become. There will be more earthquakes and more intense ones. Likewise things like famine, pestilence and war will increase in frequency and intensity.

The Mathematical Concept

In mathematics this acceleration is called an "exponential curve." This term comes from what happens when rapid growth is plotted on a chart. When graphing the growth of something, the growth is considered to be on an exponential curve when the plot line starts moving vertically because the growth is so rapid. You can see a classic example of this principle in the illustration on the next page which shows the growth of the Internet company, America Online.

Now, the point is that the Bible indicates that the exponential curve will be one of the signs of the end times, and my thesis is that we are living in the midst of the exponential curve. Therefore, we are living in the end times.

Examples of the Curve

The 20th Century was the century of the exponential curve. Let's consider some examples.

Population — Demographers estimate that the population of the world at the time of Christ was only 200 million. It took 1,650 years for the world's population to double! But thereafter it began to double very rapidly because the Industrial Revolution produced modern medicine, which, in turn, reduced infant mortality rates and increased longevity. As the statistics below indicate, the rate of doubling has now reached exponential proportions.

Time of Christ		200 million
1,650 years	1650 AD	500 million
200 years	1850	1.3 billion
100 years	1950	2.5 billion
30 years	1980	4.5 billion

Power — Throughout most of recorded history, the maximum power at man's disposal consisted of bows and arrows, spears, and catapults. Even at the beginning of the 20th Century, war was still

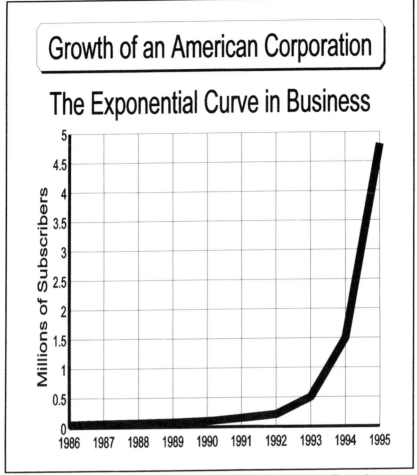

Growth of an American Corporation

The Exponential Curve in Business

The chart above shows the exponential growth during the first nine years of the Internet provider, *America Online.* In 1986 the company had 50,000 subscribers and 55 employees. At the end of 1995, it had grown to almost 5 million subscribers and had more than 3,000 employees. Source: *Dallas Morning News,* January 11, 1996.

primitive. World War I turned into a stagnant war of attrition because neither side had sufficient power to break out of the trenches.

Eighty years later, we had air power, armored power, nuclear weapons, and sophisticated bacteriological and chemical weapons. We have ICBM's that can deliver a nuclear payload half way around the world. We have laser guided missiles that can guide a bomb down a smoke stack. And we have nuclear submarines that can circle the globe without surfacing. Incredibly, just one of those subs today has more firepower than all the bombs dropped in World War II! It is no wonder the Bible says that in the end times "men will faint with fear" over the expectation of "the things which are coming upon the world" (Luke 21:26).

Transportation — In 1900 the major methods of transportation were what they had always been throughout history — namely, walking and riding a horse. Bicycles had been invented, and the steam engine had been applied to ships and trains. But steam powered transportation was too expensive for most people.

I have photos that were taken in my home town of Waco, Texas in 1912, and they clearly show that people were still getting around in horse drawn wagons and carriages.

Today we have automobiles (usually two or more to a family) and airplanes. We have bullet trains that travel 150 miles per hour and planes that travel faster than the speed of sound. And then, of course, there are rocket ships that take people into orbit around the earth.

In 1866 Mark Twain traveled to the Holy Land. It took him three months to get there. Today, a group can get on a jet plane in New York and be in Tel Aviv in 13 hours (and most will complain about how long the trip took!).

In 1900 the average number of miles traveled per year by a person inside the United States was 1,000. Today it is 25,000 miles per year, and many of us put twice that much mileage on an automobile in a year's time.

Communications — At the beginning of the 20th Century the telegraph had speeded up communications considerably, but the fundamental means which most people used to get information was still word of mouth and newspapers.

Today our communication resources are overwhelming. We have telephones, radio, and television. We have exotic devices like fax machines, pagers, and cellular phones. And we can communicate world wide through satellites.

I never cease to be amazed when I see someone use a credit card in an Arab shop in the Old City of Jerusalem. The shop may be nothing but a primitive hole in the wall, but over in some dark corner there will be a machine where the merchant can insert the card. A few moments later he receives an authorization. During those few moments, the card number has been transmitted to Tel Aviv, from Tel Aviv to New York by satellite, from New York to the credit card processing center somewhere in the States, and then back to the Arab shop in Jerusalem!

I am equally amazed at the way I can sit down at a computer at my home or office and use the Internet to send a letter in seconds to almost any place in the world.

Computers — Computer technology has contributed to the rapid acceleration of many aspects of life, but it is interesting to note that the exponential curve applies to the development of computers as well. Anyone who tries to stay on the cutting edge of what is new in computer equipment knows that it is a never ending battle that requires a lot of money. Advances are so rapid that equipment is out of date within a few months.

In 1970 I was a professor at a college where we bought an IBM computer for $100,000. The computer filled a room and generated so much heat that we had to have the room equipped with additional air conditioning. The computer's memory was 64K!

Now, if you are not a computer buff, that may not mean much to you, but keep reading because I'm going to make it understandable; and in the process, I'm going to illustrate how rapidly computer technology has developed.

Ten years later in 1980, the ministry I represent bought one of the first desk top computers made. It was a Tandy TRS 80, Model II. It cost $4,800. When I turned it on, I was astounded by the first thing that appeared on the screen: "64K Memory." In ten years time we had gone from a computer that weighed more than a ton to one that sat on a desk top, and the price had dropped 95%. But the memory was the same!

Ten years later in 1990, I went to Radio Shack and bought an electronic Rolodex small enough to fit into the palm of my hand. It cost $90. And when I turned it on, guess what? The first message that appeared on the screen was "64K Memory."

The first floppy disk that we used in the TRS 80 was eight inches in size! It held 300,000 bytes of information. A few years later the 5¼ inch disk appeared. It would hold 700,000 bytes. Then came the 3½ inch disk. Its capacity was 1.4 million bytes! The storage units kept getting smaller while their capacity continued to multiply. Then came the CD disk. I recently read an advertisement for a CD that contained 134,000 pages of theological documents, the equivalent of 1,400 pounds of books! And the capacity of a CD is nothing compared to that of a DVD!

Knowledge — The prophet Daniel was specifically told that knowledge would vastly increase in the end times, and it has. In fact, we have become so overwhelmed with the flood of new information that it is difficult to find wisdom anymore, because wisdom comes from reflection on knowledge.

When I was in graduate school in the early '60s, there were only two or three major academic journals in each field of study. Today there are dozens in each field, and they cannot begin to publish all the academic articles that are being written. Many have to limit the articles to one page abstracts, and even then most articles are rejected for a lack of space.

Encyclopedias are out of date before they can be printed. And I read recently where a research organization has determined that one Sunday issue of the *New York Times* contains more information than the normal person in the 19th Century was exposed to in a lifetime!

The most amazing thing to me in the area of information is the World Wide Web that can be accessed through the Internet. Using it, I can access the documents of the Vatican in seconds, and then in a matter of moments, I can go to the Israel Museum in Jerusalem, or I can dart back to the Library of Congress in Washington, D.C. In short, I can access information all over the world without ever leaving my office.

Violence — I don't think I have to emphasize that violence and lawlessness have been increasing. But it is hard to comprehend how rapid the increase was in the 20th Century.

It is estimated by experts that the number of people killed in all the wars fought from the time of Christ until 1939 totaled 50 million. In the next six years (1939 through 1945), 57 million people died in World War II. Since that time, almost 60 million have died in armed conflicts, either in wars between nations or civil wars within nations. The 20th Century was a century of unparalleled carnage.

Within the United States, violent crime increased 500% between 1960 and 1990. During the same period, the country's population increased only 41%.

Society — The disintegration of society has multiplied in speed as violence, wickedness, and immorality have increased exponentially. Jesus prophesied this would happen when He said that end time society would be like it was in the days of Noah (Matthew 24:37-39).

I have witnessed the decaying of society with my own eyes. I was born in 1938. When I was born, abortionists were sent to prison. Pregnancy out of wedlock was thought of as scandalous. Homosexuals were considered queer. Pornography was despised as a sickness. Marriage was sacred. Living together was taboo. Divorce was a disgrace. Homemaking was honored, and day care was provided by mothers in their homes. Child abuse was unheard of. Ladies did not curse or smoke. "Damn" was considered flagrant language in a movie. (A recent film featuring Jack Lemon had the "f-word" in it 170 times in 120 minutes!)

I could go on and on about the many ways in which our society (and societies around the world) have decided to "call evil good and good evil" (Isaiah 5:20). But the most dramatic way I can think of to illustrate how rapid the deterioration of society has become in America is to consider the results of a poll concerning public school discipline problems. Consider the differing results between the 1940's and the 1980's (and weep!):

The Top Public School Discipline Problems

1945	1985
1) Talking	1) Drug Abuse
2) Chewing gum	2) Alcohol Abuse
3) Making noise	3) Pregnancy
4) Running in the halls	4) Suicide
5) Getting out of turn in line	5) Rape
6) Wearing improper clothing	6) Robbery
7) Not putting paper in wastebaskets	7) Assault

(Source: *Time Magazine,* February 1, 1988)

The Gospel —But not all the exponential curves are bad. Modern technology has made it possible for the Gospel to be preached to billions of people through the use of such media as short wave radio, motion pictures, and satellite television.

A series of Billy Graham sermons broadcast from Puerto Rico in March 1995 were carried by satellite to 185 countries and territories in a total of 116 different languages! Plausible estimates indicate that, when network television telecasts and delayed videotape presentations were included, as many as one billion people heard at least one of Graham's sermons during this campaign, aptly titled "Global Mission." That means more people heard these sermons than had heard the gospel in all the recorded history of Christianity!

In 1800 portions of the Bible were available in only 71 languages. By 1930 the count had risen dramatically to 900. Today, there are over 2,000 languages in which at least one book of the Bible has been published. Although this figure represents less than half of the languages and dialects presently in use in the world, it nonetheless includes the primary vehicles of communication of well over 90 per cent of the world's population.

Experts on world missions estimate that 70% of all missions work in history has been done since 1900; 70% of that since 1945; and 70% of that since 1985! One of the key elements has been the "Jesus Film." Since it was produced in 1979, it has been shown to 5.1 billion people worldwide in more than 800 languages.

The results of all this mission activity are phenomenal. In 1900 there were only 10 million Christians in Africa. Today there are more than 350 million. Latin America is being swept by revival. In China, 25,000 people per day are accepting Jesus as their Savior. Among Muslims, more have been converted to Jesus in the last 20 years than in the previous 1,000 years. Jews have also been discovering their Messiah. In 1967 there was not a single Messianic congregation in existence. Today, there are more than 400 scattered around the world, with over 40 in Israel. Worldwide, Christianity is increasing at three times the rate of population growth.

World Politics — The exponential curve also applies to world events. Habakkuk 1:5 is as relevant today as if it were written yesterday: "The Lord replied, 'Look, and be amazed! You will be astounded at what I am about to do! For I am going to do something in your own lifetime that you will have to see to believe.'"

I took a sabbatical in 1987 and wrote a book called *Trusting God*. Seven years later, in 1994, I took another sabbatical and completely rewrote that book. The exercise gave me an opportunity to reflect back over the seven years between the two sabbaticals. I was astounded — even overwhelmed — by the rapidity and "stupendity" of world events.

Who could have dreamed in 1987 that within the next seven years any of the following events would have occurred? —

- The tearing down of the Berlin Wall

- The peaceful liberation of Eastern Europe from Communism

- The collapse of the Soviet Union

- The reunification of Germany

- The resurgence of Islam and its emergence as the greatest threat to world peace

- The sending of 500,000 American troops to the other side of the world to defend a country most Americans had never heard of (Kuwait)

- The handshake between Rabin and Arafat that has led to Israel surrendering its heartland to the PLO

In 1987 if you had predicted any of these developments, you would have been written off as "nuts." The rapidity of these events and their radical nature is breathtaking. They underscore the possibility of the impossible. And they certainly reveal that man is not in control.

The Significance of the Curve

So, what does all this mean to you and me? I would mention at least three things.

First, the exponential curve is proof positive that Bible prophecy is true. The Lord has told us what He is going to do in the end times, now He is doing it, and we had better pay attention to it.

Second, the fulfillment of prophecy related to the exponential curve shows that God is in control. Even when it appears that everything on this earth is out of control, we can be assured that God is orchestrating all the chaos to the ultimate triumph of His Son in history (Psalm 2).

Third, the exponential curve is very strong evidence that we are living on borrowed time. It points to the fact that Jesus is at the very gates of Heaven, waiting for the command of His Father to return.

A Warning

I want to conclude by issuing a strong warning against taking time for granted.

Many people are doing that today. They are saying, "I'm going to get serious about the Lord when I get out of school;" or "after I get a job;" or "after I'm established in my career;" or "after I get married;" or "after I get my children raised." Time is precious. There is very little left. *Now* is the time to get serious about the Lord.

Let me illustrate how critical the timing is by returning to the exponential curve. Suppose you put one bacterium in a jar, and assume it doubles every second. How many bacteria do you think would exist in the jar at the end of 30 seconds? The answer, incredibly, is over one billion — 1,073,741,824 to be exact. That's more than a billion in thirty seconds! That's the *ferocity* of the exponential curve.

Now, let's carry the illustration a step further. If at the end of 30 seconds the jar is half full, how much longer will it take for the jar to become full? The answer is one second (because it will double in the next second). That is the *suddenness* of the exponential curve.

That's what the Bible means when it states that people in the end times will be saying, "Peace and safety!" when "sudden destruction" will come upon them (1 Thessalonians 5:3).

Are you taking time for granted? Don't do it. If you are not a Christian, *now* is the time for salvation. If you are a Christian, *now* is the time for holiness.

Are we witnessing the emergence of the One World Church?

The Bible clearly prophesies that the Church of the end times will be characterized by apostasy. Paul said that the Antichrist will not be revealed until "the apostasy comes first" (2 Thessalonians 2:3). Jesus prophesied that "many will fall away" and "most people's love will grow cold" (Matthew 24:10, 12).

In the book of Revelation, chapters 2 and 3, the Apostle John records seven letters of Jesus to seven churches in the area of modern day Turkey. Among other things, these letters present a panoramic prophetic survey of the Church in history.

The last of the churches mentioned, the one that represents the Church of the end times, is the church at Laodicea. It is pictured as a church that is neither hot (healing) or cold (refreshing), but rather is lukewarm or tepid (Revelation 3:15-16). In short, it is a church that is apathetic. Jesus also pictures it as a worldly church enamored with its wealth (Revelation 3:17). The Lord is so dissatisfied with this church that He declares, "Because you are lukewarm, and neither hot or cold, I will spit you out of my mouth" (Revelation 3:16).

Clues from the Apostle Paul

Paul supplies us with some strong clues as to why the end times Church will be weak, vacillating, and full of apostasy. One of those clues can be found in 2 Timothy 4:3-4 which says that "the time will come when they [Christians] will not endure sound doctrine; but wanting to have their ears tickled, they will accumulate for themselves teachers in accordance to their own desires; and will turn away their ears from the truth, and will turn aside to myths."

Another clue is located in Paul's famous prophecy about end time society, the one in 2 Timothy 3. After describing in graphic detail how society will fall apart in the end times, Paul adds that the basic reason will be due to people "holding to a form of godliness, although they have denied its power" (2 Timothy 3:5). There will be no lack of religion, says Paul, but people will deny the true power that is able to transform society for the good, producing peace, righteousness and justice.

What is that power? First and foremost it is the power of the blood of Jesus. It is also the power that comes from accepting the Bible as the infallible Word of God. It is the power of believing in a Creator God with whom all things are possible. And certainly it includes a belief in the power of the Holy Spirit.

Today, these essential beliefs, which constitute the power of Christianity, are being subjected to an unparalleled assault from within the Church itself. The Bible says that in the end times people will mock the promise of the Lord's return (1 Peter 3:2-3). What is so shocking is that most of the mockery is coming from within the Church!

The Root of Apostasy

How have we reached this crisis point in the Church? It is rooted in the German School of Higher Criticism which invaded this country big-time in the 1920's. According to the "scientific approach" of this school of skeptics, the Bible is not the revealed Word of God. Rather, it is Man's search for God, and therefore it is filled with myth, legend and superstition.

Today this viewpoint dominates the seminaries of America. The Bible is studied not to be believed and obeyed but to be analyzed, dissected, and criticized. The result is that the Scriptures have lost their authority.

Apostate Leaders

John Spong, the former Episcopal Bishop of New Jersey, has written books in which he denies the virgin birth, denies the miracles of Jesus, denies the resurrection, denies the Second Coming, and argues that Paul and Timothy were homosexual lovers. Bishop Spong has become so enamored with other religions that he has announced he will no longer witness to those caught up in the spiritual darkness of pagan faiths!

Similar apostate thoughts were mouthed by Norman Vincent Peale in 1984 on the Phil Donahue program. Peale announced, "It's not necessary to be born-again. You have your way to God; I have mine. I found eternal peace in a Shinto shrine . . . I've been to Shinto shrines, and God is everywhere."

Phil Donahue was so shocked that he actually came to the defense of Christianity. "But you're a Christian minister," he retorted, "and you're suppose to tell me that Christ is the way and the truth and the life, aren't you?"

Peale replied, "Christ is one of the ways. God is everywhere."

Look again at Peale's incredible statement: "It's not necessary to be born again." What did Jesus say? "Truly, truly, I say to you, unless one is born again, he cannot see the kingdom of God" (John 3:3). Who are we to believe?

Schuller's Apostate Gospel

Peale's leading disciple, Robert Schuller, has outdone his teacher with the development of his "gospel of possibility thinking." In his book, *Self Esteem: The New Reformation* (1982), Schuller states that the leaders of the Reformation Movement made a mistake in centering their theology around God instead of Man!

Schuller teaches that the essence of Man's problem is low self-esteem. The Bible teaches it is pride. Schuller says that when Jesus referred in John 7:38 to "rivers of living water" flowing out of believers, He was speaking of self-esteem. The very next verse says He was speaking of the Holy Spirit. Schuller argues that sin is anything that robs us of our "divine dignity" (our "divine dignity"?). The Bible says sin is rebellion against God.

Like Spong and Peale, Schuller redefines the meaning of being born again. He says it means being "changed from a negative to a positive self-image — from inferiority to self-esteem, from fear to love, and from doubt to trust." The Bible denies that being born again is the result of changes in attitude. Rather, the Bible teaches that being born again relates to coming alive spiritually through faith in Jesus as Lord and Savior. Being born again is a spiritual phenomenon, not a psychological one. The experience will certainly result in changes in attitude, but it is not produced by them. Schuller confuses cause and effect.

An Apostate Seminar

Another modern day apostate is Robert Funk, a New Testament scholar at the University of Montana. He is the founder of the notorious Jesus Seminar which began operating in 1985.

The avowed purpose of the Seminar was "to renew the quest for the historical Jesus." The Seminar conducted this quest in a very unusual way. Meeting twice a year for six years, the group voted on each of the sayings of Jesus recorded in the Gospels. They voted by dropping colored beads in a box. A black bead meant Jesus definitely did not make the statement in question. A gray bead meant he did not say it, but it might have represented His thinking. A pink bead meant He probably said something like this, but not in the words recorded. A red bead meant He definitely made the statement.

As you can see, the very approach expressed contempt for the veracity of the Gospel accounts. What a spectacle this must have been to the Lord as He watched these so-called scholars vote on passages from His Word. "Professing to be wise, they became fools" (Romans 1:22).

The final product of the Seminar, published in 1993, was a blasphemy of God's Word. It was titled, *The Five Gospels* (1997). The title comes from the fact that the Seminar decided to grant the apocryphal Gospel of Thomas equal standing with the four traditional Gospels.

Only fifteen sayings of Jesus made it into *The Five Gospels* in red! In Matthew's account of the Lord's Prayer, the only words that made it in red were, "Our Father." Only one saying in the entire book of Mark was colored red. It is the statement of Jesus in Mark 12:17 where He told His disciples to "Render unto Caesar the things that are Caesar's, and to God the things that are God's." Likewise, only one statement from the Gospel of John qualified for the red coloring: "A prophet has no honor in his own country" (John 4:44).

The chilling thing to keep in mind is that the men who produced this spiritual pornography are professors at seminaries across America. They are the ones who are training the current generation of pastors and teachers.

Inter-Faith Apostasy

The big move at the grass roots level these days is interfaith worship services. I'm not talking about inter-denominational — rather, the emphasis is on inter-faith. Christians are inviting Muslims, Jews, Hindus, American Indian practitioners of "native religion," and others to join in worshiping "the one true god, regardless of the name you may give to him or her."

Pope John Paul II got caught up in this inter-faith fad in 1986 when he invited the leaders of the world's religions to come to Assisi, Italy to join him in praying for world peace. One hundred sixty representatives came, including the Dali Lama (who considers himself to be a god). Each representative prayed to his own god at the Pope's request! Did the Pope believe their gods were real? Or did he believe that they were all praying to the same god, but under different names?

The Most Popular Apostasy

The apostasy that is raging through Christendom today is the teaching that God has revealed Himself in many different ways to different cultures and that, therefore, all religions worship the same god, but just use different names. From this viewpoint, the Allah of Islam is the same as the Yahweh of Judaism.

The natural conclusion that is drawn from this apostate idea is that there are many different paths to God, Jesus being only one of them. This has led liberal leaders of groups like The National Council of Churches in the United States and the World Council to condemn missionary activity as "arrogant" and "anti-cultural."

The Bible teaches that these apostate Christian leaders are eventually going to succeed, at least temporarily. Their triumph will occur when the Antichrist forms his one world religion (Revelation 13:12).

The Stanford Conference

Major steps have already been taken to establish a unified world religion. In June of 1997 over 200 delegates from religious groups all over the world gathered at Stanford University to begin drafting a charter for an international interfaith institution to be called The United Religions Initiative. As one conference leader put it, "The URI is meant to be for religions what the UN is for nations."

The meeting was convened and presided over by Reverend William Swing, the Episcopal Bishop of San Francisco. Since 1993 he has been traveling worldwide to set up a network of religious leaders interested in a one world religious organization. The Bishop told the *San Francisco Chronicle*:

> I've spent a lot of time praying with Brahmins, meditating with Hindus, and chanting with Buddhists. I feel I've been enormously enriched inwardly by exposure to these folks. I've gone back and read our own scriptures, and it's amazing how they begin to read differently when you're exposed to more truth from more people in other parts of the world.

This statement is the epitome of the new tolerance that is being evidenced by Christendom's apostate leaders. (Incidentally, I wonder what "new truth" he found outside the Bible!)

The New Charter

The United Religions Charter was ratified on June 26, 2000 at a meeting held at Carnegie Mellon University in Pittsburgh, Pennsylvania. The preamble states: "The URI is a growing global community dedicated to promoting enduring, daily interfaith cooperation, ending religiously motivated violence and creating cultures of peace, justice and healing for the Earth and all living beings."

It sounds so *good!* It is all so touchy-feely and warm and fuzzy. The Charter is full of New Age type statements like the following: "We unite to celebrate the joy of blessings and the light of wisdom in both movement and stillness."

One of the key principles expressed in the Charter is worded as follows: "Members of the URI shall not be coerced to participate in any ritual or be proselytized." In other words, no member of the URI will engage in missionary activity since that would constitute an act of spiritual imperialism. It all makes sense from their viewpoint, since they believe all religions are equally valid.

The amazing thing is the degree of inclusiveness that the URI represents. In addition to the world's major faiths, the organization has embraced "neo-pagan" religions like Druids and Celtic Revivalists, Wicca and Witchcraft, and Norse Paganism.

Deceptive Tolerance

All of this is being done in the name of "tolerance." But it is a perverted tolerance. It is a subtle ploy of Satan to corrupt the Church from within.

The deception sounds so appealing: "Why draw lines of fellowship over doctrinal differences? The only thing that's important is sincerity. Reach out and embrace all those who profess to believe in God, regardless of who their god may be. Ignore doctrinal differences. Do it in the name of Christian love. Do it for the sake of religious unity."

The Coming World Religion

The Christian leaders who are advocating tolerance to the point of embracing apostasy are going to triumph in the near future, at least temporarily. The Bible makes that clear. Just as "one world" thought is dominating the political and economic scenes today, it has captivated the thinking of both Catholic and Protestant leaders regarding religion.

In that regard, I think it is significant that in 1989 the Archbishop of the Anglican Church, Robert Runcie, called for all Christians to accept the Pope as "a common leader presiding in love." Runcie made his appeal at an evening prayer service midway through his first official visit to the Vatican. "For the universal church, I renew the plea," he said. "Could not all Christians come to reconsider the kind of primacy the bishop of Rome exercised with the early church, 'a presiding in love' for the sake of the unity of the churches in the diversity of their mission?"

That kind of thinking is paving the way for the establishment of the one world government of the Antichrist (Revelation 13:1-10) which will be supported by the one world religious system of the False Prophet (Revelation 13:11-18).

I believe the harlot church of Revelation 17 will most likely be an amalgamation of the world's pagan religions, including apostate Protestants, under the leadership of the Catholic Church.

A Prophecy Fulfilled

Englishman William Booth (1829 - 1912), who founded the Salvation Army, was a man with a great zeal for the Lord and a passion for lost souls. He was also a man of vision. On the eve of the 20th Century when Christendom was caught up in euphoria about how the Church would soon take the world for Christ, Booth predicted that the gospel would not fare well in the new century. Specifically, he prophesied that by the end of the 20th Century, much of the Church would be preaching:

> Christianity without Christ
> Forgiveness without repentance
> Salvation without regeneration
> Heaven without Hell

Sad to say, we have arrived, and that fact is a sign that we are living in the season of the Lord's return.

What is its importance?

Jesus warned repeatedly that in the end times the world would witness many false Christs and false prophets. In His Olivet Discourse, when He listed the signs of the times that would point to His soon return, the very first sign He mentioned was an epidemic of false Christs. "Many will come in My name, saying, 'I am the Christ,' and will mislead many" (Matthew 24:5).

This is the only sign that He repeated in that memorable speech — and He repeated it twice. In verse 11 He focused on false prophets: "And many false prophets will arise, and will mislead many." And, again, in verse 24 He mentioned both groups: "For false Christs and false prophets will arise and will show great signs and wonders, so as to mislead, if possible, even the elect."

This latter statement is particularly chilling since it indicates that the cult leaders of the end times will have supernatural powers and will therefore be able to deceive many people through the performance of miracles.

Apostolic Warnings

The warnings of Jesus are not the only ones in the Bible concerning cults. His apostles warned repeatedly about the danger of false and deceptive teachers.

John warned that Christians are to be on guard against "antichrists" — whom he defined as those who deny that Jesus is the Christ (1 John 2:18, 22). He also challenged believers to "test the spirits to see whether they are from God; because many false prophets have gone out into the world" (1 John 4:1). The test He prescribed was to ask the questionable person to confess that "Jesus Christ has come in the flesh" (1 John 4:2).

Nearly all of John's second epistle is devoted to a warning against false teachers. As John puts it: "Many deceivers have gone out into the world" (2 John 7). He then states that "anyone who goes too far and does not abide in the teaching of Christ, does not have God," and he admonishes believers in the strongest of terms to avoid association with such people: "If anyone comes to you and does not bring this teaching [the teaching of Christ], do not receive him into your house, and do not give him a greeting; for the one who gives him a greeting participates in his evil deeds" (2 John 9-11).

Likewise, Paul speaks out strongly against false and deceptive teachers. Paul says that if an angel of God were to come with a gospel different from the one revealed in the Scriptures, we should reject his message and "let him be accursed" (Galatians 1:8-9). In his first letter to Timothy, Paul warned about deception in the end times: "The Spirit explicitly says that in later times some will fall away from the faith, paying attention to deceitful spirits and doctrines of demons" (1 Timothy 4:1).

Peter contributed to this chorus of warnings when he wrote that there will be false teachers "who will secretly introduce destructive heresies, even denying the Master who bought them" (2 Peter 2:1). He says some will be motivated by sensuality and others by greed (2 Peter 2:2-3).

Early Cults

All these apostolic warnings were much needed, for the early church was assaulted by false teachers and cultic groups from the beginning.

The first to arrive on the scene were the Judaizers who responded to the inclusion of Gentiles in the Church by demanding that they be circumcised in order to be saved (Acts 15:1). They also demanded that the Gentile converts observe the Law of Moses (Acts 15:5).

These demands caused such a crisis that a convention of church leaders was called in Jerusalem to discuss and decide the matter.

The convention reaffirmed that salvation comes "through the grace of the Lord Jesus," and not through obedience to the Law (Acts 15: 11).

The Judaizers were severely rebuffed by this decision, but they continued to plague the early church. At one point, Paul had to publicly rebuke Peter for playing politics to please what he called "the party of the circumcision" (Galatians 2:11-14). Paul also devoted much of his Galatian letter to denouncing the teachings of the Judaizers.

The Gnostics were the second major cultic group that afflicted the early church. They refused to accept the truth of the incarnation because they did not believe you could mix the holiness of God with flesh. They took this position because they considered all material things to be inherently evil. They therefore taught that Jesus was a spirit being — an angel who was neither fully God or man. In doing this they denied both the physical death of Jesus and His bodily resurrection. This is the reason that John told the early church to test all teachers by asking them to confess "that Jesus Christ has come in the flesh" (1 John 4:2).

Modern Cults

False Christs, false prophets, and their cultic groups have continued to afflict the Church throughout its history from time to time. But the acute danger of the cults that Jesus warned would characterize the end times did not begin to manifest itself until the middle of the 19th Century when an American by the name of Joseph Smith founded a religious movement that was destined to become the world's largest cult — the Church of Jesus Christ of Latter Day Saints, better known as the Mormons. Today the Mormons number more than eleven million worldwide.

Before the end of the 19th Century several more cultic organizations had been founded, including the Jehovah's Witnesses and several spiritist groups like the Church of Christ Scientists.

The 20th Century witnessed an explosion of the cults. They multiplied with great rapidity to the point that some cult-watch organizations now list more than 500 cultic groups operating in America.

The Dangers of the Cults

These cults present a clear and present danger to the true Church. That danger takes two forms. First, the cults are converting many professing Christians. One expert on the cults who grew up in a cultic group once expressed this problem to me in these terms: "Christians convert pagans. Cults convert Christians."

The statement is very true. The average cult member is thoroughly indoctrinated. He knows what he believes and why he believes it. The average Christian, by contrast, usually has little biblical knowledge. He's not sure what he believes and cannot defend his faith. The result — as cult expert Walter Martin once put it — is that "the average Jehovah's Witness can turn the average Christian into a theological pretzel in two minutes flat."

Tens of thousands of professing Christians are being deceived each year by the cults. They are being sucked into spiritual darkness by clever and deceptive peddlers of false messiahs, and the result is the damnation of their souls. The Church needs to face up to this problem and start responding to it by grounding its members in the fundamentals of the faith so that they will know what they believe and why.

Doctrinal Influence

The second danger of the cults is their penetration of the Church with their heretical doctrines. Their "doctrines of demons" (1 Timothy 4:1) are creeping into the mainline church in many forms. It is not at all unusual anymore to hear liberal denominational leaders deny the divinity of Jesus or His bodily resurrection or His Second Coming. One of the favorite liberal themes today is the teaching that there are many different roads to God — that God has revealed Himself in Buddha, Confucius, Abraham, Jesus, Mohammed, and many other persons. The natural conclusion of such thought is that it is improper for Christians to seek to convert people of other religions to Jesus.

Even fundamentalist type groups have gotten caught up in cultic doctrines. A popular fad is the teaching that the power of prayer is not to be found in faith but in the imagination, or visualization. This is a heresy straight out of Eastern mystical religion. It is a practice of

Shamanism that is being embraced by many Christian groups today.

Another cultic doctrine that has invaded the Church is the incredible teaching that our salvation was not won on the Cross by the shedding of the blood of Jesus, but was won instead at the hands of Satan as he tortured Jesus in Hell for the three days between His death and His resurrection. This nonsense ignores the fact that Jesus declared on the Cross, "It is finished!" (John 19:30). It denies the clear teaching of the Scriptures that we are saved by the blood of Jesus (1 John 1:7). And it ignores the fact that there is no mention in the Bible of any visit to Hell by Jesus or any suffering on His part after His death.

Equally incredible is the cultic doctrine that is being taught on Christian television today which holds that those who are born again are "little gods." This is the lie that Satan told to Eve in the garden of Eden, and it is the same lie that is taught by many cultic groups like the Mormons.

Christian Involvement

Additional evidence of cultic influence on the Church is to be found in the growing acceptance of the cults by some church leaders.

A very well known Charismatic leader has stated that he felt it was time for the Church to embrace Mormons as brothers in Christ! Another endorsement of a cultic group occurred when Christendom's leading televangelist served as the featured speaker at the dedication of the new international headquarters of the Unity Church, a classic cult that teaches reincarnation! He even conducted a seminar for them on church growth.

Definition

What is a cult? The typical dictionary definition is so vague and general that the term could be applied to any religious group. For example, The American College Dictionary defines a cult as "a particular system of religious worship." In practice the term is used in many different ways and is usually used in a very indiscriminate manner.

Often the word is used in a very broad sense to refer to any religious group that is non-Christian in nature. Thus, people lump together pseudo-Christian movements (like Armstrongism and Mormonism) with completely non-Christian groups (like Muslims and Hindus).

I prefer to give the term a more technical meaning. To me, a cult is a religious group that masquerades as being Christian. It employs Christian terms, quotes the Bible, and uses Christian symbols. But it is not a true expression of the Christian faith.

The Distinguishing Feature

The fundamental thing that sets a cult apart from orthodox Christianity is its concept of Jesus. That concept is always distorted and perverted. In short, cults present a false Jesus.

This is a very serious matter because our salvation depends upon our relationship with Jesus — the true Jesus of Nazareth who revealed Himself to the world as God in the flesh (John 14:9-11). There is salvation in no other person (Acts 4:10-12). There is salvation in no other way (John 14:6).

We can be wrong about many things, but if we are right about Jesus, we can be saved. Likewise, we can be right about many things, but if we are wrong about Jesus, we can be lost. To be saved, we must put our faith in Jesus — the Jesus revealed by the Word of God (John 17:3).

As you can see in the chart on the next page, the identity of Jesus is terribly distorted by the cults. For one, He is an angel; for another, He is a minor god; for many He was just a remarkable man who manifested the Christ consciousness. None view Him biblically as God in the flesh.

Cultic Views of Jesus

Cultic Group	View of Jesus
1) Church of Jesus Christ of Latter Day Saints (Mormons)	Jesus is the brother of Lucifer. He is one of several gods created by the super god, Adam, an exalted man.
2) Jehovah's Witnesses	Jesus is Michael the Archangel.
3) The Unification Church (Moonies)	Jesus was only a spiritual redeemer who failed to provide the physical redemption that the new messiah, Reverend Moon, will supply.
4) The Armstrongites	Jesus is part of a Godhead that is open to perfected men.
5) The Way International	Jesus was a created being who was sent by God to die for the sins of Mankind.
6) The Unitarian Church	Jesus is a good moral man.
7) The Mind Sciences (Christian Science, Religious Science, Unity, Theosophy, etc.)	Jesus was only a man who manifested the Christ potential that resides in each person. He neither died for sins, nor was He resurrected. One spiritist group has referred to Jesus as "a medium of the sixth sphere of the astro-projection"!
8) Church Universal and Triumphant	Jesus was just another "avatar" or Ascended Master, along with such people as Buddha, Enoch and Elijah.
9) Freemasonry	Jesus was not God, nor is salvation available only through Him. He was a man who attained the state of Christ-consciousness.

"Jesus is the name of the man who, more than all other men, has presented Christ, the true idea of God . . . Jesus is the human man, and Christ is the divine idea; hence the duality of Jesus the Christ." — Mary Baker Eddy

Other Characteristics

With respect to organization and operation, there are two types of cultic groups.

One type — the rarer form — operates openly and encourages freedom of thought. The Unitarian Church and the Mind Science Churches are examples of this type. These usually teach universalism — the ultimate salvation of all people.

The more common type of cult are those that operate in some degree of secrecy and which exercise a large degree of thought control over their members. These groups share six characteristics:

1) **Leadership** — There is usually a dynamic, charismatic founder or leader who considers himself to be either the true Christ or the last prophet of God. Examples are Joseph Smith, the founder of the Mormons, and Sun Myung Moon, the leader of the Moonies.

2) **Writings** — There are always some extra-Biblical writings which are considered equal to or superior to the Bible. The Mormons have their Pearl of Great Price. The Children of God look to the letters of their founder, Moses David (David Berg). The prophetic proclamations of Herbert W. Armstrong are revered as scripture by many Armstrongites. The Jehovah's Witnesses have their own eccentric "translation" of the Scriptures. It is actually a version that simply rewords all the verses that conflict with their theology!

3) **Salvation** — There is always a perverted view of salvation. Cults emphasize salvation by works. Their faithful followers are therefore zealous about knocking on doors or giving their time or money.

4) **Doctrine** — Cults always have some weird doctrines that are not biblically based. Many of the Mind Science groups teach reincarnation, and all of them deny the reality of evil, disease, and death. Nearly all the cults deny the existence of Hell. The Children of God practice sexual permissiveness. Mormons believe in baptism for the dead. The Armstrongites teach that the Anglo-Saxon peoples are the true Jews.

5) **Attitude** — The groups are exclusivistic and sectarian, usually viewing themselves as God's only true church. They therefore refuse to have anything to do with any other group. They are often very secretive in nature — as evidenced by the secret temple rites of the Mormons.

6) **Government** — The groups are almost always authoritarian in nature, and some are even totalitarian in the control they try to exercise over their members. Someone at the top — either an individual or a collective leadership — calls all the shots.

Borderline Groups

There are a number of religious groups that manifest many of the characteristics listed above, but I do not consider them to be cults because they have an orthodox view of Jesus as God in the flesh.

These groups tend to be sectarian, legalistic, and exclusivistic to the point that each of them consider their particular group to be the one and only true church. Accordingly, they have almost nothing to do with other Christian groups.

I classify these groups as sects. They include, among others, the non-instrumental Churches of Christ, the United Pentecostals, the Seventh Day Adventists, and Catholics.

Like the cults, the sects manifest many unorthodox beliefs. The Seventh Day Adventists observe the Jewish Sabbath and the Jewish dietary laws. The Churches of Christ believe instrumental music in worship is sinful. They also believe in water regeneration, and many of their members equate the Holy Spirit with the Bible. United Pentecostals believe you must speak in tongues in order to be saved. They are also unitarian in their view of God. And the Catholics believe in papal infallibility, purgatory, prayer to saints — and other such unbiblical concepts.

The rest of Christendom falls into the category of denominations like the Baptists, Methodists, and Assemblies of God. These are orthodox Christian groups who are non-sectarian and thus consider themselves to be a part of the body of Christ — but only a part. These groups view the true Church as being composed of all born again people, regardless of their denominational or sectarian label.

The Transformed Cult

There is only one example in history of a cult transforming itself into a mainline, orthodox Christian fellowship — and that is the Worldwide Church of God of Herbert W. Armstrong.

When Armstrong died in 1986 at the age of 94, he was succeeded as General Pastor by Joseph W. Tckach (pronounced Ta-koch).

Pastor Tckach immediately began to lead the group away from its cultic doctrines. He affirmed the traditional Christian concept of the Trinity, rejected the doctrine of British-Israelism, and renounced Sabbath-keeping as a requirement for salvation.

In the spring of 1997 the church was admitted to the membership of the National Association of Evangelicals, becoming the first cult in history to make the transition to mainline Christianity.

The membership of the church has since dropped from 145,000 worldwide in 1988 to 75,000, and approximately 50 splinter groups have formed, many of which still teach the cultic doctrines of the founder.

The Invisible Cult

Most modern day cults operate outside the Church, attempting to convert Christians to their perverse doctrines and their false messiahs.

The cult that presents the greatest danger to Christianity is the one that operates inside the Church. It seems to present no challenge to the Church. It does not attempt to draw members out of the Church. Most people are oblivious to its presence and its influence, which is why I refer to it as "the invisible cult."

I am speaking of the Masons. These are well-meaning men who have given their allegiance to a secret organization that teaches doctrines that run counter to the gospel. They pray to the "Great Architect of the Universe" without mentioning Jesus. They subscribe to demonic oaths. Their official publications teach salvation through good works, and they therefore believe that people of all religions can be saved.

No Christian has any business being a member of a secret organization that teaches unbiblical doctrines. It diverts his energy and resources from his church, and it compromises his spiritual growth.

An Attractive Facade

Cults are incredibly deceptive. They not only use Christian language and symbols, but they also display worthy attributes like zeal, dedication, and concern for the individual.

Another thing that makes them attractive is that they usually exhibit very fine moral qualities. Take the Mormons for example. They are a people committed to personal holiness, and they put great importance on the value of the family.

To put it another way, the cults are full of very sincere and religious people. But no one can be saved by sincerity or by being religious. No one can earn salvation. Again, salvation comes by grace through faith in a person; and that person is Jesus — the true Jesus revealed in the Bible.

Cults are a perfect example of what the Bible means when it says that "Satan disguises himself as an Angel of light . . . and his servants as servants of righteousness" (2 Corinthians 11:14-15). They are like the white washed tombs which Jesus said were full of dead men's bones — beautiful to behold, but full of spiritual death.

A Challenge

The Word of God challenges us to test everything because we are all subject to deception. We are told to "test the spirits to see whether they are from God; because many false prophets have gone out into the world" (1 John 4:1).

We are even exhorted to test ourselves. Here's how Paul puts it: "Test yourselves to see if you are in the faith; examine yourselves!" (2 Corinthians 13:5).

The test of all teaching and all doctrine is the Word itself. We are called to be like the Bereans who tested everything Paul taught by the Word of God (Acts 17:10-11).

How is it manifested?

One hundred years ago, as the 20th Century began, the Holy Spirit was not alive and well in the Church. Christendom was in bondage to the theology of Deism which held that miracles had ceased, all aspects of the supernatural (such as angels and demons) had been laid to rest, and that God was a grand old man in the sky, best identified as "The Great I Was."

A Deceptive Doctrine

The Church had been deceived into adopting a theological argument which had the effect of stifling and quenching the Holy Spirit. The argument was based on a statement in 1 Corinthians 13:10 — ". . . when the perfect comes, the partial will be done away." It was argued that the "perfect" was the completion of the perfect, inerrant Word of God. Thus, it was argued, all supernatural gifts of the Spirit, as well as other manifestations of the supernatural, ended with the completion of the New Testament canon around 95 AD.

To this was added the argument that gifts of the Spirit could only be passed along to others by the apostles through the laying on of hands. Therefore, when the last apostle died (John in about 95 AD), the gifts ceased.

Flawed Arguments

The arguments were so neat. But they were full of holes. For one thing, they flew in the face of experience. Throughout Church history, there is abundant evidence of spiritual gifts being experienced on the part of the small minority who continued to believe in them. There had also been major outbreaks of the supernatural, as in the camp meetings on the American frontier in the early 1800's.

The argument revolving around 1 Corinthians 13:10 was faulty because it denied the contextual meaning of the word "perfect." In context, the word refers to the return of Jesus. This is made clear in verse 12: "For now we see in a mirror dimly, but then [when the perfect comes] face to face; now I know in part, but then I shall know fully . . ." The argument also overlooked the clear teaching of 1 Corinthians 1:7 that all the gifts of the Spirit will continue to be operative until Jesus returns: ". . . you are not lacking in any gift, awaiting eagerly the revelation of our Lord Jesus Christ."

Finally, the argument about the apostles passing the gifts along to others was a sham because it attempted to convert the gifts of the Spirit into gifts of the apostles. The apostles may have been able to lay their hands on people and pray for them to receive certain gifts, but the gifts came from the Holy Spirit, not from the apostles. Furthermore, every believer receives at least one supernatural gift of the Spirit at the time of his or her salvation (1 Corinthians 12:4-11). Paul put it this way: "To each one is given the manifestation of the Spirit for the common good" (1 Corinthians 12:7).

An Important Prophecy

The anti-Holy Spirit mentality of the Church in 1900 also ignored the clear teaching of Bible prophecy that the end times would be characterized by a great outpouring of God's Spirit. The key passage is found in Joel 2:28-29:

> 28 And it will come about after this
> That I will pour out My Spirit on all mankind;
> And your sons and daughters will prophesy,
> Your old men will dream dreams,
> Your young men will see visions.

> 29 Even on the male and female servants
> I will pour out My Spirit in those days.

The Church's position in 1900 was that this prophecy had been fulfilled on the Day of Pentecost in 31 AD and was no longer applicable. It was argued that the "last days" began at Pentecost when the Church was established (Hebrews 1:2 and 1 Peter 1:20). Also, it was pointed out that the apostles themselves quoted this passage from Joel when they were asked what was going on as they began "to speak with other tongues" (Acts 2:4).

More Flawed Arguments

But again, these arguments about Joel 2:28-29 ignored the context of the passage. Note that the passage beings with the words, "And it will come about after this . ." After what? If you back up and read verses 18 through 27 you will see that the chapter is talking about the regathering and resettlement of the Jews in the land of Israel — something that did not occur until the 20th Century.

Also, the preceding verses speak of the outpouring of the Spirit symbolically as the "early and latter rain," referring to the two rainy seasons of Israel. In other words, the prophet was saying there will be two great outpourings of the Spirit. The "early rain" was at Pentecost and continued throughout the early history of the Church, as recorded in the book of Acts. The "latter rain" would immediately precede the return of the Messiah in judgment. This is made clear again by the passage itself in verses 30-31: "And I will display wonders in the sky and on the earth, blood, fire, and columns of smoke. The sun will be turned into darkness and the moon into blood, before the great and awesome day of the Lord comes." This is classic language about the Second Coming of Jesus.

Yes, the Bible speaks of the Church Age as the last days: "He [Jesus] was foreknown before the foundation of the world, but has appeared in these last times for the sake of you" (1 Peter 1:20). But it also speaks of the Lord's return as the last days when it says Christians are being protected "by the power of God through faith for a salvation ready to be revealed in the last time . . . at the revelation of Jesus Christ" (1 Peter 1:5, 7).

We have been in the "last times" since the Day of Pentecost. We are now in the latter part of the last times.

Joel 2:28-29 was fulfilled in part on the Day of Pentecost. Its total fulfillment was yet future in 1900, awaiting the "latter rain" that would be one of the signs of the Lord's soon return.

A Move of God

The Church had its jaw set against the Holy Spirit as the 20th Century began. But God was ready to burst on the scene with a great move of the Spirit in order to prepare the way for the return of His Son. That move began at a poverty-stricken school in Topeka, Kansas in January 1901 when a student named Agnes Ozman received the gift of tongues. Three years later a great Holy Spirit revival broke out in the English area of Wales, led by a remarkable young man named Evan Roberts. Then, in 1906, the Spirit fell with great power on a home meeting in Los Angeles led by a black preacher named William J. Seymour (1870-1922).

At Seymour's meeting, spiritual gifts were manifested, spectacular healings occurred, people were "slain in the Spirit," and sinners were saved. The meeting grew quickly and had to be moved to a dilapidated building on Azusa Street. It continued for almost four years, with preaching every day, three times a day!

The Azusa Street meeting gave birth to the Pentecostal Movement. The latter rain had begun. But it was only a sprinkle in terms of its impact on Christendom at large. The Pentecostals were written off as "Holy Rollers," and their religion was considered appropriate only for the superstitious and uneducated. But they were paving the way for a rediscovery of the Spirit.

The Latter Rain

The latter rain did not become a downpour until after the regathering of the Jewish people to the land of Israel (1900-1945) and the re-establishment of the state (May 14, 1948). Then, just as Joel had prophesied, the heavens opened and the downpour began — first, with the anointing of Billy Graham's ministry in 1949 and then with the emergence of the Charismatic Movement in the 1950's and 60's.

Today, much of Christendom is caught up in the Third Wave Movement that grew out of the Charismatic Movement in the 1970's and 80's. It is made up of churches that fully recognize the ministry of the Holy Spirit, including the significance of Spirit-led worship, the continuing validity of spiritual gifts, the reality of spiritual warfare, and the importance of a Spirit-filled life in winning that warfare. However, unlike the Pentecostals and Charismatics, the Third Wave Movement does not put an emphasis on the gift of tongues as the sign of having been baptized in the Spirit.

Confusion About the Spirit

The 20th Century was the century of the rediscovery of the Holy Spirit. Yet, widespread ignorance and confusion about the Holy Spirit still characterizes the Church. A 1997 poll by the Barna Research Group showed that only 40% of Americans believe in the existence of the Holy Spirit (as opposed to 90% who believe in the existence of God). But what was even more stunning was the response of "born-again Christians." More than 5 out of 10 born-again Christians (55%) agreed that the Holy Spirit is a symbol of God's presence or power but not a living entity! It appears that Christians have been brainwashed into believing that the Holy Spirit is an impersonal power like "The Force" in Star Wars.

Why is there so much continuing confusion about the Spirit? I think it relates in part to the self-effacing role of the Spirit. As we will see, one of the primary roles of the Spirit is to point people to Jesus as Savior and Lord. He does not draw attention to Himself. He works behind the scenes. Another factor relates to the many symbols that are used of the Spirit in Scripture — things like wind, rain, and fire. These symbols seem to communicate an impersonal force.

Our Creator God has been revealed to us as our Father. That is a concept we can grasp. Jesus took on a human body and lived among us. We have biographies of Him by eye witnesses. But for most people, the Holy Spirit is a shadowy entity difficult to grasp. Trying to get hold of the concept for many is like trying to nail jello to a wall.

The Identity of the Spirit

So, let's look for a moment at the identify of the Holy Spirit. The first thing you need to keep in mind is that the Spirit is never referred to as an "it." The Spirit is not an inanimate object. The Spirit is not, for example, the Bible, as some contend. The Spirit is intimately related to the Bible because it was the Spirit who inspired the biblical writers (2 Timothy 3:16), but the Bible is the "sword of the

Spirit," not the Spirit Himself (Ephesians 6:17). The Spirit works through the Bible to draw people to Jesus, although the work of the Spirit is not confined to the testimony of the Scriptures. The Spirit can witness directly to our spirits (Romans 8:16).

The Holy Spirit is a person. The Spirit is always referred to directly in the Scriptures as "He." Referring to the Spirit, Jesus told His disciples that when He left, He would send a "Helper." ("Paracletos" in Greek, meaning a helper or intercessor.) Jesus added, "And He, when He comes, will convict the world concerning sin, and righteousness, and judgment" (John 16:7-8). To Jesus, the Holy Spirit was "He" not "it."

The Bible says the Holy Spirit can be lied to (Acts 5:3-4). It also says the Holy Spirit can be quenched (1 Thessalonians 5:19) and grieved (Ephesians 4:30). These are characteristics of a personality. You cannot lie to a chair, or quench a wall, or grieve a light fixture.

The Holy Spirit is the supernatural presence of God in the world today. Paul put it this way: "The Lord is the Spirit" (2 Corinthians 3:17). Luke stated that the Holy Spirit is "the Spirit of Jesus" (Acts 16:6-7). Peter equated the Holy Spirit with God the Father when he told Ananias and Sapphira that they had lied to the Holy Spirit (Acts 5:3) and then added, "You have not lied to men but to God" (Acts 5:4). Remember that old axiom in geometry: "Things equal to the same thing are equal to each other."

The Holy Spirit is one of the three persons who constitute the One God. That's the reason we are told to be baptized "in the name of the Father and the Son and the Holy Spirit" (Matthew 28:19). As such He is co-equal to Jesus and the Father, but He plays a different role.

The Work of the Spirit

This brings us to the work of the Spirit. The Holy Spirit has two roles — one toward the unbeliever and another within the believer. With regard to the unbeliever, the Holy Spirit is the Father's Evangelist. With regard to the believer, He is the Father's Potter. Let's consider these two roles in detail.

Jesus summarized the work of the Spirit regarding unbelievers. He said that the Holy Spirit would "convict the world concerning sin, and righteousness, and judgment" (John 16:8). Specifically, the Spirit convicts unbelievers of their sinfulness, impresses upon them the righteousness of Jesus, and points them to the judgment of Satan (John 16:9-11). The Bible makes it clear that no person can come to Jesus apart from the testimony of the Holy Spirit. Jesus put it this way: "No one can come to Me, unless the Father who sent Me draws him" (John 6:44). And how does the Father draw unbelievers to Jesus? Through the Holy Spirit who bears witness of Jesus as the Father's only begotten Son (John 15:26 and 1 John 5:7).

When a person responds to the witness of the Spirit by accepting Jesus as Lord and Savior, he is "born-again" (John 3:3), and the Father gives that person a very special birthday present — the Holy Spirit! That's right, the Holy Spirit ceases to be on the outside drawing the person to Jesus. Instead, He moves inside the person and takes up residence within him (Romans 8:9). And when He does so, His role changes.

The Spirit in the Believer

Within the believer, the Holy Spirit is the Father's Potter. His role is to shape each believer into the image of Jesus (Romans 8:29 and Galatians 4:19), a process which the Bible refers to as sanctification (Romans 6:22 and 2 Thessalonians 2:13). The Spirit does this by first of all gifting us. Each person, when he or she is born again, is given at least one gift of the Spirit, and sometimes more than one (1 Corinthians 12:4-11). And if we are good stewards of our gifts, using them to advance the Lord's kingdom, we may be given additional gifts during our spiritual walk with the Lord.

The Spirit also accomplishes His work of sanctification by guiding us (Romans 8:14), comforting us (Acts 9:31), strengthening us (Philippians 4:13 and 1 John 4:4), praying for us (Romans 8:26-27), encouraging us (Romans 15:5), defending us (Luke 12:11-12), and illuminating us as we study the Word (1 John 2:27).

The work of sanctification is life long. It continues until we die or we are raptured to meet the Lord in the sky. The Holy Spirit wants to fine tune us into the image of Jesus because the Father is interested in nothing less than perfection in our lives (James 1:4 and 1 Peter 1:13-16). Yes, He is a God of grace who will accept us in all our imperfections, but He desires that we be perfected (Matthew 5:48).

Think of it this way — when a child takes his first step, his father rejoices. But no father is going to be satisfied with that one step. He will not be satisfied until the child can walk and then run without falling. For this reason, Christians are commanded to "be filled with the Spirit" (Ephesians 5:18).

A Special Work

In these end times the Spirit is doing a unique work as mentioned in Joel 2:28-29. He is giving believers a special anointing to witness Jesus to the world in preparation for the Second Coming. This special work is motivated by the fact that God "does not wish that any should perish, but that all should come to repentance" (2 Peter 3:9).

There are several manifestations of this end time anointing of the Spirit. The first is the one I have already mentioned — namely, the rediscovery of the Holy Spirit that occurred in the 20th Century and which opened the Church to the gifts of the Spirit.

As the Church has become newly empowered by the Spirit, it has become bolder and more effective in its evangelistic outreach. Missionaries have been sent out to the remotest parts of the earth, and the gospel is being proclaimed not only through them but through every imaginable type of modern technology — from radio to satellite television, to the Internet.

Worldwide Evangelism

Seventy per cent of all evangelism in the history of Christianity has been done since 1900, and 70% of that has been accomplished since the end of World War II, and 70% of that has been done since 1985! The results are phenomenal:

- **Missions** — There are more than 400,000 missionaries scattered all over the earth.

- **Africa** — In 1900 Christianity was almost non-existent in Africa (3% of the population). Today, over 350 million Africans are Christians (45%).

- **China** — Despite all the restrictions on Christianity that exist in China, 25,000 people a day are accepting Christ.

- **Latin America** — Christianity is growing exponentially. At the beginning of the 1980's there were only 18.5 million Evangelical Christians in Latin America. Today, there are more than 60 million! Brazil now has more Evangelical Christians than practicing Catholics.

- **The Muslim World** — More Muslims have been converted to Christ in the last 20 years than in the previous 1,000 years. Much of this success is due to the emphasis on that part of the world by the 10/40 Window prayer campaign.

- **Jews** — In 1967 when the Six Day War occurred, there was not one Messianic congregation in existence. Today, there are more than 400, with more than 40 in Israel.

- **Jesus Film** — Since the "Jesus Film" was released in 1979, it has been shown worldwide in 228 countries, in 839 languages. More than 5 billion people have seen the film (counting multiple viewings).

- **Conversions** — Worldwide, one million people per week are accepting Jesus as Lord and Savior. Evangelical Christianity is multiplying at 3½ times the growth of the world's population.

An Unrecognized Manifestation

A third manifestation of the Holy Spirit's special work in paving the way for the return of Jesus is one that many people have not realized. It is the re-establishment of the Tabernacle of David through the Holy Spirit's revival of Davidic praise worship. This work of the Spirit is directed toward believers with the purpose of drawing them into a closer relationship with the Lord and motivating them to holiness. Jesus is about to return, and the Father wants Him to return on a cloud of praise.

This particular manifestation is so significant and yet so little understood and appreciated, that the next chapter is devoted to exploring it in detail.

What About You?

Are you filled with the Spirit? Are you living your life daily in the power of the Spirit? Are you fully aware of your spiritual gifts, and are you using them to advance the Lord's kingdom?

If you can't answer these questions with a confident "Yes!" then I would urge you to contact your pastor and get involved in a Bible study that will introduce you to the gifts of the Spirit and help you identify yours. The time we have remaining is short, and you need to be utilizing your spiritual gifts to the maximum in the Lord's service.

How does it relate to the end times?

> 11 "In that day I will raise up the fallen
>   tabernacle of David,
>   And wall up its breaches;
>   I will also raise up its ruins,
>   And rebuild it as in the days of old;
>
> 12 That they may possess the remnant of
>   Edom and all the Gentiles
>   Who are called by My name,"
>   Declares the Lord who does this.

Most Christians are familiar with this prophecy from Amos 9:11-12 because it is quoted in Acts 15. The occasion was a special conference of church leaders that was called in Jerusalem to consider the momentous implications of Gentiles being added to the Church. In the midst of the debate, James, the leader of the Jerusalem church, quoted this prophecy from Amos to prove that it was God's intention to someday include the Gentiles in His scheme of redemption.

This usage of the prophecy has historically led to the conclusion that the term, "the tabernacle of David," refers to the Church. And perhaps it does in a spiritual sense. But the context of the passage in the book of Amos makes it clear that the prophecy will find its ultimate fulfillment in something other than the establishment of the Church.

Note that the prophecy begins with the words, "In that day." What day? A quick glance at the prophecy in its context shows that the "day" being referred to is the period of time when the Jews are regathered to the land of Israel (see Amos 9:14-15). That process began in the 20th Century. There were 40,000 Jews in 1900. Today, there are more than five million. They re-established their state on May 14, 1948, and they have regathered their people from the four corners of the earth.

Has anything happened since 1948 that could constitute a literal fulfillment of the restoration of the "tabernacle of David"? To answer this question we must first seek to understand the meaning of the term, "tabernacle of David." What did Amos have in mind when he used this term?

The Tabernacle of Moses

To fully understand the Tabernacle of David, we must first begin with a consideration of the Tabernacle of Moses. It was a nomadic temple that moved with the Children of Israel as they crossed the Wilderness of Sinai in search of the Promised Land. Its Holy of Holies contained the Ark of the Covenant where the Shekinah Glory of God resided.

When the Children of Israel entered the Promised Land, they settled the Tabernacle of Moses at Shiloh in Samaria. There the sacrificial ceremonies were conducted for 400 years during the period of the Judges. By the end of that chaotic period, the Children of Israel were engulfed in spiritual darkness, having fallen victim to idolatry and immorality.

One day, during the judgeship of Samuel, as the Israelites were preparing to fight the Philistines, they decided to take the Ark of the Covenant into battle with them, as if it were some sort of good luck charm. They evidently reasoned that God would never allow the Philistines to capture the Ark, and therefore they would win the battle.

The Lord was not pleased by this action, so He allowed the Philistines to defeat the Israelites and capture the sacred Ark (1 Samuel 4:1-11). They also proceeded to destroy the Tabernacle of Moses at Shiloh (Jeremiah 7:12). Israel had become "Ichabod," (meaning, "no glory") for the glory of God had departed (1 Samuel 4:21).

The Odyssey of the Ark

Plagues afflicted the Philistines, so they sent the Ark back to Israel on an ox cart. It finally came to rest eight miles west of Jerusalem in a town called Kiriath-jearim (named Abu Gosh today) where it stayed for approximately 70 years (20 years under Samuel's judgeship, 40 years under Saul's kingship, and almost 10 years into David's kingship).

Meanwhile, the Tabernacle of Moses was moved to Nob for a while (1 Samuel 21:1) and then on to Gibeon (about ten miles northwest of Jerusalem) where it remained until the Temple of Solomon was built (2 Chronicles 1:3).

Now note something very important. During this 70 year period of transition between the Judges and the Kings, there was no Shekinah Glory in the Tabernacle of Moses located at Gibeon. The Holy of Holies was empty. The priests continued to minister at the tabernacle, offering daily sacrifices, but it was all dead ritual, for the glory had departed.

The astounding thing is that the Ark was located in a farmhouse situated only about five miles from Gibeon. It would have been very easy to restore the Ark to the Tabernacle of Moses, but no one cared enough to do so. The Ark was ignored, and it became a symbol of Israel's apostasy.

Saul vs David

Saul did not have a heart for the Lord, so he ignored the estrangement of the Ark from its proper resting place. But when David became king, he was determined to correct this situation, for he was a man after God's own heart (1 Samuel 13:14). David had to wait seven and a half years until he became king of all Israel (he was king of only Judah during his first years in power — see 2 Samuel 5:5).

David was determined to bring God back into the heart of his nation, and he recognized the symbolic significance of the Ark in accomplishing this purpose. He was so determined to provide a proper resting place for the Ark that it became the top priority of his kingship. In this regard, we are told in Psalm 132 that when David became king of all of Israel, he "swore to the Lord" that he would not sleep in a bed until he could provide a proper "dwelling place for the Mighty One of Jacob" (Psalm 132:1-5).

The Tabernacle of David

The amazing thing is that David brought the Ark to Jerusalem rather than returning it to the Holy of Holies in the Tabernacle of Moses at Gibeon. David pitched a tent in Jerusalem (probably on a slope of Mt. Moriah), placed the Ark inside, and instituted a whole new concept of praise worship. Instruments of worship were introduced. Special psalms of praise were written and sung. And, incredibly, special priests were appointed to minister music before the ark *continually* (1 Chronicles 16:6, 37) — whereas only the High Priest had been allowed to minister before the Ark once a year in the Tabernacle of Moses.

In fact, the Scriptures indicate that there was such great intimacy with the Lord, that David would actually lounge before the Ark (1 Chronicles 17:16). It is probably during these times of intimacy that he wrote new songs to the Lord (Psalm 40:3).

David's revolution in worship was very radical. There was no singing or celebration at the Tabernacle of Moses. The worship there was one of solemn ritual focused on sacrifices. The only joy that had ever been evidenced in the worship of the Israelites had occurred spontaneously, as when Miriam danced with a tambourine and rejoiced over the destruction of Pharaoh and his army (Exodus 15).

The Psalms make it clear that the praise worship inaugurated by David was a worship of great joy that was characterized by hand clapping (Psalm 47:1), shouting (Psalm 47:1), singing (Psalm 47:6-7), dancing (Psalm 149:3), hand waving (Psalm 134:2), and the display of banners (Psalm 20:5). The worshipers were encouraged to praise God with every form of musical instrument, from the gentle lyre to the "loud crashing cymbals" (Psalm 150:3, 5).

The Davidic Revolution

But why? Why did David so radically change the worship of Israel? We are told in 2 Chronicles 29:25 that he did so in response to commands of God given to him through the prophets Nathan and Gad. But why didn't the Lord simply tell David to put the Ark back in the Holy of Holies in Gibeon? Why did God tell him to revolutionize the worship of Israel?

The Bible does not tell us why. We can only guess. My guess is that God wanted to give David a prophetic glimpse of the glorious Church Age to come when animal sacrifices would cease, worshipers would have direct access to God, and worshipers would come before the Lord in rejoicing with a sacrifice of praise.

I think there was also another reason. I believe the Lord wanted to give the Church a model for Spirit-filled worship.

For one generation (about 30 years under David and 12 years into Solomon's reign), two tabernacles existed in Israel. In Gibeon there was the dead, liturgical worship that characterized the Tabernacle of Moses. In Jerusalem, there was the lively, spontaneous worship that characterized the Tabernacle of David.

The worship in Gibeon was the performance of ritualistic symbolism. The worship in Zion was the experience of the presence of God. At Gibeon, the priests offered the sacrifice of animals. At Zion, the offering was the sacrifice of praise: "Come before Him with joyful singing . . . Enter His gates with thanksgiving and His courts with praise" (Psalm 100:2,4).

The Prophetic Significance

The Tabernacle of David served as a joyous bridge between the spiritual deadness that had come to characterize the Tabernacle of Moses and the Spirit-filled glory that would characterize the Temple of Solomon.

In like manner, since the re-establishment of the nation of Israel in 1948, God has been raising up the Tabernacle of David again to serve as a joyous bridge of transition between the dead worship of mainline Christendom and the glorious worship that will characterize the Millennial Temple of Jesus Christ. God wants His Son to return on a cloud of praise.

The Worldwide Spread

Appropriately, God began to focus His revival of the Tabernacle of David in the city of Jerusalem in the early 1980's. It occurred when the International Christian Embassy in Jerusalem decided to host a celebration of the Feast of Tabernacles.

Zechariah 14 says that during the millennial reign of Jesus the nations will send representatives to Jerusalem each year to celebrate this feast and that any nation that fails to do so will not receive rain. The Embassy decided it would be appropriate for Gentiles to start rehearsing for the Millennium, so they sent out a call worldwide for Christians to come to Jerusalem to celebrate the feast and to show their support of Israel.

The Embassy also decided to give an emphasis to Davidic praise worship which was springing up all over the world at that time through a sovereign move of the Holy Spirit. They brought together Christendom's best practitioners of celebratory worship.

The result was an explosion of Davidic worship worldwide as the thousands of Christians who came to Jerusalem took what they had experienced back home with them in their hearts and on videos. The Embassy's celebration has continued to this day, with 4,000 to 6,000 Christians attending annually from every continent.

A Move of the Spirit

The Tabernacle of David today consists of those churches that have rediscovered the true meaning of worship and have given their people the freedom in Christ to worship God with all their energy, resources, gifts and talents.

The renewal in worship that is sweeping Christendom worldwide is a move of the Spirit. It is a fulfillment of prophecy. It is a mark of the end times. It is a sign of the soon return of Jesus. And it is preparation for that day very soon when:

> The ransomed of the Lord will return,
> And come with joyful shouting to Zion,
> With everlasting joy upon their heads,
> They will find gladness and joy,
> And sorrow and sighing will flee away.
> — Isaiah 35:10

What do you think it is?

One hundred years ago there was not one definite, tangible, objective sign that we were living in the season of the Lord's return. Today, the signs are everywhere. A person would have to be spiritually blind to be unaware of them. There are so many, and they are so intense, that they are like a neon sign flashing in the sky proclaiming, "Jesus is coming soon!"

Several years ago I participated in a prophecy conference in Orlando, Florida. One of the speakers was Elbert Peak, a great man of God from Abilene, Texas, who is in his 80's. His topic was "The Signs of the Times." He began his presentation by saying, "I have been speaking on the signs of the times for over 60 years. When I first began, I had to scratch around like a chicken to find even one sign. Today, there are so many that I am no longer looking for signs. Instead, I am listening for sounds — the shout of an archangel and the blowing of a trumpet."

The Key Development

Yes, we are surrounded today by signs of the times, all of which burst on the scene during the 20th Century. Looking back on that century, what would you identify as the most important prophetic development? There are certainly a lot of crucial events to chose from:

- Word Wars I and II.

- The Invention of Television.

- The Development of Atomic Power.

- The Advent of Space Travel.

- The Collapse of Communism.

- The Reunification of Europe.

- The Resurgence of Islam.

All of these events were very important, and all had prophetic significance. But none of them was the most important prophetic development. In fact, all of them put together were not as important as the event that dominated the century from a biblical perspective. That event was **the regathering of the Jewish people to their homeland from the four corners of the earth**.

Scriptural Proof

Now, lest you think I am exaggerating, let me prove this point to you from the Scriptures.

In Jeremiah 16:14-15 there is a statement that is mind-boggling from a Jewish perspective. Read it below and see if you can detect why it is so revolutionary:

14 "Therefore, days are coming," declares the Lord, "when it will no longer be said, 'As the Lord lives, who brought up the sons of Israel out of the land of Egypt,'

15 but, 'As the Lord lives, who brought up the sons of Israel from the land of the north and from all the countries where He had banished them.' For I will restore them to their own land which I gave to their fathers."

For 3,500 years the Jews have annually celebrated the Feast of Passover which commemorates what they believe to be the greatest miracle God has ever performed — namely, their deliverance from Egyptian captivity. Yet, this passage from Jeremiah 16 (repeated verbatim in Jeremiah 23:7-8) says that when history is completed, the Jewish people will look back and consider their worldwide regathering to be a greater miracle than their deliverance from Egypt!

Accordingly, the Jewish people will no longer swear by the God who brought them out of Egypt; rather, they will point to the God who gathered them out of all the nations where they had been scattered. Same God, but a greater miracle.

A Second Prophecy

Another significant prophecy can be found in Isaiah 11:10-12:

10 Then it will come about in that day
That the nations will resort to the root of Jesse;
Who will stand as a signal for the peoples;
And His resting place will be glorious.

11 Then it will happen on that day that the Lord
Will again recover the second time with His hand
The remnant of His people, who will remain,
From Assyria, Egypt, Pathros, Cush, Elam, Shinar,
   Hamath,
And from the islands of the sea.

12 And He will lift up a standard for the nations,
And will assemble the banished ones of Israel,
And will gather the dispersed of Judah
From the four corners of the earth.

I discovered this prophecy when I was a teenager. I took it to my pastor and asked him what it meant. He told me it had been fulfilled in the return of the Jews from Babylonian captivity.

But this passage has nothing to do with the return from Babylon. First, it speaks of "in that day," which is the term Isaiah uses throughout his book for the end times. Then it speaks of a "second" regathering. Babylon was the first. Further, it describes the regathering as being from "the four corners of the earth." Finally, it says the regathering will include both Israel (the ten northern tribes) and Judah (the two southern tribes). The regathering from Babylon involved only Judah.

A Third Prophecy

Another important prophecy can be found in Ezekiel 37:1-12. This is the famous prophecy of the "Valley of the Dry Bones." This passage has been spiritualized to death by applying it to the Church, despite the fact that it is clearly talking about the Jewish people.

In this passage, the prophet Ezekiel is given a vision. He sees himself standing in a valley full of dry bones. He is told to preach to the bones. He does so, and the bones start moving! They come together, flesh forms on them, but the reconstituted bodies have no breath. Ezekiel is told to keep preaching, and as he does, breath comes, and the bodies come alive and stand up, constituting a great army of people.

The Lord then gave Ezekiel an explanation of the meaning of the vision (Ezekiel 37:11-12):

11 Then He said to me, "Son of man, these bones are the whole house of Israel; behold, they say, 'Our bones are dried up, and our hope has perished. We are completely cut off.'

12 Therefore, prophesy, and say to them, 'Thus says the Lord God, "Behold, I will open your graves and cause you to come up out of your graves, My people; and I will bring you into the land of Israel."'"

What the Lord is saying is that a day will come when He will open up the "graves" of the Jews — that is, the nations where they have been dispersed — and He will bring them back to their homeland of Israel.

Even though the Jews were in Babylonian captivity at the time, the regathering promised in this vision applies to the worldwide regathering in the end times. That is made clear by the subsequent verses that speak of both Israel and Judah returning to the land (verses 19-22).

Other Prophecies

The final specific prophecy I would like to bring to your attention is one that was written *after* the return from Babylonian captivity. It is contained in Zechariah 8:7-8:

7 Thus says the Lord of Hosts, "Behold, I am going to save My people from the land of the east and from

the land of the west;

8 and I will bring them back, and they will live in the midst of Jerusalem, and they will be My people and I will be their God in truth and righteousness."

There can be no doubt that this prophecy is speaking about a regathering other than the one from Babylon.

The prophecies I have quoted above are only four of dozens that exist in the Hebrew Scriptures concerning a great end time regathering of the Jewish people, right before the return of the Messiah. The regathering prophecies are, in fact, the most prolific ones in the Old Testament.

A Latter Day Visionary

Almost 2,500 years after these prophecies were written, God raised up a visionary to lay the ground work for their fulfillment. His name was Theodore Herzl (1860-1904).

Herzl was an Hungarian Jew who became a Viennese journalist. In 1894 he was sent to Paris the cover the trial of a Jewish army officer who had been falsely accused of treason. When Herzl arrived, he was astonished over the virulent anti-Semitism which he witnessed as the people of Paris surrounded the courthouse and chanted, "Death to the Jews!"

Previous to this experience, Herzl had assumed that the Jews of Europe could be assimilated into European culture. His Paris experience convinced him otherwise. It also convinced him that a holocaust was coming. When he returned home, he wrote a brief booklet in which he argued it was time for the Jews to return to their homeland in Israel.

Herzl's vision ignited the hearts of Jews all over the world. It led to the convening of the First Zionist Congress in Basel, Switzerland in 1897. At that conference Herzl proclaimed his belief that a Jewish state would come into existence within 50 years. His words proved to be prophetic, for 50 years later in November 1947, the United Nations voted to allow the creation of the state of Israel.

Herzl died in 1906 at the age of 44, so he did not live to see his vision become a reality. His efforts prompted only a handful of Jews to return to Israel. Still, the vision had been proclaimed and had become implanted in Jewish hearts. What was needed was a major stimulus.

The Balfour Declaration

That stimulus came on November 2, 1917 in the form of a proclamation by the British government called The Balfour Declaration. This important document became the very first, tangible sign pointing to the soon return of Jesus. It took the form of a letter addressed to Lord Rothschild, president of the British Zionist Federation. The letter was from Arthur Balfour, the Foreign Minister in the government of Lloyd George. It read as follows:

> I have much pleasure in conveying to you, on behalf of His Majesty's Government, the following declaration of sympathy with Jewish Zionist aspirations which has been submitted to, and approved by, the Cabinet.

> His Majesty's Government view with favour the establishment in Palestine of a national home for the Jewish people, and will use their best endeavours to facilitate the achievement of this object, it being clearly understood that nothing shall be done which may prejudice the civil and religious rights of existing non-Jewish communities in Palestine . . .

Arthur Koestler, in his book, *Promise and Fulfillment* (1949), characterized this letter as "unorthodox, unpolitic, and freakish." His analysis was right on target, for the British government was promising the Jews a land that belonged at the time to the Ottoman Empire!

Why would the British be so audacious? Well, what most Americans do not remember is that the Turks sided with the Germans in World War I, and thus the Allies intended to divide up the Ottoman Empire after they defeated the German-Turkish Alliance.

A Key Personality

The Declaration had been urged upon the British government by Dr. Chaim Weizmann, a Russian Jew who was later to serve as the first president of Israel.

At the outbreak of World War I, Weizmann was 40 years old and living in England where he was serving as a chemistry professor at the University of Manchester. He was also the leader of a committee of Zionists who were seeking a homeland for the Jews.

Because of his political interests, Weizmann made contacts with all the key British political leaders, many of whom, including Lloyd George and Arthur Balfour, were evangelical Christians. These men knew Bible prophecy and were sympathetic to Jewish desires to return to their homeland which was then called Palestine — a land which had been under Turkish control for 400 years.

Weizmann endeared himself to the British leaders when he solved a critical shortage of acetone, an ingredient necessary for the production of a propellant for artillery shells. After two years of research, Weizmann invented a method of producing synthetic acetone.

A Fulfillment of Prophecy

What I want to emphasize is that the Declaration started a series of events that were to lead to the re-establishment of the state of Israel, in fulfillment of Bible prophecy.

British evangelicals in the 19th Century were well aware of these prophecies. They believed in them and looked forward to their fulfillment. That's what prompted them to build the first Protestant church in the city of Jerusalem. It was called Christ Church. It was constructed near the Jaffa Gate and dedicated in 1849. The church was built in anticipation of the worldwide regathering of the Jews prophesied in the Hebrew Scriptures. It was even designed to look like a synagogue.

The Declaration's Impact

With such expectations long established, it is no wonder that the Balfour Declaration electrified the British evangelical community. The person who seemed to be impacted by it the most was Dr. F. B.

Meyer, one of the best known and most highly respected evangelical leaders of the time. He quickly huddled with other English evangelicals and issued a manifesto to the press on the 8th of November (just six days after the issuance of the Declaration). Entitled "The Significance of the Hour," it included the following points:

1) That the signs of the times point towards the close of the times of the Gentiles.

2) That the return of the Lord may be expected at any moment when He will be manifested as evidently as to His disciples on the evening of His resurrection.

3) That the completed church will be translated to meet the Lord in the air, and to be forever with the Lord.

4) That Israel will be restored to their own land in unbelief, and be afterwards converted by the manifestation of Jesus as their Messiah.

Meyer's group also called for an all-day meeting to be held on December 13 at Queens Hall in London. The purpose of the meeting was to provide an opportunity to emphasize that "the times of the Gentiles" (Luke 21:24) were clearly drawing to a close and that consequently the return of Jesus for His church might be expected imminently.

The Liberation of Jerusalem

Before the meeting could be held, General Edmund Allenby liberated the city of Jerusalem from 400 years of Turkish rule. Allenby was a devout Christian, and on the day he entered the city — December 11, 1917 — he refused to ride his horse. He walked in because the Scriptures say that the Messiah is the one who will enter Jerusalem on a white horse at the time of His Second Coming (Revelation 19:11).

The Arab world initially looked upon Allenby's capture of Jerusalem as a matter of divine intervention. This was due to the mistaken impression that the name, Allenby, was a combination of Allah (God) and Neby (prophet), and that he was, therefore, a prophet of God.

Evangelicals in England also considered the liberation of Jerusalem to be a divine act, as did Bible-believing Christians worldwide. As one minister put it, "Christianity the world over put on her garments of praise. Songs were sung, poetry was recited, prayers offered, and sermons preached."

Birth of a Ministry

By the time Dr. Meyer and his colleagues gathered at Queens Hall on December 13, the atmosphere was electric. There was an overwhelming consensus that God had begun the implementation of His end time program for regathering the Jews to their homeland. A dozen preachers spoke that day to a packed house. Included among them was Dr. G. Campbell Morgan who asserted: "We all feel that never in the history of the Church have the signs seemed so definite to point to the fulfilling of Gentile times as they do today. Our loins should be girt about, and our lamps should be burning. We should be occupying until He comes."

The meeting resulted in the formation of an organization called The Advent Testimony Movement. Dr. Meyer was appointed the president. The organization immediately launched a series of Bible prophecy conferences which were held throughout England.

The conferences rapidly spread to the Continent, to Australia and South Africa, and to the United States. In America, the meetings were so large that it was impossible to find buildings big enough to accommodate the crowds. When a conference was held in Philadelphia, it filled the largest hall in the city and four other churches at the same time!

The ministry founded by Dr. Meyer in 1917 continues to this day under the name, The Prophetic Witness Movement International. It is the oldest Bible prophecy ministry in the world.

British Duplicity

At the end of World War I, Britain was given Palestine as a League of Nations Mandate, meaning that the English were responsible for tutoring the people within the area toward self-rule. Palestine at that time included all of present day Jordan. The Jews looked forward to the day when this territory would become their home.

But they were severely disappointed in 1922 when the British government suddenly issued a White Paper in which it announced that two-thirds of Palestine would be set aside for an Arab state to be known as Trans-Jordan. This decision was prompted by a desire to placate the Arabs in the area who opposed the Balfour Declaration. And this is the reason that to this very day Israeli leaders point out that a Palestinian state already exists — the state of Jordan, as it is known today. In fact, over 70% of its population is made up of Palestinians.

William Hull, in his landmark book, ***The Fall and Rise of Israel*** (1954), states that British policy between 1917 and 1939 toward the establishment of a Jewish Home in Palestine could be summed up in one word: *whittling.* When the Jews were first promised a national home, the area included Trans-Jordan — a total of 45,000 square miles. In 1922 when Trans-Jordan was given to the Arabs, only 10,000 square miles were left for the Jewish home. The partition plan of the Peel Commission in 1937 would have given the Jews only 2,000 square miles. New regulations under a 1939 British White Paper tried to cut the area to 260 square miles!

Jewish Aid and Opposition

Despite the double-dealing of the British, Jews worldwide rallied to the British cause during World War II, doing everything they could to help the Allies defeat the Nazis. The Arabs sat on the sidelines, and the Grand Mufti of Jerusalem actually collaborated with Hitler, encouraging his policy of Jewish genocide.

When the war ended, the Jews expected to be rewarded by the British with a lifting of the restrictions of the 1939 White Paper. This failed to happen, despite the fact that hundreds of thousands of Holocaust survivors were clamoring to get into Palestine. The result was the birth of the Jewish Revolt headed up by Menachen Begin.

Begin's revolt proved effective. Besieged by both sides, the British decided the time had come to terminate the Mandate. A United Nations committee recommended a Solomonic solution: "Cut the baby in half." The committee recommended that the remaining sliver of Palestine be divided between the Jews and Arabs, creating two patch-work states intermingled with each other. The UN General Assembly agreed with the plan, and on November 29, 1947, the United Nations voted by a two-thirds majority to partition Palestine. Again, the Jews were disappointed with another division of their land, but they agreed to the partition. The Arabs denounced the resolution and prepared for war.

The True Arab Intent

On May 14, 1948, the Jewish state was proclaimed, and the Arabs launched an all-out war to destroy it. And war it has been ever since, simply because the Arab desire is not for the creation of an Arab state within Palestine, but rather, the incorporation of all Palestine into an Arab state. Or, to put it another way, the true aim of the Arabs is to annihilate the state of Israel and drive the Jews into the sea.

The Arab goal will never be achieved. The Bible says that once the Jews are re-established in the land, they will never be rooted up again (Amos 9:15). The Bible clearly prophesies that the Arabs will lust after the land of Israel in the end times (Ezekiel 35:1 - 36:7) and try to take it for themselves. But God promises that He will intervene and make the Arab lands a desolation (Ezekiel 35: 15).

Recognizing the Season

Noah preached for 120 years that his generation was living in the season of the pouring out of God's wrath. We have been in the season of the Lord's return since November 2, 1917.

The Bible says the generation that witnesses the rebirth of Israel is the one that will witness the return of the Lord (Matthew 24:32-35). The Bible also says that in the end times, right before the return of the Lord, the Jews will be back in their land and their city, and the whole world will come against them over the issue of the control of Jerusalem (Zechariah 12:1-4).

That's exactly where we are today on the prophetic time line. We are living on borrowed time. The crucial question for every person is this one: "Are you ready for the Lord's return?"

He Will Come Back

Lanny Wolfe

On the third day Jesus came back.
He arose from the dead.
Not until then did believers believe
Everything He had said.
Then they heard Jesus say,
"I must go away to prepare you a place,
And if I go, don't doubt it,
Just know that I will come back."

(Chorus)

And He will come back,
Just wait and see.
He will come back
Just like He said for you and me.
He came back the first time
From the grave.
He came back.
God cannot lie.
If He said He'd return,
Then He will come back.

Well, it's been so long
Since He's been gone.
Some doubters may ask,
"Is His Word really true?
What He said will He do?
Will He really come back?"

Then I ask a question,
"Has God ever failed you?
Has He ever let you down?"
If the answer is, "No!"
Get ready to go,
Soon the trumpet will sound.

Part Five

Prophetic Hope

"[We are to live] looking for the
blessed hope and the appearing of the
glory of our great God and Savior, Christ Jesus."
Titus 2:13

What happens when you die?

If several years ago you had asked me what happens when you die, I would have given you a pathetic answer.

I would have told you that when you die your soul goes to sleep until the Lord returns. At the return of the Lord, the universe explodes and cease to exit, your soul is resurrected and judged, and you are either consigned to Hell or allowed to enter Heaven.

My conception of Heaven was that of a spirit world where the saved spend eternity as disembodied spirits, floating around on clouds, playing harps.

A Mistaken View

Needless to say, I couldn't get very excited about all that. I sure didn't like the idea of being unconscious for eons of time. The idea of the universe ending in a big bang scared me to death. Nor could I develop any enthusiasm for the prospect of being a disembodied spirit with no particular identity or personality.

And the idea of playing a harp for all eternity was downright scandalous, for I had been taught that instrumental music in worship was an abomination!

You can imagine, therefore, the sense of shock I felt when I started studying Bible prophecy and discovered that all these ideas of mine about life after death were foreign to God's Word. But my shock quickly gave way to exhilaration when I discovered what the Lord really has in store for me.

The Biblical View

I learned from God's Word that when those of us who are Christians die, our spirits never lose their consciousness. Instead, our fully conscious spirits are immediately ushered into the presence of Jesus by His holy angels.

We receive an intermediate spirit bodies and remain in the Lord's presence until He appears for His Church. At that time, He brings our spirits with Him, resurrects our bodies, reunites our spirits with our bodies, and then glorifies our bodies, perfecting them and rendering them eternal.

We return with Him to Heaven in our glorified bodies where we are judged for our works to determine our degrees of rewards. When this judgment is completed, we participate in a glorious wedding feast to celebrate the union of Jesus and His Bride, the Church.

Witnesses of Glory

At the conclusion of the feast, we burst from the heavens with Jesus, returning with Him to the earth in glory. We witness His victory at Armageddon, we shout "Hallelujah!" as He is crowned King of kings and Lord of lords, and we revel in His glory as He begins to reign over all the earth from Mt. Zion in Jerusalem.

For a thousand years we participate in that reign, assisting Him with the instruction, administration, and enforcement of His perfect laws. We see the earth regenerated and nature reconciled. We see holiness abound and the earth flooded with peace, righteousness and justice.

At the end of the Millennium we witness the release of Satan to deceive the nations. We see the truly despicable nature of the heart of Man as millions rally to Satan in his attempt to overthrow the throne of Jesus. But we will shout "Hallelujah!" again when we witness God's supernatural destruction of Satan's armies and see Satan himself cast into Hell where he will be tormented forever.

We will next witness the Great White Throne Judgment when the unrighteous are resurrected to stand before God. We will see perfect holiness and justice in action as God pronounces His terrible judgment upon this congregation of the damned who have rejected His gift of love and mercy in Jesus Christ.

Jesus will be fully vindicated as every knee shall bow and every tongue confess that He is Lord. Then the unrighteous will receive their just reward as they are cast into Hell.

Witnesses of a New Creation

We will then witness the most spectacular fireworks display in all of history.

We will be taken to the New Jerusalem, the eternal mansion prepared by Jesus for His Bride, and from there we will watch as God renovates this earth with fire, burning away all the filth and pollution left by Satan's last battle.

Just as the angels rejoiced when God created the universe, we will rejoice as we watch God superheat this earth and reshape it like a hot ball of wax into the New Earth, the eternal earth, the paradise where we will live forever in the presence of God.

What a glorious moment it will be when we are lowered to the New Earth inside the fabulous New Jerusalem. God will come down from Heaven to dwell with us. He will proclaim: "Behold, I make all things new." We will see God face to face. He will wipe away all our tears. Death will be no more. We will be given new names and we will exist as individual personalities encased in perfect bodies. And we will grow eternally in knowledge and love of our infinite Creator, honoring Him with our talents and gifts.

Now, I can get excited about that!

The Word vs. Tradition

Isn't it amazing how far we can drift away from the Word of God when we stop reading His Word and start mouthing the traditions of men?

As I kept making one discovery after another in God's Prophetic Word that ran contrary to what I had been taught, I began to wonder about the origin of the doctrines I had learned. It didn't take me long to discover that the source was Greek philosophy.

The first attempt to mix the concepts of Greek philosophy with the teachings of God's Word came very early in the history of the Church. The attempt was called Gnosticism. The Gnostic heresy arose among the first Gentile converts because they tried to Hellenize the Scriptures; that is, they tried to make the Scriptures conform to the basic tenets of Greek philosophy.

The Greeks believed that the material universe, including the human body, was evil. This negative view of the creation was diametrically opposed to Hebrew thought, as revealed in the Bible. To the Hebrew mind, the world was created good (Genesis 1:31). And even though the goodness of the creation was corrupted by the sin of Man (Isaiah 24:5-6), the creation still reflects to some degree the glory of God (Psalms 19:1). Most important, the creation will someday be redeemed by God (Romans 8:18-23).

The Gnostic Heresy

When the first Gentiles were converted to the gospel, their Greek mind set immediately collided with some of the fundamental teachings of Christianity. For example, they wondered, "How could Jesus have come in the flesh if He was God? God is holy. How can He who is holy be encased in a body which is evil?"

In short, because they viewed the material universe as evil, they could not accept the Bible's teaching that God became incarnate in the flesh. Their response was to develop the Gnostic heresy that Jesus was a spirit being or phantom who never took on the flesh and therefore never experienced physical death.

This heresy is denounced strongly in Scripture. In 1 John 4:1-2 we are told to test those who seek our spiritual fellowship by asking them to confess "that Jesus Christ has come in the flesh."

The Augustinian Corruption

About 400 AD a remarkable theologian by the name of St. Augustine attempted to Hellenize what the Scriptures taught about end time events and life after death. Augustine was very successful in his attempt. His views were endorsed by the Council of Ephesus in 431 AD and have remained Catholic dogma to this day.

The influence of Greek philosophy would not allow Augustine to accept what the Bible taught about life after death.

For example, the Bible says the saints will spend eternity in glorified bodies on a new earth (Revelation 21:1-7). Such a concept was anathema to the Greek mind of Augustine. If the material world is evil, then he reasoned that the material world must cease to exist when the Lord returns. Augustine solved the problem by spiritualizing what the Bible said. He did this by arguing that the "new earth" of Revelation 21 is just symbolic language for Heaven.

Augustine's views are held by most professing Christians today, both Catholic and Protestant. That means that most of Christianity today teaches Greek philosophy rather than the Word of God when it comes to the realm of end time prophecy and life after death.

The Fallacy of Soul Sleep

When I started seriously studying what the Bible says about life after death, one of the first discoveries I made concerned "soul sleep." I found out that it is an unbiblical concept. It is true that when we die, our bodies "sleep" metaphorically, because at the time of the resurrection, they will be awakened. But the spirits of the dead never lose their consciousness.

Jesus clearly taught this in His story about the rich man and Lazarus (Luke 16:19-31). When they died, their spirits went to Hades. The rich man's spirit went to a compartment in Hades called "Torments." The spirit of Lazarus went to a compartment named "Abraham's bosom." On the Cross, Jesus referred to Abraham's bosom as "Paradise" (Luke 23:43). The two compartments were separated by a "great chasm" which could not be crossed.

In Jesus' story both men are pictured as fully conscious. They even carry on a conversation with each other. Their souls are not asleep.

Further evidence of consciousness after death can be found in Revelation 7. John is taken up to Heaven and is given a tour of the throne room of God. He sees "a great multitude . . . from every nation and all tribes and peoples and tongues," standing before the throne of God "clothed in white robes" and waving palm branches in worship (Revelation 7:9). They are fully conscious as they sing, "Salvation to our God who sits on the throne and to the Lamb" (Revelation 7:10).

John wants to know the identity of these people. He is told that they are martyrs for Christ coming out of the "great tribulation" (Revelation 7:14).

Here are two scenes in Scripture of people after death who are fully conscious. But note that there is one very important difference in the two scenes. In Jesus' story, the saved are in Hades in a compartment called "Abraham's bosom" or "Paradise." In John's vision the saved are in Heaven. Why the two different locations?

Hades and Heaven

The answer is that before the Cross, the souls of the saved did not go directly to Heaven. They could not go there because their sins were not forgiven. Their sins were only covered by their faith, not forgiven. There can be no forgiveness of sins without the shedding of blood (Leviticus 17:11 and Hebrews 9:22). Forgiveness for those who died in faith before the Cross had to await the shedding of the blood of the Messiah.

That's the reason Jesus descended into Hades after His death on the Cross (1 Peter 3:19-20). He went there to proclaim the shedding of His blood for the sins of Mankind.

There must have been great shouts of rejoicing by the Old Testament saints who had been waiting for this good news. Now their sins were not only covered by their faith, they were forgiven by the blood of Jesus. That made them candidates to be ushered into the presence of the Father in Heaven.

And that's exactly what happened when Jesus later ascended into Heaven. He took with Him "a host of captives" (Ephesians 4:8), referring to the saved who had been retained in Hades, awaiting the shed blood of the Messiah.

Hades and Hell

A lot of misunderstanding about all this has existed throughout the history of Christianity because translators confused Hades with

Hell. The two are not the same. Hades (called Sheol in the Old Testament) is a temporary holding place of the spirits of the dead. Hell is the ultimate destiny of the unsaved.

No one is in Hell today. The first to go to Hell will be the Antichrist and his False Prophet (Revelation 19:20). They will be joined by Satan at the end of the Millennium when he will be thrown into the lake of fire (Revelation 20:10).

The unsaved are currently in Hades in the compartment called Torments. At the end of the Lord's millennial reign, they will be resurrected, judged, condemned, and consigned to the "lake of fire," which is Hell (Revelation 20:11-15). Notice that in Revelation 20:14 the text specifically says that both "death and Hades" will be thrown into the lake of fire. This means both the body (death) and the soul (Hades) will be assigned to Hell.

Paul's Affirmations

Since the Cross, the spirits of the saved have been ushered immediately into the Lord's presence in Heaven by His holy angels. Paul affirms that Paradise was moved from Hades to Heaven. In 2 Corinthians 12:2-4 he states that he was taken up to the "third heaven," which he identifies as "Paradise." The first heaven is the atmosphere of this planet. The second heaven is outer space. The third heaven is where God resides.

Paul also affirms consciousness after death. In 2 Corinthians 5:8 he wrote that he would prefer to be "absent from the body and to be at home with the Lord." He repeated this sentiment in his Philippian letter where he wrote, "to live is Christ, and to die is gain" (Philippians 1:21). He elaborated on the meaning of this statement by adding that his desire was "to depart and be with Christ" (Philippians 1:23).

The Intermediate State

My second discovery was that we are not destined to an ethereal existence as disembodied spirits. Immediately after death both the saved and the lost receive a body that I am going to call an "intermediate spirit body." I have given it that name because it is a body that is intermediate between our current fleshly body and the ultimate, glorified body that saints will receive at the time of their resurrection.

The Bible does not tell us much about this body except that it is tangible and recognizable. An example of it is found in 1 Samuel 28 where we are told that King Saul, in his rebellion against God, sought the counsel of a witch. She, in turn, attempted to call up her familiar demon spirit. Instead, the Lord sent Samuel who had died some time before. The moment Samuel appeared, both the witch and Saul recognized him. Samuel proceeded to pronounce judgment upon Saul, telling him that his kingdom would be given to David and that the next day, "you and your sons will be with me" (1 Samuel 28:8-19). The next day Saul and his three sons, including Jonathan, were killed by the Philistines (1 Samuel 31:1-6).

Another example of the intermediate spirit body can be found in Matthew 17 where the story is told of Jesus' transfiguration. This was when His disciples were given a glimpse of His coming glory. As they witnessed this marvelous event, suddenly two people appeared and began talking with them. The two were Moses and Elijah (Matthew 17:1-5).

It is quite possible that these two appeared again at the ascension of Jesus. Luke tells us that as the disciples gazed intently at Jesus while He was ascending into Heaven, two men in white suddenly appeared and told them, "This Jesus, who has been taken up from you into heaven, will come in just the same way as you have watched Him go into heaven" (Acts 1:9-11). The men are not identified. They could have been angels, but they might also have been Elijah and Moses.

Glorification

When Jesus returns, the Bible says He will bring with Him the spirits of the saved (1 Thessalonians 4:13-14). He will resurrect their bodies in a great miracle of re-creation (whether their bodies are preserved, rotted, cremated, or dissolved in the ocean). In the twinkling of an eye, He will reunite their spirits with their resurrected bodies and will then glorify their bodies (1 Thessalonians 4:15-16). Then, those saints who are alive will be caught up (raptured) to meet the Lord in the sky, and they will be transformed on the way up (1

Thessalonians 4:17).

All my life I have heard people say, "There are two things in life that no one can avoid: death and taxes." That statement is wrong. The only thing we cannot avoid is taxes and more taxes. A whole generation of believers will avoid death — the generation living when the Lord returns for His Church. It's no wonder that Paul concluded this great passage in 1 Thessalonians by saying, "Therefore, comfort one another with these words" (1 Thessalonians 4:18).

A Third Discovery

My first discovery was that there is no such thing as "soul sleep." We remain conscious after death. My second discovery was that we are not destined to be disembodied spirits. We continue to have a body — first, an intermediate spirit body, and then a glorified body. My third discovery was that we are not going to be bored stiff playing harps for eternity. We are going to be engaged in some meaningful activities.

If you are a believer and you die before the Lord returns, you will go to Heaven where you will be involved in worship (Revelation 7:9-14) and service (Revelation 7:15). Admittedly, the Bible does not get specific about our worship and service, but we can be assured that we will find both to be fulfilling and edifying. It could also be that this will be a time of rest, preparing us for the time of vigorous service that will follow, when the Lord returns to earth.

During the Lord's reign, the redeemed are going to be doing anything but floating around on clouds playing harps. We are going to reign with Jesus over those who are allowed to enter the Millennium in the flesh (which will be those believers who are alive at the end of the Tribulation). Jesus will reign over all the earth from Jerusalem (Isaiah 2:1-4) as King of kings and Lord of lords (Revelation 19:16). David, in his glorified body, will reign as king of Israel (Ezekiel 37:24). Those of us who will be glorified saints will be scattered all over the earth to assist with Jesus' reign (2 Timothy 2:12).

Think of it — every person on earth who is in a position of governing authority will be a glorified saint. Some of us will be in ad-

ministrative positions, sharing in Jesus' reign as presidents, governors, or mayors (Luke 19:11-27). Others will serve as judges (1 Corinthians 6:3). Most of us will serve as "shepherds," or teachers,
trying to bring those who are born during the Millennium to faith in
Jesus (Isaiah 66:18-21 and Jeremiah 3:15).

None of us will serve as legislators because the law will be given
by Jesus Himself, and it will be perfect (Isaiah 2:1-4). There will be
no abomination known as the Texas Legislature or the United States
Congress. Nor will there be any lobbyists or political parties.

The Lord will rule with "a rod of iron" (Psalm 2:9 and Revelation 2:27). The government of the world will be a theocracy, with
Jesus serving as both the spiritual and political leader. "He will be a
priest on His throne, and the counsel of peace will be between the
two offices" (Zechariah 6:13).

We will be given the blessing of seeing this old sin-sick world
flooded with peace, righteousness and justice, "as the waters cover
the sea" (Isaiah 11:9). There will be no homeless people or hungry
people (Isaiah 65:21-22 and Micah 4:4). Peace will envelope the
earth (Isaiah 2:4). The Lord's reign will be characterized by righteousness, fairness, and faithfulness (Isaiah 11:4-5). "The whole
earth will acknowledge the Lord and return to Him. People from
every nation will bow down before Him" (Psalm 22:27).

The Eternal State

When the Millennium ends and we move into the Eternal State,
the Bible does not go into detail as to what our activities will be. It
tells us only three things: we will see the face of God (Revelation
22:4); we will serve the Lord (Revelation 22:3); and we will reign
with Him forever (Revelation 22:5).

Seeing the face of God is an exciting prospect, for the Bible says
that no one has ever seen His face (Exodus 33:20 and 1 Timothy
6:16). I believe the promise of seeing God's face means we are going to enjoy intimacy with Him forever. Much of that, undoubtedly
will be in the form of worship. I think it also means we will grow in
our knowledge of the Lord forever. He is infinite, and no matter how
much we come to know Him, there will be just that much more for

us to experience. I feel certain that one aspect of this will be the eternal study of His Word. I get excited over all this as I think of singing the Psalms with David and studying the book of Romans with Paul.

As for service, I would imagine, for one thing, our gifts and talents will be magnified and that we will use them to glorify the Lord. Thus, a singer will be able to sing with a perfection and range never before achieved, and a painter will be able to paint with a glory never imagined.

Reigning with the Lord forever implies that we will be reigning over someone. Who that will be, I do not know. Perhaps it will be the mysterious "nations" referred to in Revelation that seem to inhabit the new earth (Revelation 21:24-27 and 22:2).

My Final Discovery

This brings me to the final discovery I made when the Holy Spirit led me into an in-depth study of Bible prophecy. I discovered that the redeemed are not going to live eternally in an ethereal world called Heaven. I learned, instead, that our eternal home is going to be on a new earth. Most Christians are amazed by this truth, which shows how little Bible prophecy is taught in the Church today.

Since the Bible teaches that the current earth is eternal (Psalm 78:69 and Psalm 148:6), I have concluded that the "new earth" will be the current earth renovated by fire. It is true that Peter said that the current earth will be "destroyed" by fire (2 Peter 3:10,12), but in the context, it is clear that he is referring to a radical transformation of the current earth. Earlier in the same passage he referred to the original earth as having been "destroyed" by water, speaking of the Noahic flood. The earth of Noah's day did not cease to exist, but the flood "destroyed" it in the sense that it radically changed the nature of the earth — tilting it on it axis, splitting the continents apart, laying down the fossil record, depositing the marine organisms that would become petroleum deposits, and creating the ocean depths and the mountain heights.

At the end of the Millennium, fire will be used by God to burn away the pollution of Satan's last revolt (2 Peter 3:12). In the midst of that fiery inferno, God will reshape the earth like a hot ball of wax. He will refresh it and restore it to its original perfection (Acts 3:21). He will then lower the new Jerusalem down to the new earth, with the redeemed inside (Revelation 21:1-2). Then, He Himself will come to earth to live in our presence eternally! "The tabernacle of God is among men, and He shall dwell among them, and they shall be His people, and God Himself shall be among them" (Revelation 21:3).

Heaven is where God resides. When the new earth is supplied, Heaven will descend to earth as God takes up residence on this new earth. So, it is true that the redeemed will live eternally in Heaven, but Heaven will be on earth.

The Redemption of All Creation

God loves His creation, and He intends to redeem it — all of it — and not destroy it with some mystical "big bang." Jesus died on the Cross not only to redeem Mankind but also to redeem the creation. That's the reason the High Priest in Old Testament times sprinkled the blood not only on the mercy seat of the Ark, but also on the ground in front of the Ark (Leviticus 16:15).

The blood on the mercy seat of the Ark was a symbolic prophecy pointing to the fact that the blood of the Messiah would cover the law of God (the tablets inside the Ark) with the mercy and grace of God. The blood on the ground was a reminder that the sacrifice of the Messiah would make it possible for the curse to be lifted and for the animal and plant kingdoms to be returned to their original perfection (Isaiah 11:6-9 and Romans 8:18-23).

An Unjustified Fear

Many people are afraid of Bible prophecy. They say it is full of "doom and gloom." That is true for those who have rejected the Lord. But for those who know Him and love Him, there is only good news. The Old Testament ends with an example of what I'm talking about. It says, "For behold, the day is coming, burning like a furnace; and all the arrogant and every evildoer will be chaff; and the day that is coming will set them ablaze" (Malachi 4:1). That is bad news. But the very next verse contains incredibly good news for believers: "But for you who fear My name, the sun of righteousness will rise with healing in its wings; and you will go forth and skip about like calves released from the stall" (Malachi 4:2).

Bible prophecy is full of glorious promises that are designed to give God's people a strong sense of hope as they live as strangers and pilgrims in the midst of an increasingly evil, God-rejecting world. When you read these wonderful promises, you can understand why Paul wrote these words (1 Corinthians 2:9):

> No eye has seen,
> No ear heard,
> Nor the heart of man conceived,
> What God has prepared for those who love Him.

A God of Hope

As this verse indicates, we cannot even begin to imagine the marvelous blessings God has in store for the redeemed. But the very next verse says that the Holy Spirit has revealed those blessings to us in God's Word (1 Corinthians 2:10). The sad thing is that most Christians are ignorant of those promises and therefore have no idea what Paul meant when he wrote: "For I consider that the sufferings of this present time are not worthy to be compared with the glory that is to be revealed to us" (Romans 8:18).

How many will occur and when?

My boyhood church always taught that there would be one resurrection and one judgment. Everyone who had ever lived would be resurrected at one time, and all of us — the just and the unjust — would be judged at the same time. The sheep would be separated from the goats at the Great White Throne Judgment pictured in Revelation 20:11-15.

But this concept is all wrong. The Bible reveals that there will be more than one resurrection and more than one judgment.

Multiple Resurrections

Concerning resurrection, Jesus clearly taught that there would be more than one resurrection. In John 5:29 He refers to a "resurrection of life" and a "resurrection of judgment." The apostle Paul confirmed this concept in his defense before Felix when he stated that he believed the teaching of the prophets "that there shall certainly be a resurrection of both the righteous and the wicked" (Acts 24:15).

Of course, it could be argued that the two resurrections referred to in these scriptures will occur at the same time. Thus, because they will happen simultaneously, there is, in effect, only one resurrection. However, the Scriptures establish the fact that the resurrection of the righteous will occur in stages.

In other words, the Bible does not teach one resurrection or even two resurrections in *number*. Rather, it teaches that there will be two resurrections in *type* which will be conducted in stages, resulting in several resurrections — at least four, to be specific.

The Resurrection of the Just

That the resurrection of the righteous will occur in stages is clearly taught in 1 Corinthians 15:20-24. In fact, the first stage of the resurrection of the righteous has already happened, for verse 20 says that "Christ has been raised from the dead, the first fruits of those who are asleep."

Verses 22 and 23 go on to explain that all who have died in Christ shall be made alive, "but each in his own order: Christ, the first fruits, after that those who are Christ's at His coming."

The imagery of the harvest that is used in these verses is a key to understanding the first resurrection — the resurrection of the righteous.

The Harvest Imagery

In Bible times the harvest was conducted in three stages. It began with the gathering of the first fruits which were offered as a sacrifice of thanksgiving to God.

It proceeded with the general harvest. But not all was taken in this harvest. Some of the crop was left in the field to be gathered by the poor and the needy. This was called the gleanings (Leviticus 19:9-10).

Using this imagery, the Bible presents the resurrection of Jesus as the "first fruits" of the resurrection of the righteous. The gathering of the Church Age saints, living and dead, at the appearing of the Lord (the Rapture) is thus the general harvest stage of the resurrection of the righteous (John 14:1-3 and 1 Thessalonians 4:13-18).

But there is a third and final stage to this resurrection of the righteous. It is the gleanings, and it occurs at the end of the Tribulation when the Lord's Second Coming takes place. At that time two final groups of the righteous will be resurrected: the Tribulation martyrs (Revelation 20:4), and the Old Testament saints (Dan 12:2).

Some people are startled by the thought that the Old Testament saints will not be resurrected until the end of the Tribulation. But keep in mind that the Rapture is a promise to the Church, and the Church only. Also, the book of Daniel makes it clear that the Old

Testament saints will be resurrected at the end of the "time of distress" (Daniel 12:1-2).

So the first resurrection, the resurrection of the righteous, occurs in three stages, beginning with Christ, continuing with the Church at the Rapture, and culminating with the Tribulation martyrs and the Old Testament saints at the return of Jesus.

The Resurrection of the Unjust

The second type of resurrection, "the resurrection of the wicked" (Acts 24:15), will take place all at one time at the end of the millennial reign of Jesus. This is at the time of the Great White Throne Judgment, the judgment of the damned (Revelation 20:11-15).

Every person who ever failed to relate to God in faith will be resurrected at this time, regardless of when he or she may have lived and died — whether before or after the Cross. This resurrection will also include the unjust who died during the Tribulation and the Millennium.

There will be no need for an additional resurrection of the righteous at the end of the Millennium, because all those born during that time who accept Jesus as their Savior will live to the end of the Lord's reign (Isaiah 65:19-20). "'As the lifetime of a tree, so shall be the days of My people,'. . . says the Lord" (Isaiah 65:22, 25). In other words, life spans during the Millennium will be returned to what they were at the beginning of time, before the flood.

The Certainty of Judgment

Resurrection will be followed by judgment. Solomon wrote, "Fear God and keep His commandments . . . For God will bring every act to judgment, everything which is hidden, whether it is good or evil" (Ecclesiastes 12:13-14).

The apostle Paul emphasized the certainty of judgment. In Romans 2:16 he wrote, "God will judge the secrets of men through Christ Jesus." And in Romans 14:10, 12 he stated, "We shall all stand before the judgment seat of God . . . So then each one of us shall give account of himself to God." The writer to the Hebrews summed it up succinctly: "It is appointed for men to die once and after this comes judgment" (Hebrews 9:27).

The Completed Judgment

But not all people are going to be judged at the same time. Just as there are going to be several resurrections, there are also going to be several judgments.

One judgment has already taken place. It is the judgment of believers for their sins.

This comes as a surprise to most Christians. Some find it hard to believe. I'll never forget when I realized it from my study of Scripture. I became filled with so much joy that I felt like jumping pews all day!

Let me put it to you in another way. If you are truly born again, then you will never stand before the Lord and be judged of your sins. That's because the judgment for your sins took place at the Cross.

You see, all your sins, and mine, were placed upon Jesus as He hung upon the Cross, and the wrath we deserve was poured out upon Him (2 Corinthians 5:21). He became our substitute. He took our judgment for sin (Romans 8:3 and Galatians 3:13).

If you have appropriated the blood of Jesus to your life by accepting Him as your Lord and Savior, then your sins have been forgiven. They have also been forgotten in the sense that God will never remember them against you again (Isaiah 43:25 and Hebrews 8:12).

Think of it — forgiven and forgotten! That is grace!

The Judgment of the Just

If the Redeemed will never be judged of their sins, then what will they be judged of, and when will the judgment take place?

The Bible teaches that the Redeemed will be judged of their works, not to determine their eternal destiny, but to determine their degrees of reward.

Christians do not work to be saved; they work because they are saved. In fact, the Bible says they are saved to do good works (Ephesians 2:10 and Titus 2:14). Such good works, if properly done, will be done in the power of the Holy Spirit (1 Peter 4:11) and for the glory of God (1 Corinthians 10:31).

The Significance of Spiritual Gifts

Paul says in 1 Corinthians 12 that every person who is born again receives at least one supernatural spiritual gift from the Holy Spirit. A person may receive more than one gift. And, if you are a good steward of the gifts you receive, then you may receive additional gifts as you develop spiritually (Luke 19:26).

God expects us to use our spiritual gifts to advance His kingdom. This is what the judgment of works will be all about. Each of us who are redeemed will stand before the Lord Jesus and give an accounting of how we used our gifts to advance the kingdom of God on earth.

We will be judged as to the *quantity* of our works (Luke 19:11-27 and Romans 2:6-7). We will be judged as to the *quality* of our works (1 Corinthians 3:10-14). Finally, we will be judged as to the *motivation* of our works (1 Corinthians 4:5).

I can imagine some famous evangelist being brought before the Lord for judgment.

"How did you use your spiritual gifts to advance my kingdom?" asks the Lord.

"I used my gifts as a teacher and evangelist to preach the gospel to millions," replies the preacher.

"Yes," says the Lord, "you certainly did that. But, I know your heart, and thus I know your motivation. You preached not because you loved Me but because you wanted to become famous. You wanted to have your picture published on the cover of *Time* magazine. You accomplished that in February of 1953. Here's your picture. That's all the reward I have for you!"

And then I can imagine the Lord calling up a little old lady that no one has ever heard of.

"Dear, on the day you accepted Me as your Lord and Savior, I gave you one gift — the gift of mercy. And every time someone was ill, you were the first to offer comfort and encouragement. You were the one who organized the prayer chain. Every time someone went to the hospital, you were the first to visit them. Every time someone died, you were the one who organized the meals. And you did all of these things simply because you loved me."

The Lord will give her a crown full of so many jewels that she will have a neck ache for eternity!

Seriously, there will be degrees of rewards. They will be manifested in the crowns we receive (2 Timothy 4:7-8), the robes we wear (Revelation 19:8), and the degrees of ruling authority which we exercise with the Lord (Luke 19:11-27).

The Timing of the Judgments

When and where will the judgment of the Redeemed take place? The Bible indicates the judgment of believers who have lived and died during the Church Age will occur in Heaven before the judgment seat of Jesus, immediately following the Rapture of the Church (2 Corinthians 5:10 and Revelation 19:6-9).

Those who are saved and martyred during the Tribulation will be judged at the end of that period when they are resurrected at the Second Coming of Christ (Revelation 20:4). The Tribulation saints who live to the end of that terrible period are another group that will be judged at the Second Coming of Jesus in "the sheep and goat judgment" portrayed in Matthew 25:31-46. The Old Testament saints will also be judged at the time of the Second Coming (Ezekiel 20:34-38).

All the unrighteous who have ever lived will be resurrected and judged at the end of the millennial reign of Jesus.

The Judgment of the Unjust

The terrible judgment of the unrighteous is pictured in Revelation 20:11-15. It is called the "Great White Throne" judgment.

We are told that the wicked also will be judged of their works. But their judgment will be radically different from the judgment of the Redeemed. Whereas the Redeemed are judged of their works to determine their degrees of reward, the lost are judged of their works to determine their eternal destiny.

And since no one can be justified before God by their works (Isaiah 64:6 and Ephesians 2:8-10), all will be condemned to Hell. That's why I call this judgment "the judgment of the damned."

The unjust are also judged for another reason. There are going to be degrees of punishment (Luke 12:35-48 and 20:45-47).

There is a popular myth in Christendom that says, "All sin is equal in the eyes of God." That is not true. The only way in which all sin is equal is that *any* sin, whether a white lie or murder, condemns us before God and necessitates a Savior.

But all sin is not equal in the eyes of God. For example, Proverbs 6:16-19 lists seven sins that the Lord particularly hates, including "hands that shed innocent blood." And the Bible makes it very clear that idolatry is a sin that is especially heinous in the eyes of God (Exodus 20:3-5).

Because God considers some sins worse than others, there will be degrees of punishment (Revelation 22:12), and these degrees will be specified at the Great White Throne judgment.

A Call to Repentance

Where do you stand with respect to the inevitable judgment which you will face before the Lord?

If you are a Christian, do you know what spiritual gifts you have been given? Are you using them to advance the Lord's kingdom? Is your motivation a love of the Lord?

If you have never confessed Jesus as your Lord and Savior, do you really want to participate in the judgment of the damned? Do you realize that the Bible says, "Every knee shall bow and every tongue confess that Jesus is Lord"? That means Hitler and every vile person like him who has ever lived will one day make the confession of Jesus' lordship. You will too.

I urge you to make that confession *now* so that you can participate in the resurrection and judgment of the righteous. As you consider your decision, weigh carefully the following words from the book of Hebrews:

> Christ also, having been offered once to bear the sins of many, shall appear a second time for salvation without reference to sin, to those who eagerly await Him — Hebrews 9:28

Notice carefully that this verse promises that for those who are ready for Him, Jesus will come "without reference to sin." That is a wonderful promise.

What rewards can believers look forward to?

19 Do not lay up for yourselves treasures upon earth, where moth and rust destroy, and where thieves break in and steal.

20 But lay up for yourselves treasures in heaven, where neither moth nor rust destroys, and where thieves do not break in or steal;

21 for where your treasure is, there will your heart be also.

Matthew 6:19-21

What does this passage mean when it speaks of "treasures in heaven"? Certainly it is referring to promises that God has made to all believers. But in addition, I believe it refers to special rewards that we are earning right now as a result of our good works.

The Significance of Good Works

Now don't panic! I'm not saying that we earn our salvation. Nor am I saying that we are saved by good works. We are not.

The Bible clearly teaches that we are saved by grace through faith in Jesus as our Lord and Savior — and not by our own works (Ephesians 2:8-9). Salvation is a "gift of God" (Ephesians 2:8).

But we often stress this truth to the point that we forget that the Bible also teaches that we are saved to do good works: "We are His workmanship, created in Christ Jesus for good works, which God prepared beforehand, that we should walk in them" (Ephesians 2: 10).

The apostle Paul stressed this important point in his letter to Titus. He wrote that Jesus has redeemed us in order to "purify for Himself a people for His own possession, zealous for good deeds" (Titus 2:14). Paul proceeded to emphasize that "He saved us, not on the basis of deeds which we have done in righteousness, but according to His mercy . . . being justified by His grace" (Titus 3:5,7). But then he added that those who have believed must "be careful to engage in good deeds" (Titus 3:8).

To summarize, we do not work to be saved; we work because we are saved. Our good works are a manifestation of our salvation. That's what James, the brother of Jesus, meant when he wrote, "What use is it, my brethren, if a man says he has faith, but he has no works?" He then added that "faith without works is useless" (James 2:20).

Besides manifesting our salvation, our good works bring honor and glory to God: "Let your light shine before men in such a way that they may see your good works, and glorify your Father who is in heaven" (Matthew 5:16). That's why it is important to perform good deeds in the name of Jesus: "And whatever you do in word or deed, do all in the name of the Lord Jesus, giving thanks through Him to God the Father" (Colossians 3:17).

The Judgment of Good Works

Our good works are so important that God is keeping a record of them because one day all believers are going to stand before Jesus and be judged of their works to determine their degrees of reward. Speaking of believers, Paul wrote, "For we must all appear before the judgment seat of Christ, that each one may be recompensed for his deeds in the body, according to what he has done, whether good or bad" (2 Corinthians 5:10).

There is both good news and bad news about this judgment. The good news is so incredible that many Christians find it hard to believe. It is the fact that believers will not be judged of their sins to determine their eternal destiny. The reason is that they have already been judged of their sins! That judgment took place at the Cross where every sin we have ever committed and ever will commit was placed upon Jesus, and He received the wrath of God that we deserve (2 Corinthians 5:21 and 2 Peter 2:24).

Because of the work that Jesus did on the Cross, the sins of those who have placed their faith in Him have been forgiven and forgotten: "For I will be merciful to their iniquities, and I will remember their sins no more" (Hebrews 8:12). Our sins have been forgotten in the sense that God will never hold them against us again. Thus, the book of Hebrews says, "So Christ, having been offered once to bear the sins of many, shall appear a second time for salvation without reference to sin, to those who eagerly await Him" (Hebrews 9:28).

What a gracious God! When we place our faith in His Son, He forgets our evil deeds, but He remembers all our good works: "For God is not unjust so as to forget your work and the love which you have shown toward His name, in having ministered and in still ministering to the saints" (Hebrews 6:10).

The Criteria of Judgment

So, the good news is that believers will not be judged of their sins to determine their eternal destiny. The bad news is that they will be judged of their works to determine their degrees of reward.

Let's consider how our works will be judged. First of all, they are going to be judged in relation to our spiritual gifts. Every person receives one or more spiritual gifts when he or she places their faith in Jesus and are born again (1 Corinthians 12:4-11 and 1 Peter 4:10-11). We are expected to use those gifts to advance the Lord's kingdom. That's why it is so important for all believers to study the spiritual gifts and determine which ones they have received.

To those to whom much is given, much will be expected (Luke 12:48). But we will not be judged solely on the quantity of our works. We will also be judged as to quality (1 Corinthians 3:13) and motive (1 Corinthians 4:5).

When this judgment is completed, some will be laden with rewards, but others will be stripped naked. The apostle Paul described it in this manner in 1 Corinthians 3:13-15:

13 Each man's work will become evident; for the day will show it, because it is to be revealed with fire; and the fire itself will test the quality of each man's work.

14 If any man's work which he has built upon it [the foundation of Jesus Christ] remains, he shall receive a reward.

15 If any man's work is burned up, he shall suffer loss; but he himself shall be saved so as through fire.

What an image verse 15 presents of a person saved with his tail feathers smoking! This passage makes it clear that some who are saved will receive no special rewards whatsoever. In short, some believers will experience embarrassment at the judgment seat of Jesus. Since they will fail to receive any special rewards, they also will not have anything to place at the feet of Jesus to honor Him.

Take a look at the heavenly scene portrayed in Revelation 4. The 24 Elders, representative of the Church, cast their golden crowns at the feet of Jesus and then bow before Him in worship (Revelation 4:4-11). What a tragedy it will be for those who have no special rewards to offer back to Jesus in honor of Him.

Degrees of Reward

Some people have difficulty with the concept that there will be degrees of reward, but this principle is clearly taught in the Scriptures. Consider the following promises:

• Whatever a person gives up for the Lord, he will receive back one hundred times over (Mark 10:29-30).

• Those who are hated and persecuted for Christ will receive a great reward in Heaven (Matthew 5:11-12).

• Those who show kindness to the poor, the maimed, the lame and the blind will be rewarded at the resurrection of the Righteous (Luke 14:12-14).

Types of Rewards

There are two types of rewards that believers will receive. The first category consists of the general rewards all believers will receive because they are associated with their salvation. These include such things as resurrection, glorification, and eternal life in the presence of God on a new earth.

The special rewards will be related to believers' utilization of their spiritual gifts to advance the kingdom. These will include such things as customized robes and crowns — as well as differing degrees of ruling authority during the Millennium.

Let's take a look at both general and special rewards in the chronological order in which they will be distributed.

Rewards at the Rapture

The Rapture itself is referred to in the Scriptures as a reward for believers: "I [Paul] press on toward the goal for the prize of the upward call of God in Jesus Christ" (Philippians 3:14).

Both the living and dead in Christ will receive deliverance from death (John 11:25-26). Our bodies will be glorified (1 Corinthians 15:35-53), and our souls will be conformed to the image of Jesus (Romans 8:29-30).

Glorified Bodies

What will it mean to receive a glorified body? Paul wrote a whole chapter about the topic in 1 Corinthians 15. According to him, our glorified bodies will be imperishable, gloriously pure, powerful, and spiritual (1 Corinthians 15:42-44).

Paul further states that the glorified body will be immortal, and as such will no longer be subject to death (1 Corinthians 15:53-55). This is an important point. Many in Christendom believe in the immortality of the soul. That is not a biblical concept. It comes from the writings of Plato, a Greek philosopher. The Bible says that God alone possesses immortality (1 Timothy 6:16). We do not receive immortality until we are given our glorified bodies. Immortality is a gift of grace to the redeemed.

The Nature of the Glorified Body

Paul made a statement in his letter to the Philippians that I think provides us with the best framework for understanding what our glorified bodies will be like. He wrote that when Jesus returns, He "will transform the body of our humble state into conformity with the body of His glory, by the exertion of the power that He has even to subject all things to Himself" (Philippians 3:20-21). In other words, our glorified bodies are going to be like Jesus' resurrection body.

Now, think about that for a moment. After His resurrection, Jesus had a tangible body that could be touched and recognized (Luke 24:41-43 and John 20:27-28). People had difficulty recognizing Him at first, but that is understandable. If you buried your best friend one day, and he knocked on your door the next, would you recognize him? Wouldn't you assume he was someone who looked like your friend? Once the disciples realized that Jesus had truly been resurrected, they had no more difficulty recognizing Him, even at a distance (John 21:1-7).

So, Jesus had a body similar to the ones we have now. It was tangible and recognizable. It was also a body that ate food. Jesus is pictured eating with His disciples several times, including a meal of fish on the shore of the Sea of Galilee (Luke 24:30-31, 41-42, and John 21:10-13). I must admit that I get excited when I read these accounts of Jesus eating, and also when I read about our eating with Him in Heaven at the "marriage supper of the Lamb (Revelation 19:7-9). I have this fantasy that we will be able to eat all we want in our glorified bodies and not have to worry about gaining weight! (That should be sufficient to prompt many of you to shout, "Maranatha!")

A Different Dimension

The resurrected body of Jesus was similar to ours in many respects, but there were also some differences. Jesus' body seemed to have a different dimension to it, for He could pass through a wall into a locked room (John 20:26), and He could move from one place to another almost instantly (Luke 24:30-36). One moment He was on the road to Emmaus, the next He was in Jerusalem, and then He would appear in the Galilee area.

His disciples were so startled and frightened by His ability to vanish and reappear suddenly at another place that they thought they were seeing a spirit. But Jesus countered that idea immediately by telling them, "Touch Me and see, for a spirit does not have flesh and bones as you see that I have" (Luke 24:39). When the Word says that our glorified bodies will be "spiritual" in nature (1 Corinthians 15:44), it does not mean we will be ethereal spirits. It says our natural body will be raised a spiritual *body*, not a spirit. We will still have a body, but it will no longer be controlled by the old sin nature, the flesh. Rather, it will be a body yielded completely to the control of the Holy Spirit.

There is one other thing the Bible reveals about the glorified body that should be a source of great comfort. The glorified body will be a perfected body. That means the blind will see, the deaf will hear, the lame will walk, and the mute will speak. Those who are mentally impaired will have their minds healed (Isaiah 29:18-19, 32:3-4, and 35:5-6). There will no longer be any pain or death (Revelation 21:4). God will "wipe away every tear," and "there shall no longer be any mourning, or crying, or pain" (Revelation 21:4).

The Throne of God in Heaven

The first event for believers after the Rapture will be their presentation to God the Father before His throne in Heaven (Jude 24).

They will appear without blemish and with rejoicing (Jude 24). Jesus will confess each one before His Father and the angels (Revelation 3:5), and each one will be honored by the Father by being perfected, confirmed, strengthened, and established (John 12:26 and 1 Peter 5:10). It is at this point that the Redeemed will be formally adopted as children of God (Romans 8:23).

Comfort will be granted to the those who mourned (Matthew 5:4). Those who hungered for righteousness will experience satisfaction (Matthew 5:6). The merciful will receive mercy (Matthew 5:7). A great reward of praise, honor and glory will be given to those who were persecuted for Christ's sake (Matthew 5:10-12).

Those who were sacrificial will receive back a hundred times more than what they surrendered (Matthew 19:29). Those who were humble will be exalted (Matthew 18:4). Special blessings will be given to those who rendered special services to the Church (2 Timothy 1:16-18).

The Judgment Seat of Christ

Following their welcome to Heaven, the Redeemed will appear before the judgment seat of Christ to be judged of their works to determine their degrees of rewards (2 Corinthians 5:10). Among the rewards that will be given are the following:

- An imperishable wreath for those who exercised self-control (1 Corinthians 9:24-27).

- A crown of exaltation for those who were soul winners (1 Thessalonians 2:19-20).

- A crown of righteousness for those who lived with the love of the Lord's appearing in their hearts (2 Timothy 4:8).

- A crown of life for those who endured trials (James 1:12).

- An unfading crown of glory for those who served as elders (1 Peter 5:1-4).

The Marriage Feast of the Lamb

At the end of the Tribulation, each redeemed person will receive an invitation to attend the greatest feast in the history of the cosmos — what the Bible calls 'the marriage feast of the Lamb" (Revelation 19:7).

This will be the joyous occasion when Jesus, the Bridegroom, will celebrate His union with His bride, the Church. The Redeemed will be given special robes of fine linen, clean and bright (Revelation 3:5 and 19:8). The robes will be decorated in a manner that will reflect the righteous deeds of the each person.

The Second Coming

When the great marriage feast celebration ends, Jesus will return to earth to reign. The Redeemed will return with Him (Revelation

19:8) and will inherit the earth (Matthew 5:5) and the kingdom (James 2:5). They will reign with Jesus over the world (2 Timothy 2:12 and Revelation 2:26-27), exercising various degrees of ruling power (Luke 19:1-27). And during this time, the Redeemed will be glorified along with Jesus (Matthew 13:43 and Romans 8:17).

We will be blessed to see the whole world flooded with peace, righteousness and justice, as the waters cover the seas (Isaiah 11:1-9).

Rewards Beyond Comprehension

What I have catalogues here is by no means all the rewards promised to believers. But it will give you an idea of the wonderful blessings that lie in store for us.

It will also help you to understand what the apostle Paul meant when he wrote: "I consider that the sufferings of this present time are not worthy to be compared with the glory that is to be revealed to us" (Romans 8:18). That's a mouthful! Paul reaffirms it in 1 Corinthians 2:9 (RSV):

> No eye has seen,
> No ear has heard,
> Nor has the mind of Man conceived,
> What God has prepared
> For those who love Him.

A Crucial Question

Do you have an invitation to the "marriage feast of the Lamb"? If not, then you will be at the "supper of God" described in Revelation 19:17-18).

What a contrast the Bible presents between these two feasts! The "marriage feast of the Lamb" will occur in Heaven at the end of the Tribulation, right before the return of Jesus to earth. It will be a celebration of great joy, as the Redeemed are united with their Savior and express their thanks to Him for the salvation He provided on the Cross.

The "supper of God," in contrast, will occur on earth after the Second Coming of Jesus. All those who have rejected Jesus will be gathered, consigned to death, and fed to the vultures (Luke 17:34-37 and Revelation 19:18).

Those invited to the "marriage feast of the Lamb" will be honored guests. Those invited to the "supper of God" will serve as the meal!

The invitation to the "marriage feast of the Lamb" is free of charge. To secure an invitation, all you have to do is repent of your sins and accept Jesus as your Lord and Savior (Romans 10:8-11).

If you have never done that, then pray this simple prayer:

> Heavenly Father, I confess to You that I am a sinner and that my sins have separated me from You. I desire to be reconciled to you by accepting Your Son, Jesus, as my Lord and Savior. I believe that He died on the cross for my sins and rose from the dead. Give me the gift of your Holy Spirit that I might be born again and sealed for redemption. Thank You, Lord. In Jesus' name, Amen.

If you prayed that prayer, please seek out a Bible believing church where Jesus is honored as Lord and Savior. Make a public confession of your faith, and manifest your faith in water baptism.

Then, with the help of fellow Christians, start studying God's Word and growing in the image of Jesus.

Are you living with an eternal perspective?

One of the greatest public servants in the history of England was William Gladstone (1809-1898) who served as Prime Minister four times during the latter half of the 19th Century.

Gladstone was a committed Christian who always attended church. Gladstone also taught a Sunday School class throughout his adult life. In fact, his aim early in his life was to become an Anglican clergyman, but after his graduation from Oxford, his strong-willed father insisted that he enter politics.

Shortly before he died, Gladstone gave a speech in which he told about being visited by an ambitious young man who sought his advice about life. The lad told the elder statesman that he admired him more than anyone living and wanted to seek his advice regarding his career.

A Remarkable Interview

"What do you hope to do when you graduate from college?" Gladstone asked.

The young man replied, "I hope to attend law school, sir, just as you did."

"That's a noble goal," said Gladstone, "Then what?"

"I hope to practice law and make a good name for myself defending the poor and the outcasts of society, just as you did."

"That's a noble purpose," replied Gladstone. "Then what?"

"Well, sir, I hope one day to stand for Parliament and become a servant of the people, even as you did."

"That too is a noble hope. What then?" asked Gladstone.

"I would hope to be able to serve in the Parliament with great distinction, evidencing integrity and a concern for justice — even as you did."

"What then?" asked Gladstone.

"I would hope to serve the government as Prime Minister with the same vigor, dedication, vision, and integrity as you did."

"And what then?" asked Gladstone.

"I would hope to retire with honors and write my memoirs — even as you are presently doing — so that others could learn from my mistakes and triumphs."

"All of that is very noble," said Gladstone, "and then what?"

The young man thought for a moment. "Well, sir, I suppose I will then die."

"That's correct," said Gladstone. "And then what?"

The young man looked puzzled. "Well, sir," he answered hesitantly, "I've never given that any thought."

"Young man," Gladstone responded, "the only advice I have for you is for you to go home, read your Bible, and *think about eternity.*"

Good Advice

Think about eternity! What good advice. Life goes by so quickly. It is like a vapor that is here one moment and evaporates the next. We are preparing for eternity. Are you ready?

Or, are you living like you expect to live forever? Are you focused on this life, determined to accumulate all the money, power and fame you possibly can? Are you like the young man who visited Gladstone — are you a person who has never given eternity a thought? If so, the Word of God has a stern warning for you (James 4:13-15 — *The Message*):

13 And now I have a word for you who brashly announce, "Today — at the latest, tomorrow — we're off to such and such a city for the year. We're going to start a business and make a lot of money."

14 You don't know the first thing about tomorrow. You're nothing but a wisp of fog, catching a brief bit of sun before disappearing.

15 Instead, make it a habit to say, "If the Master wills it and we're still alive, we'll do this or that."

The Fleeting Nature of Life

This passage always reminds me of an incident that occurred in my life several years ago. A dear friend of mine whom I had taught with in a Texas college called me one day and told me he had been diagnosed with prostate cancer.

"The doctor has given me only six months to live," he reported.

I told him I was very sorry to hear the news, and I promised to pray for him and his family. Then, I added, "But keep in mind, I may be dead before you."

"Oh? Do you have cancer too?" he asked.

"No," I responded, "it's just that I do not have the promise of even one day of life, much less six months."

We all tend to live like we are going to live forever, when the fact is that we are all mortal and can die at any moment from a thousand different causes, natural or accidental. Ironically, the Bible tells us that we are to live like we are going to live forever — but not on this earth. We are to live in preparation for eternity, hopefully an eternity with God.

A Constant Battle

Most likely you are a born again believer who has given serious thought to eternity, but who finds it difficult to maintain an eternal perspective. You repeatedly find yourself caught up with the problems of life, and the result is stress, anxiety, and even depression.

Living with an eternal perspective is one of the keys to living as an overcomer. It is a virtue that is going to become increasingly important as society continues to disintegrate and Christians come under increasing attack.

What is the secret to maintaining an eternal perspective? Much of the answer lies in your attitude about this world.

Your Attitude Toward the World

Stop for a moment and think. What is your attitude about this world? Are you enthusiastic about it? Or do you feel uncomfortable with it? Do you love the world? Or do you often feel alienated from it? Are you at home in this world? Or do you feel like a stranger?

There's an old Negro Spiritual that always challenges me to examine my attitude toward the world. The first verse goes as follows:

> This world is not my home,
> I'm just a passing through.
> My treasures are laid up
> Somewhere beyond the blue.
>
> The angels beckon me
> From heaven's open door,
> And I can't feel at home
> In this world anymore.

Do those words express your feeling about this world? What word would you use to summarize your feeling? Zealous? Anxious? Enamored? Estranged? Are you comfortable or do you feel ill-at-ease?

My Attitude

Let me ask your indulgence for a moment as I share my personal feeling about this world. The word I would use is "hate." Yes, I hate this world. I hate it with a passion so strong and so intense that I find it difficult to express in words.

Now, let me hasten to clarify my feeling by stating that I do not hate God's beautiful and marvelous creation. I have been privileged to marvel over the majesty of the Alps. I have been awed by the rugged beauty of Alaska. I never cease to be amazed by the creative wonders of God in the great American Southwest. I have been blessed to see the incredible beauty of Cape Town, South Africa. And I have been overwhelmed time and time again by the stark and almost mystical bareness of the Judean wilderness in Israel.

When I say that I "hate" this world, I'm not speaking of God's creation. I'm speaking, instead, of the evil world system that we live in. Let me give you some examples of what I'm talking about:

- I hate a world where thousands of babies are murdered every day in their mother's wombs.

- I hate a world where young people in the prime of life have their lives destroyed by illicit drugs.

- I hate a world that coddles criminals and makes a mockery of justice.

- I hate a world that glorifies crime in its movies and television programs.

- I hate a world that applauds indecent and vulgar performers like Madonna.

- I hate a world where government tries to convert gambling from a vice to a virtue.

- I hate a world in which professional athletes are paid millions of dollars a year while hundreds of thousands sleep homeless in the streets every night.

- I hate a world where people judge and condemn one another on the basis of skin color.

- I hate a world that calls evil good by demanding that homosexuality be recognized as a legitimate, alternative lifestyle.

- I hate a world in which mothers are forced to work while their children grow up in impersonal day care centers.

- I hate a world in which people die agonizing deaths from diseases like cancer and AIDS.

- I hate a world where families are torn apart by alcohol abuse.

- I hate a world where every night I see reports on the television news of child abuse, muggings, kidnappings, murders, terrorism, wars, and rumors of wars.

- I hate a world that uses the name of my God, Jesus, as a curse word.

I hope you understand now what I mean when I say, "I hate this world!"

Jesus' Viewpoint

But how I personally feel about this world is not important. The crucial point for you to consider is the biblical view. Let's look at it, and as we do so, compare the biblical view with your own.

Let's begin with the viewpoint that Jesus told us we should have. It is recorded in John 12:25 — "He who loves his life loses it, and he who hates his life in this world shall keep it to life eternal."

Those are strong words. They are the kind that cause us to wince and think, "Surely He didn't mean what He said." But the context indicates that Jesus meant exactly what He said. So, what about it? Do you hate your life in this world or do you love it?

The Viewpoint of the Apostles

The apostle Paul gave a very strong warning about getting comfortable with the world. In Romans 12:2 he wrote: "Do not be conformed to this world, but be transformed by the renewing of your mind." How do you measure up to this exhortation?

Are you conformed to the world? Have you adopted the world's way of dress? What about the world's way of speech or the world's love of money? Are your goals the goals of the world — power, success, fame, and riches?

The brother of Jesus expressed the matter in very pointed language. He said, "Do you not know that friendship with the world is hostility toward God? Therefore, whoever wishes to be a friend of the world makes himself an enemy of God" (James 4:4).

Are you a friend of the world? Are you comfortable with what the world has to offer in music, movies, television programs and best selling books? Friendship with the world is hostility toward God!

In fact, James puts it even stronger than that, for at the beginning of the passage I previously quoted (James 4:4), he says that those who are friendly with the world are spiritual adulterers.

The apostle John makes the same point just as strongly in 1 John 2:15-16:

15 Do not love the world, nor the things in the world. If anyone loves the world, the love of the Father is not in him.

16 For all that is in the world, the lust of the flesh, and the lust of the eyes, and the boastful pride of life, is not from the Father, but is from the world.

There is no way to escape the sobering reality of these words. Do you love the world? If so, the love of the Father is not in you!

The Focus of Your Mind

Paul tells us how to guard against becoming comfortable with the world. In Colossians 3:2 he says, "Set your mind on the things above, not on the things that are on earth." In Philippians 4:8 he expresses the same admonition in these words:

Finally, brethren, whatever is true, whatever is honorable, whatever is right, whatever is pure, whatever is lovely, whatever is of good repute, if there is any excellence and if anything worthy of praise, let your mind dwell on these things.

As these verses indicate, one of the keys to living a triumphant life in Christ — to living a joyous and victorious life in the midst of a world wallowing in despair — is to live with a conscious eternal perspective.

What does that mean? In the words of Peter, that means living as "aliens and strangers" in this world (1 Peter 2:11). Similarly, in the words of the writer of Hebrews, it means living as "strangers and exiles." (Hebrews 11:13). Paul put it this way: "Do not set your minds on earthly things, for our citizenship is in heaven" (Philippians 3:19-20).

The great Christian writer, C. S. Lewis, explained that to live with an eternal perspective means "living as commandos operating behind the enemy lines, preparing the way for the coming of the Commander-in-Chief."

Another Test of Attitude

Let me give you one last test for determining whether or not you are living with an eternal perspective: How do you feel about the Lord's return? This is an acid test that will determine whether you are in love with the world or the Lord.

The attitude of the person who is in love with the world can best be expressed in these words: "I want the Lord to return, but . . ." There is always a "but."

- "I want the Lord to return, but I want Him to come after I have made a million dollars."

- "I want the Lord to come, but I want Him to come after I've written a great novel."

- "I want the Lord to come, but I want Him to come after I've made the cover of *Time.*"

- "I want the Lord to come, but I want Him to come after I've built a great church."

- "I want the Lord to come, but I want Him to come after I'm 85 years old and have experienced all that life has to offer."

What these people are really saying is, "I want Jesus to come, but I don't want Him messing up my life!" They are in love with the world.

An Evidence of True Love

You see, when you are in love with someone, you want to be with them. That's a fact of life. Watch people who have just fallen in love. They want to be with each other all the time. When they are apart, they are constantly on the phone talking about when they will be together again!

The same is true of the Lord. If you truly love Jesus, you will want to be with Him. You will talk with Him in prayer. You will fellowship with Him in His Word and in worship. But these forms of communication will never satisfy your longing to be in His presence, to have personal, intimate fellowship with Him, face to face.

The Biblical Attitude

You will be like Paul, willing to stay on in this world serving the Lord, but yearning for the day when you will be united with Him, either through death or His return (2 Corinthians 5:8 and Philippians 1:23-24).

A sense of yearning is characteristic of those who live with an eternal perspective. It can be found expressed throughout the Bible:

> The patriarch Job stated that he looked forward to the day when his Redeemer would stand upon the earth because he knew that when that happened, he, Job, would receive a new body and would see the Lord. He added that the very thought was enough to cause him to faint! (Job 19:25-27)

> Abraham "lived as an alien in the land of promise" because he yearned for "the city which has foundations, whose architect and builder is God" (Hebrews 11:9-10).

> Moses thought it was better to be ill-treated for the promised Messiah's sake than to own all the riches of Egypt because he was looking forward to his heavenly reward (Hebrews 11:26).

> David relished the promise of God that one day He will send His Son to terrify the nations with His wrath and reign as King on Mt. Zion (Psalm 2:5-6).

> Isaiah's heart was so filled with desire to be with the Lord that he cried out, "Oh, that You would rend the heavens and come on down . . . to make Your name known to Your adversaries, that the nations may tremble at Your presence!" (Isaiah 64:1-2).

Jeremiah dreamed of when the Lord would "roar from on high, and utter His voice from His holy habitation" (Jeremiah 25: 30).

Ezekiel spent nine chapters (40-48) describing in detail the glorious Millennial Temple of the Lord, obviously yearning for the day it would be built. He concluded the description with the reason for his yearning. He revealed that the city will have a new name: "Yahweh Shammah," which means, "The Lord is there" (Ezekiel 48:35).

Daniel had visions about the Lord returning to reign over all the earth, together with His saints (Daniel 7:13-14, 18, 27).

Micah cried out for the day when the Lord will dwell once again in Jerusalem and will "teach us about His ways" and "we will walk in His paths" (Micah 4:2).

The Old Testament ends with Malachi looking forward to the day when the "sun of righteousness will rise with healing in its wings." He says his response will be to "go forth and skip about" like a calf released from a stall! (Malachi 4:2).

This yearning to be with the Lord continues throughout the New Testament. Peter exhorted us to live with our hope fixed confidently on the return of Jesus (1 Peter 1:13-16).

Paul urged us to live with the love of the Lord's appearing in our hearts (2 Timothy 4:8). He also told the Church to pray, "Maranatha!" meaning, "Our Lord come!" (1 Corinthians 16:22).

The New Testament ends with the words of John crying out, "Amen. Come Lord Jesus!" (Revelation 22:20).

Are You Yearning or Yawning?

From beginning of the Bible to its end, we find people who are in love with God and who are expressing that love by yearning to be with Him. In contrast, we find the Church of the 21st Century yawning about the Lord's return.

We are the church of Laodicea: penetrated by the world, rich and in need of nothing — not even the Lord who stands at the door knocking, asking to be let in (Revelation 3:14-17). Like that church, we are "neither cold nor hot." We are lukewarm. And the result is that we are apathetic and worldly. We desperately need to have our eternal perspective restored.

A number of years ago I was given the blessing of meeting a great man of God named Leonard Ravenhill, a prophetic preacher from England. After our meeting, we corresponded briefly. Right before he died, in the last letter he sent me, he enclosed a small card containing a brief, one sentence message. He urged me to memorize the message and live it daily.

That was July of 1988. I still have the card. It is worn and tattered because I have made it a point to keep it in my shirt pocket at all times. The message printed on it is simple but profound: *"Lord, keep me eternity conscious."*

Are you yearning or yawning about the Lord's return?

Many scholars believe that one of the earliest prayers of the Church was "Maranatha!" (1 Corinthians 16:22).

That word is actually an Aramaic phrase that means "Our Lord come!" This prayer expresses a fact that is confirmed by many other scriptures; namely, that the First Century Church had an ardent desire for the soon return of Jesus.

The Yawning of the Church

The 21st Century Church seems to have lost that desire. The average Christian today does not pray "Maranatha!" Most Christians do not yearn for the return of the Lord.

Instead of yearning, they are yawning. Christendom at large is caught up in apathy regarding the return of Jesus. And that is sad, for the Word says that the return of the Lord is our "Blessed Hope" (Titus 2:13).

Also, we are constantly admonished in the Scriptures to watch for the Lord's coming and to be ready. As Jesus Himself put it, "Be dressed in readiness, and keep your lamps alight" (Luke 12: 35).

Reasons for Yearning

There are at least six reasons why every Christian should earnestly desire the soon return of Jesus:

1) **Glory for Jesus** — When Jesus returns He will get what He deserves — honor, glory and power. He was humiliated in history, and

He will be vindicated and glorified in history. He will be coronated the King of kings and Lord of lords, and He will reign over all the world from Mt. Zion in Jerusalem (Isaiah 24:21-23).

2) Defeat for Satan — When Jesus returns, Satan will receive what he deserves — defeat, dishonor and humiliation. The fate of Satan was sealed by the Cross, but his nefarious activities will not cease until the Lord returns. At that time, he will be crushed (Romans 16:20 and Revelation 20:1-3).

3) Refreshment for the Earth — When Jesus returns, the creation will receive what it has been promised — restoration. The earth will be renovated by earthquakes and supernatural phenomena in the heavens. The result will be a beautified earth. The destructive forces of nature will be curtailed. Deserts will bloom. The plant and animal kingdoms will be redeemed. Poisonous plants and animals will cease to be poisonous. Carnivorous animals will become herbivorous. All of nature will cease to strive against itself. Instead, it will work together harmoniously to the benefit of Mankind and the glory of God. (See Isaiah 11:6-9; Isaiah 35:1-10; Isaiah 65:17-25; Acts 3:19-21; and Romans 8:18-23.)

4) Peace for the Nations — When Jesus returns, the nations will receive what they have been promised — peace, righteousness and justice. (See Isaiah 9:6-7; 11:3-5; and Micah 4:1-7.)

5) Primacy for the Jews — When Jesus returns, the Jews will receive what they have been promised — salvation and primacy. Near the end of the Tribulation, a remnant of the Jews will accept Jesus as their Messiah. This remnant will be gathered and established in Israel as the prime nation of the world. (See Hosea 2:14-20; Isaiah 60-62; and Romans 9-11.)

6) Blessings for the Church — When Jesus returns, the saints will receive what they have been promised — glorified bodies, a redeemed earth, ruling power over the nations, and reunification with loved ones who are already with the Lord. (See Philippians 3:20-21; Matthew 5:5; Revelation 2:26-27; and 1 Thessalonians 4: 14.)

These six reasons make it clear that every Christian should be earnestly desiring the return of the Lord. Yet apathy prevails. Why?

Reasons for Apathy

I have found four reasons for the apathy and indifference that characterize the Christian community concerning the return of Jesus: 1) Unbelief; 2) Ignorance; 3) Fear; and 4) Carnality.

Many professing Christians simply do not believe that Jesus will ever return. Most of these are people with a liberal view of Scripture. They have spiritualized away the meaning of the Second Coming, just as they have spiritualized the virgin birth of Jesus and His miracles.

Probably most Christians are just ignorant about what will happen when the Lord returns. As a result, they cannot get excited about an event they know nothing about. I was in this category for 30 years. Although I attended church faithfully, my church ignored the teaching and preaching of the Prophetic Word.

Some Christians fear the return of Jesus, and so they try to repress the thought that He might break from the heavens at any moment. They fear He might return on one of their "bad" days or when they have an "unconfessed sin" on their conscience. These people are caught up in works salvation. They do not understand that they are saved by grace and that "there is therefore now no condemnation for those who are in Christ Jesus" (Romans 8:1).

Finally, there are many carnal Christians who cannot get excited about the coming of the Lord because they are in love with the world. They are walking with one foot in the Church and one foot in the country club. They want the Lord to come, but they want Him to come when they are 80 years old and have experienced all that this world has to offer. In other words, they want Him to come, but they don't want Him to mess up their lives.

Implications of the Message

The message that Jesus is coming soon is like a two edged sword. It speaks to both believers and unbelievers.

The message to unbelievers is "flee from the wrath that is to come" (Matthew 3:7) by fleeing into the loving arms of Jesus now (Matthew 11:28-30). The message to believers is to stop playing church and get serious about their Christian commitment by dedicating their lives to holiness (1 Peter 1:13-16).

The Challenge to Unbelievers

If you are an unbeliever who is still struggling with God, I urge you to carefully contemplate the evidence of fulfilled prophecy that has been presented in this book. Consider how it validates the Bible as the Word of God and confirms Jesus as the Son of God.

God loves you (John 3:16). He wants you to become an heir of the promises contained in His master plan (2 Peter 3:9). I appeal to you to reach out in faith to Him (Hebrews 11:6). Humble yourself before Him (2 Peter 5:6-7). Confess your sins (Romans 10:9). Ask Him to forgive you and save you (Acts 2:21). Receive His Son, Jesus, as your Lord and Savior (John 14:6). And then seek out a fellowship of believers where you can manifest your faith in baptism and begin to grow in the Lord (Hebrews 10:25).

Receiving Jesus into your life is not just a way of preparing for His soon return. It will have an impact upon your life here and now. He will give you the gift of His Holy Spirit (Romans 5:5), and the Spirit will begin to empower and strengthen you for victorious living as an "overcomer" (1 John 5:1-5).

The Challenge to Believers

If you are a believer, you are going to have to face the fact that after reading this book you can no longer plead ignorance regarding the marvelous promises of God that will be fulfilled when Jesus returns. You now know God's plan for the ages.

Hopefully, this book has also dispelled any fear that you might have had about the certainty of your salvation. I have repeatedly emphasized the amazing grace of God. You need to trust in the Lord's faithfulness.

So, let me ask you: Are you still apathetic? If so, why? If it's not due to fear or ignorance, is it then due to unbelief or carnality?

I challenge you to allow the spotlight of the Holy Spirit to shine upon your heart and reveal to you the reason for any apathy you may still have regarding the soon return of Jesus.

If your problem is unbelief regarding Bible prophecy, then I challenge you to accept in faith the validity of all God's Word — and not just the truth of the gospel message (2 Timothy 3:16-17). Consider the fact that when you call into question any of God's Word, you challenge the validity of all of it. We are not free to pick and choose what we want to believe in God's Word. We are called to accept all of it in faith (Habakkuk 2:4 and Romans 1:17).

If your problem is carnality because you have compromised with the world, then I challenge you to commit your life to holiness by making Jesus the Lord of every aspect of your being (Romans 13:12-14). Take an inventory of your life and ask: Is Jesus the Lord of your movies? Is He the Lord of your TV? What about your music and your reading material? Is He the Lord of your job? Your marriage? Your recreation? Is He the Lord of anything in your life?

I can think of one other concern about the return of Jesus that may be prompting an apathetic attitude on your part. Perhaps you are saying to yourself, "I want the Lord to come, but I want to see certain family members or friends give their lives to Jesus first."

If that is your attitude, please don't feel bad about it. It is a spiritually legitimate attitude. You should be concerned about the eternal destiny of your family members and friends.

Just keep in mind that the Lord's timing for His return will be perfect, so turn your concern for family and friends over to the Lord and let Him deal with it. He wants your heart to be filled with unqualified anticipation for His soon return (2 Timothy 4:7-8).

Something Personal

I have presented many reasons why every Christian should earnestly desire the soon return of Jesus.

In addition to those reasons, I want to add a personal one. I want Jesus to come back because :
I want to be with Him.
I want to bask in the presence of His love and holiness.
I want to see the glory of God in His face.
I want to kiss the nail-scarred hands and say "Thank You"
for dying for me,

for forgiving me,
for changing me,
for guiding me,
for comforting me,
for giving my life meaning and purpose.
And I want to join the Saints and the Heavenly
Host in singing: "Worthy is the Lamb."

MARANATHA!

Part Six

Prophetic Epilogue

"The Lord will be king over all
the earth; in that day the Lord
will be the only one, and His
name the only one."
Zechariah 14:9"

Psalm 2: The King is Coming

A glorious summary of a rock solid guarantee

> And there will be signs in sun and moon and stars,
> and upon the earth dismay among nations . . . men
> fainting from fear and the expectation of the things
> which are coming upon the world; for the powers of
> the heavens will be shaken. — Luke 21:25-26

We live in a world gripped by fear. Among all segments of society and all nations of the world, there is a foreboding sense that we are marching toward some cataclysmic consummation of history.

The news is filled with reports of increasing violence — muggings, kidnapings, child abuse, terrorism, wars, and rumors of wars. We seem to be bombarded by a endless stream of natural calamities such as earthquakes, famines, hurricanes, floods, and fires. And the increasing immorality continues to spawn new diseases that threaten Mankind's very existence.

Significant too is the fact that all these frightful trends are taking place within the context of a world armed to the teeth with nuclear weapons. And to make things worse, these weapons of mass destruction are now spreading to irresponsible outlaw nations like Syria, Iran, and North Korea. We have giant weapons in the hands of moral pygmies.

All the while, the nations of the world continue on their spending binge, piling debt on debt, preparing the way for a colossal worldwide economic collapse.

The Reality of Fear

In the midst of the Great Depression, President Franklin Roosevelt tried to rally a despondent nation by declaring, "There is nothing to fear but fear itself." Those words ring hollow today as we face a multiplicity of very real and unprecedented fears.

It is no wonder that people are scared. They are afraid of losing their jobs, their homes, and their life savings. They fear for their personal well-being, the safety of their children, and the security of their nation. They are frightened by the prospect of menacing plagues and the potential for devastating civil disorder. And lurking in the background is always the possibility of nuclear holocaust.

People are desperately searching for security. They are buying guns and securing their houses with electronic devices. They are altering their lifestyles to protect themselves against the violence of muggers and diseases like AIDS. They are turning to eastern religions and pop psychology to find solace for their souls.

Increasing Questions

As the world disintegrates before our eyes, even Christians are beginning to question the trends. Increasingly, Christians are asking: "Is God in control? Is evil going to triumph? Is there really any hope?"

The good news is that God in His grace and mercy gave the answers to these questions almost three thousand years ago when He spoke to the heart of a shepherd boy by the name of David ben Jesse. He gave the boy a poem that was short, sweet, powerful, and full of hope. It contains a message that a fearful world desperately needs to hear today.

The poem is found in the Hebrew Bible. It is called Psalm 2. Let's take a look at it.

RULERS SCOFF

Unlike most of the psalms, Psalm 2 does not have a superscription that identifies its author. But we know it was written by David ben Jesse because Luke, by inspiration of the Holy Spirit, identified David as the author in Acts 4:25.

The psalm was placed near the beginning of the collection of psalms because Jewish scholars were convinced that it was one of David's earliest psalms, possibly written while he was still a shepherd boy, long before he became the king of Israel.

The psalm begins with the author lamenting the world's condition:

1 Why are the nations in an uproar,
And the peoples devising a vain thing?

2 The kings of the earth take their stand,
And the rulers take counsel together
Against the Lord and against His Anointed:

3 "Let us tear their fetters apart,
And cast away their cords from us!"

The language of these verses is rather stilted in the English translation, so let me try to put the words into modern English for you.

The psalmist is asking: "Lord, why is it that everywhere I look in the world the nations are in turmoil? Why are they always devising some vain thing to the glory of Man — things like the tower of Babel, the Roman Empire, the League of Nations, and the United Nations? Why is it, Lord, that the presidents, and prime ministers, and kings of the earth are always conspiring against You and Your Anointed One, Jesus? Why is it that the world's political leaders are always saying, 'Let's put aside the limitations of God's Word and cast away His laws and do what we please!'"

As you can see, nothing has changed in three thousand years. As in the time of David, the nations of the world today are still in full revolt against the Lord. And so it is that Psalm 2 is just as relevant as if it were written yesterday.

Probing Questions

One thing you must understand about Psalm 2 is that the questions which David poses at the beginning were not asked for the purpose of eliciting answers from God. David already knew the answers.

These are rhetorical questions, asked for the purpose of provoking thought. They are designed to motivate the reader to think about the nature of the world in which he lives, and to do so in response to what God's Word reveals about that world.

I say David knew the answers to the questions because the answers are provided in the book of Genesis, and David must have been familiar with that book as well as all the Torah — the first five books of the Hebrew Scriptures — if only by oral tradition.

A Phenomenal Gift

If you will think back for a moment to the opening pages of Genesis, you will remember that God presented an incredible gift to Adam and Eve shortly after their creation.

God gave them something on a silver platter that Hitler lusted for. He gave them something that Stalin dreamed of, that the Romans yearned for, and that Alexander the Great almost achieved. God gave them dominion over all the earth (Genesis 1:27-28).

But almost as soon as Adam and Eve had been given this gift, they lost it. When they rebelled against God, Satan stepped forward and stole the dominion that was intended for Man.

Satan became the prince of this earth. That is the reason Jesus referred to him as "the ruler of this world" (John 12:31). That is the reason that Satan could tempt Jesus by offering Him "all the kingdoms of the world" if Jesus would only worship him (Matthew 4:8-10). That would not have been a legitimate temptation if the kingdoms were not Satan's to give.

Even after the Cross, the apostle John stated that "the whole world lies in the power of the evil one" (1 John 5:19). The Cross sealed the ultimate fate of Satan, but that fate will not be experienced until Jesus returns and Satan is crushed beneath the feet of the

Lord's people (Romans 16:20).

Satan continues to this day to serve as the prince of this world, exercising the dominion that God intended for Man.

God's Sovereignty

The fact that Satan rules as the prince of this earth does not mean that God has lost control. Satan is not omnipotent. He has always operated within limits prescribed by God.

The oldest book in the Bible, the book of Job, begins by picturing Satan before the throne of God asking permission to afflict Job (Job 1:6-11). God gives him permission to touch all that Job has but denies him permission to take Job's life (Job 1:12).

Satan was further limited by the Cross, for since that time believers have been indwelt by the Holy Spirit, and "He who is in us is greater than he who is in the world" (1 John 4:4).

The book of Daniel makes it clear that God is the one who raises up nations and puts them down. As Daniel put it, "He [God] removes kings and establishes kings" (Daniel 2:21). Paul affirms this in the New Testament when he speaks of "governing authorities" and states that "there is no authority except from God" (Romans 13:1).

But the other side of the coin is the fact that the moment God puts someone in a position of governing authority, Satan comes against that person and attempts in every way possible to corrupt and compromise the person so that he ends up serving Satan's purposes.

It doesn't matter whether the person is a school board member, the governor of a province, or the president of a nation, Satan attempts to control all governing authorities. That is why we are so strongly urged to pray "for kings and all who are in authority" (1 Timothy 2:1).

Satan's Havoc

The Bible attests to this never-ending cycle of God appointing and Satan attacking. I think, for example, of the tragic story of Saul, the first king of Israel. He began with such promise, having received a special anointing of God's Spirit that even enabled him to prophesy with the prophets (1 Samuel 10:1, 6, 9-11).

But Satan immediately encouraged Saul's pride and attacked him with a spirit of melancholy that drove him into fits of depression. Out of pride Saul began to "act foolishly," assuming for himself the duties of the priests (1 Samuel 13:8-13). In depression, he turned to mediums and witches for advice rather than relying on the prophets of God. The tragic result was that the Spirit of God departed from him (I Samuel 16:4), and Saul committed suicide on the battlefield (I Samuel 31:4).

In like manner, Solomon began his reign on his knees before the Lord, receiving a special anointing of wisdom and knowledge (2 Chronicles 1:7-12). His future looked so bright.

But Satan came against him, tempting him with worldly riches. Solomon's turning point came in the year when he received 666 talents of gold (I Kings 10:14). From that point on, he became obsessed with three things: riches, women, and military power (I Kings 11:1-8). He ended up doing "what was evil in the sight of the Lord" (I Kings 11:6).

The empire divided following Solomon's death, and during the 209 year history of the northern kingdom of Israel, there was not one king who was considered good in God's sight. The southern kingdom of Judah lasted a hundred years longer, but during its three hundred years, only 8 of its 20 kings were considered righteous by the Lord.

The Continuing Struggle

When the New Testament opens, we find the tug of war between God and Satan continuing. Satan inspires King Herod to slaughter all the babies of Bethlehem in an attempt to cut off the Messiah at His birth.

Later, Satan orchestrates a conspiracy between governing authorities who hated each other. He brings together the Roman governor and the Jewish Sanhedrin, and through their joint efforts he accomplishes the murder of the Messiah.

Satan's triumph was, of course, short lived, for it was overcome by the victory of the Messiah's resurrection. But Satan was not to be deterred for long. He renewed his relentless attacks on God's sovereignty by launching an all out persecution of the Messiah's followers.

When Satan realized that this persecution of the Church was only spreading it and increasing its strength, he shifted to a new strategy — the wedding of the Church and the State so that the Church could be compromised. This occurred around 331 AD, and it marked the beginning of the Dark Ages when the Church became subservient to the State. The Church quickly became penetrated by the world, and its testimony for Christ became secondary to the pursuit of politics.

But, thank God, Jesus had made an important promise concerning His Church. He had promised that "the gates of Hades shall not overpower it" (Matthew 16:18). So, even during the darkest years of the Middle Ages, there was always a faithful remnant preserved by the Spirit of God.

Finally, the day came when Martin Luther nailed his theses to the door and called for a return to God's Word. Satan was put on the defensive once again as the Church experienced reformation and began to send out missionaries all over the world.

The Conflict in Our Time

As the 20th Century dawned, Satan went back on the offensive. He orchestrated one of his greatest victories with the birth of Communism in Russia in 1917. Satanism became incarnate in the atheistic ideology of the Communists as they attempted to exterminate both the Church and God's Word.

Simultaneously, Satan launched an internal attack on the Western democracies by energizing the philosophy of Secular Humanism. The Judaic-Christian foundation of Western Civilization came under direct attack from within while the Communists hammered at it from without.

The Communist threat has collapsed from the weight of its own internal inconsistencies. But Satan has provided no breathing space.

He continues to promote the advance of Secular Humanism, and he has brought about a resurgence of Islam.

The Focus of the Conflict

Perhaps the clearest example of Satan's determination to exert his dominion in defiance of God's will is to be found in his opposition to the re-establishment of the nation of Israel.

Throughout the Old Testament God promises repeatedly that in the end times He will regather the Jewish people from the four corners of the earth to the land of Israel (see Isaiah 11:10-12 and Ezekiel 36:22 - 37:12). God reveals that His purpose is to do a mighty work in the hearts of the Jews that will result in a remnant accepting His son as their Messiah (Zechariah 12:10, 13:1 and Romans 9:27, 11:1-6, 25-32).

Satan hates this purpose of God because he hates the Jewish people with a passion. His hatred is fueled by the fact that God has used the Jewish people as a vehicle to bless all the nations of the world. Through the Jews, God gave the world the Scriptures. Through the Jews, God gave the Messiah.

Satan is determined to destroy the Jewish people so that God cannot keep His promise to bring a remnant to salvation. This is the reason that Satan is orchestrating all the nations of the earth against Israel today. God has raised up a nation that Satan, as the prince of this world, is determined to destroy.

Rage vs. Laughter

I am personally outraged by Satan's many attempts to frustrate and defeat the will of God in Israel and throughout the earth today. I often feel so frustrated that I want to shout, "How long, O Lord, holy and true, will You refrain from judging and avenging" by sending your Son back to reign in glory and majesty and righteousness and justice? (Revelation 6:10)

The only way I am able to restrain my anger is to remind myself of what God is doing in Heaven while I fume over Satan's plots on this earth. Do you know what the Scriptures say God is doing?

He is laughing! Yes, God is sitting on His throne laughing — not because He doesn't care, but because He has the world's events under control. This may be hard to believe, but I can prove it to you. Let's return to Psalm 2.

GOD LAUGHS

4   **He who sits in the heavens laughs,**
    The Lord scoffs at them.

5   **Then He will speak to them in His anger**
    And terrify them in His fury:

6   **"But as for Me, I have installed My King**
    Upon Zion, My holy mountain."

God laughs at Satan and all the politicians in league with him as they attempt to thwart God's purposes in history. He laughs for three reasons.

First, the passage says, "The Lord scoffs at them." The Hebrew here means literally that "the Lord has them in derision."

This means that God has the wisdom and power to orchestrate all the evil of Satan and his henchmen to the ultimate victory of Jesus. In short, it means that no matter what Satan does, God sees to it that it backfires in his face to the glory of Jesus. Psalm 76:10 says that even "the wrath of Man" shall go to the praise of God.

Satan's Frustration

In this regard, Satan has got to be the most frustrated personality on planet earth. All his schemes ultimately fail. All his plots sooner or later unravel.

The Cross is the classic example. Satan thought he had gained his greatest victory. Instead, it proved to be a defeat. God took history's most dastardly event and converted it into something majestic through the power of the resurrection.

In World War I Satan managed to put together a conflict of unparalleled carnage, but God worked through the evil of that war to accomplish a spiritual purpose. He liberated the land of Israel from the Turks and delivered it into the hands of the British who immediately proclaimed it to be a homeland for the Jews.

Likewise, during World War II, God worked through the incredible evil of Satan's Holocaust to prepare the Jewish people for their homeland. They came out of the Holocaust saying, "Never again! Never again! We are going to have our own land, our own nation, our own state." Accordingly, they began to return to Israel by the hundreds of thousands.

God used World War I to prepare the land for the people. He worked through World War II to prepare the people for the land.

God sits in the heavens and laughs while Satan writhes in frustration.

A Day of Wrath

The second reason God is laughing is because "He will speak to them in His anger and terrify them in His fury" (Psalm 2:5). This statement refers to the fact that God has appointed a day when He will deal with all the kingdoms of the earth and their political leaders by pouring out His wrath through the return of His Son, Jesus the Messiah.

Paul spoke of this momentous day during his sermon on Mar's Hill in Athens: "God is now declaring to men that all everywhere should repent because He has fixed a day in which He will judge the world in righteousness through a Man whom He has appointed, having furnished proof to all men by raising Him from the dead" (Acts 17:30-31).

This day is often mentioned by the Old Testament prophets. They called it "the day of the Lord" (Joel 2:1). The prophet Zephaniah described it as "a day of wrath, trouble, distress, destruction, desolation, darkness and gloom" (Zephaniah 1:15). He said that the Lord will bring such distress upon people that they will reel about, walking like blind men (Zephaniah 1:17).

Isaiah characterized it as "a day of reckoning against everyone who is proud and lofty" (Isaiah 2:12). He said that "men will crawl into caves of the rocks and into holes in the ground" as they experience "the terror of the Lord" (Isaiah 2:19).

This same scene is echoed in the book of Revelation where we are told that on the day the Lord returns, "the kings of the earth and the great men and the commanders and the rich and strong . . . will hide themselves in the caves and among the rocks of the mountains," and they will cry out to rocks and mountains: "Fall on us and hide us from the presence of Him who sits on the throne and from the wrath of the Lamb" (Revelation 6:15-16).

Satan's False God

This day of wrath that God has reserved for the rebellious nations of the world and their leaders is one of the best kept secrets in the universe. Satan doesn't want anyone to know about it. In his attempt to cover it up, he has created a false image of God that has been bought by both Christians and unbelievers.

The false god Satan wants us to believe in is a push-over that could be characterized as "the cosmic teddy bear." He is big and warm and soft and cuddly, and He winks at sin.

No such namby-pamby god exists. He is a cruel hoax created by Satan. All of us stand condemned before the true God, for "all of us like sheep have gone astray" (Isaiah 53:6). Our only hope is through faith in Jesus (Romans 3:21-24). God does not grade on the curve nor is He some patsy who can be easily hoodwinked. God cannot be deceived or mocked (Galatians 6:7).

Yes, God is full of grace and mercy (Psalm 86:15), and He does not desire that any should perish (2 Peter 3:9), but He is also a God of perfect righteousness, holiness, and justice — and as such, He cannot countenance sin.

God must deal with sin, and He does so with either grace or wrath. That is why John the Baptist declared that every person on earth is under either the grace of God or His wrath (John 3:36).

God sits in the heavens and laughs because Man thinks he can thumb his nose at God and get away with it. A "day of reckoning" is coming when God will deal decisively with Satan's kingdom.

A Coming Reign

The passage in Psalm 2 indicates a third reason that God is laughing. God explains it by saying, "As for Me, I have installed My King upon Zion My holy mountain" (Psalm 2:6).

The wording here is very interesting. God speaks of a future event — the millennial reign of Jesus — as if it were an accomplished historical fact. This strange manner of speaking of the future as if it were past is a very common feature of Bible prophecy — so common, in fact, that theologians have coined a word for it. They call it "proleptic" speech.

Such speech is particularly characteristic of God in the Scriptures. The reason is that God is not in time as we are. We are on a time line. We have a past, a present, and a future. God is outside of time. If He wills something, it is accomplished, whether or not it has yet happened in history as we know it.

Take for example the crucifixion of Jesus. We think of it as happening 2,000 years ago on the outskirts of Jerusalem — and it did, as we perceive time. But when did the crucifixion take place as God sees time? The Bible says that Jesus was slain "from the foundation of the world" (Revelation 13:8) because that is when God willed it.

The proleptic principle is best expressed by God Himself in 2 Kings 19:25 —

> Have you not heard?
> Long ago I did it;
> From ancient times I planned it.
> Now I have brought it to pass

But let's get back to our point. The point is that God sits in the heavens and laughs at the rebellious kingdoms of the earth because He has ordained that one day soon His Son will return as "King of kings and Lord of lords" (Revelation 19:16) to reign over all the earth and bring it into submission to God's perfect will.

An Unfulfilled Promise

How do we know this is a proleptic statement — that although it is stated in the past tense, it is a promise yet to be fulfilled?

The answer is obvious — namely, there is no fulfillment in history. Does Jesus reign today as King of kings from Mount Zion in Jerusalem? Has He ever?

There are those who argue that He is spiritually reigning over the nations of the earth. If so, then He is doing a very poor job, for the earth is dominated by evil rebellion against God.

When you consider what the Bible says will be the characteristics of the Lord's reign over the earth, it is easy to see that the reign is yet future. Isaiah 11 says the reign will be characterized by righteousness, fairness, and faithfulness. Are these the characteristics of national governments today? In that same chapter Isaiah says "the earth will be full of the knowledge of the Lord as the waters cover the sea" (Isaiah 11:9). How could anyone argue that such a prophecy has been fulfilled?

Missing Characteristics

In Isaiah 2:4 we are told that during the reign of Jesus the nations "will hammer their swords into plowshares and their spears into pruning hooks, and nation will not lift up sword against nation, and never again will they learn war." Does that sound like the world we are living in?

Revelation 20:3 says that when the Lord begins His reign, Satan will be bound so that he cannot "deceive the nations any longer." Has Satan been bound in this way? If the nations of the world are no longer deceived, then why are they still rebelling against the Lord? And why does the apostle John say (long after the Cross) that "the whole world lies in the power of the evil one"? (1 John 5:19). Likewise, Peter states that Satan still "prowls about like a roaring lion, seeking someone to devour" (1 Peter 5:8). If Satan is bound now, then he is bound on a very long chain!

The promise of God in Psalm 2 that His Son will one day rule over all the earth is yet future. The King is coming! The kings of the earth are living on borrowed time. They plot and connive, but their fate is sealed. So, God sits in the heavens and laughs.

JESUS PROCLAIMS

The next spokesman in Psalm 2 is Jesus Himself. He makes a glorious proclamation about the future in which He confirms His Father's intention to establish Him as the King of kings:

> 7 I will surely tell of the decree of the Lord:
>   He said to Me, "You are My Son,
>   Today I have begotten You.
>
> 8 Ask of Me, and I will surely give the nations
>   as Your inheritance,
>   And the very ends of the earth as Your possession.
>
> 9 You shall break them with a rod of iron,
>   You shall shatter them like earthenware."

The Begotten One

Jesus begins His proclamation by repeating the Father's promise to Him that He will one day rule from Mount Zion over "the very ends of the earth." It is a promise that undoubtedly dates back to the foundation of the world itself. I say that because the Bible tells us that Jesus was foreknown as the Savior who would shed His blood "from before the foundation of the world" (1 Peter 1:19-20, Revelation 13:8, and Ephesians 1:4).

Because Jesus is the Worthy Lamb who was slain for the sins of Man (Revelation 5:9), He is the only one eligible to assert dominion over God's creation. In that sense, He is the "only begotten" (John 1:14,18) — the only Anointed One of God who is authorized to act in the Father's behalf as the Regent of planet earth.

This sense of meaning is reflected in the Living Bible's paraphrase of Jesus' proclamation:

> I will reveal the everlasting purposes of God, for the
> Lord has said to me, "You are my Son. This is your
> Coronation Day. Today I am giving you your glory.
> Only ask, and I will give you all the nations of the world."
> — Psalm 2:7-8

Note that the statement, "Today I have begotten You," is para-phrased to present the real meaning: "This is your Coronation Day." That is why Jesus could address Himself to the church at Philadelphia as the one "who has the key of David" (Revelation 3:7). He is the fulfillment of the Davidic Covenant and its promise:

> I have made a covenant with My chosen;
> I have sworn to David My servant,
> I will establish your seed forever,
> And build up your throne to all generations.
> — Psalm 89:3-4

Once again, keep in mind that the Father's promise to Jesus is yet to be fulfilled. Remember, Jesus was "slain from the foundation of the world" (Revelation 13:8) because that is when the Father willed it to happen. But the Father's will did not become an historical reality until thousands of years later. In like manner, Jesus was crowned from the foundation of the world — also because the Father willed it then — but it is an event that is yet to take place in history.

The Roles of Jesus

The first time Jesus came, He came as our Suffering Savior (Isaiah 53). After His resurrection, He became our High Priest (Hebrews 4:14-16). He continues in that capacity today, ministering as the mediator of our prayers before the throne of God (Hebrews 8:1-2). But one day very soon He will return, and when He does so, He will return as our King to reign over all the nations of the world (Revelation 19:16).

Jesus is not serving as a king now. He is never pictured as currently being the king of this world or the king of the Church. His relationship to the Church is portrayed as being like the head to the body (Ephesians 5:23) or a bridegroom to a bride (Revelation 19:6-9).

Jesus is a king-in-waiting. The situation is like that which prevailed in the life of David for many years. David was anointed the King of Israel by Samuel. But David had to wait many years before he was coronated. Likewise, Jesus has been anointed King of kings and Lord of lords, but He will not be crowned as such in history until He returns to earth.

An Incredible Inheritance

When Jesus does return, the promises of Psalm 2 will be fulfilled to Him. The first of those promises is that He will inherit the earth — "the very ends of the earth" will become His possession (Psalm 2:8).

There is a popular myth that when Jesus returns the earth will burn up and cease to exist. That can't be true because the Bible affirms that the earth is "eternal" (Psalm 148:6, Psalm 78:69, and Ecclesiastes 1:4).

It is true that the earth will be radically changed when the Lord returns. The change agents will be earthquakes and supernatural phenomena in the heavens (Revelation 6:12-13). We are told that every island will be moved and that every mountain will be lowered and every valley raised (Revelation 6:14 and Isaiah 40:4). The image that is portrayed is one of the earth's surface being smoothed out, with Jerusalem being lifted up to become the highest point on the face of the planet (Micah 4:1).

The earth will also be refreshed. The deserts will bloom (Isaiah 35:1, 6-7). The hills will "drip with sweet wine" and "flow with milk" (Joel 3:18). The abundance of agriculture will be so great that "the plowman will overtake the reaper" in the sense that a new crop will be planted as fast as the old crop can be harvested (Amos 9:13). Even the Dead Sea will come alive and teem with fish (Ezekiel 47:8-9).

The animal kingdom will also be restored. We are told that the carnivorous animals will become herbivorous. Thus, "the lion will eat straw like the ox" (Isaiah 11:7). This change will enable the animals to live together in peace with each other and with Man. "The wolf will dwell with the lamb" (Isaiah 11:6), and a "nursing child will play by the hole of the cobra" because the cobra will no longer be poisonous (Isaiah 11:8).

A Personal Hope

I don't know about you, but I get excited about these promises. One time when I was preaching a whole sermon on the millennial earth, I got carried away with my descriptions and said: "One of the reasons I want the Lord to return is because He will do away with the chiggers!"

For those of you who fortunately are not familiar with chiggers, let me explain. They are microscopic creatures that look like a tiny red dot. They live in tall grass and weeds in the South and abound in the summer time. They crawl up your legs, find a nice tender spot, and then drill in. The result is a big red welt that itches like mad for about three days. They are a scourge, and I hate them.

The night I mentioned them in my sermon, my wife happened to be in the audience. As we were driving home, I noticed she was unusually quiet.

"Is something wrong?" I asked

"I couldn't believe what you said tonight about the chiggers," she replied.

"You're right," I admitted, "I got a little carried away."

"That's not the point" she retorted.

"Oh? Well then, what is the point," I asked.

With a twinkle in her eye, she replied: "The point is that the Lord is not going to 'do away with the chiggers;' He is going to make you lie down with them!"

Maybe so, but I hope he defangs those little buggers first!

The Eternal Earth

Even when the Millennium ends, the earth will not cease to exist. Instead, its fundamental nature will be changed once again. This time the change agent will be fire.

God will take the redeemed off this planet and put us in the New Jerusalem. From that vantage point we will watch as the Lord super-heats the earth and burns away the pollution of Satan's last revolt.

Then, working with the earth like a hot ball of wax, the Lord will reshape it, and out of that flaming inferno will come a new earth, a perfected earth, an earth which will serve as our home eternally (Revelation 21:1).

Cessation vs. Destruction

The concept that the earth will be burned up and cease to exist is based on a statement in 2 Peter 3:10: "The day of the Lord will come like a thief, in which the heavens will pass away with a roar and the elements will be destroyed with intense heat, and the earth and its works will be burned up."

But when this verse speaks of destruction, it is speaking of a basic change in nature, not a cessation of existence. This is made clear by what is said in the passage, both before and after the verse.

For example, in 2 Peter 3:6, the writer refers to the earth of Noah's time being "destroyed" by water. That does not mean that the earth ceased to exist. It means that the earth's fundamental nature was changed by the flood. And in 2 Peter 3:13 the writer affirms that a new earth is coming, the one renovated by fire.

God loves His creation. He has no intention of destroying it. His purpose, instead, is to redeem it by returning it to its original perfection — the perfection that existed before the sin of Man and the consequent curse of God (Romans 8:18-23).

Joint Heirs

God has promised to give that redeemed planet to His Son and to His joint heirs — namely, those who have received Jesus as their Lord and Savior. In Psalm 2, He promises the earth to His Son. In Psalm 37:11, He extends that promise to the redeemed: "The humble will inherit the earth." That promise is repeated in verses 22, 29, and 34.

These promises are the ones that Jesus referred to in His Sermon on the Mount when He said: "Blessed are the meek, for they shall inherit the earth" (Matthew 5:5). Paul recognized that the same promise was inferred in the Abrahamic Covenant when he wrote that God's promise to Abraham and his descendants (by faith) is that they would "inherit the world" (Romans 4:13).

A Worldwide Reign

The second promise that the Father makes to His Son in Psalm 2 is a natural corollary of the first. Not only will Jesus inherit the earth, but He will also reign over it: "I will surely give the nations as Your inheritance . . . You shall break them with a rod of iron" (Psalm 2:8-9).

Jesus is coming to reign. That is one of the most persistent themes of the Scriptures from beginning to end. And again, the Redeemed will be joint heirs of this promise. We will reign with Jesus.

These truths were graphically portrayed to Daniel in a series of night visions. In one he saw the "Son of Man" appear before the "Ancient of Days" and receive dominion and a kingdom that included "all the peoples, nations, and men of every language" (Daniel 7:13-14). Then Daniel was told that "the saints of the Highest One" would receive the kingdom and would exercise "the sovereignty, the dominion, and the greatness of all the kingdoms under the whole heaven" (Daniel 7:18, 27).

In the book of Revelation Jesus promises that He will give overcomers "authority over the nations" and they will rule over the nations "with a rod of iron" (Revelation 2:26, 27). An overcomer is defined in 1 John 5:5 as any person "who believes that Jesus is the Son of God."

In Revelation 4, when John is raptured to Heaven and finds himself in the throne room of God, he hears the heavenly host singing a song of praise to Jesus. In the song the statement is made that those who have been redeemed by the blood of the Lamb have been made a kingdom, and "they will reign upon the earth" (Revelation 5:9-10).

Co-Regents

Have you ever stopped to think what that means for you and me — for the redeemed? In what way will we reign with the Lord?

Some of us will serve as administrators. Jesus Himself made this clear in a parable He told about the kingdom. The parable is recorded in Luke 19:11-27.

Jesus taught in this parable that there would be degrees of reward in the kingdom based upon our faithfulness to Him in this life. Part of those rewards would be the degree of our participation with Him in His ruling authority. He pointed out that some would rule over ten cities, while others would rule over only five.

The image that emerges from this and parallel passages is that Jesus will reign as King of the world from Mount Zion in Jerusalem (Isaiah 24:21-23). David, in his resurrected body, will reign under Jesus as King of Israel (Ezekiel 34:23-24). And we — the Redeemed in our glorified bodies — will be scattered across the face of the earth to serve as mayors, governors, presidents, and kings. Every person on planet earth who will be in a position of governing authority — whether a school board member or the head of a nation — will be a redeemed saint in a glorified body.

Some of us will be judges (1 Corinthians 6:2). Think of it! Every judge in the world will be a born again child of God in a glorified body with the mind of Christ.

Justice for those in the flesh will be sure, swift, and just. The first decision made in any court case will be the final one because it will be perfect. There will be no need for endless appeals.

Education

Some of us will serve as administrators, some as judges, but most of us will likely participate in the Lord's reign as educators. Yes, the entire educational system of the world will be in the hands of glorified saints. We will be the "shepherds" of the world (Jeremiah 3:15 and 23:3-4). We will declare the Lord's glory among the nations (Isaiah 66:19), and we will try to bring those who are in the flesh to a saving faith in Jesus.

It is an exciting thought. The artificial separation of church and state will come to an end. The Bible will be in every classroom on the teacher's desk, and it will serve as the basic textbook for everything: history, geography, science, morals, literature — you name it. And no one will be able to cry, "Separation of Church and State!" because there will be no such separation in the theocracy that Jesus will establish.

It is no wonder that "the earth will be full of the knowledge of the Lord as the waters cover the sea" (Isaiah 11:9).

A Significant Absence

There is one activity that none of us will be involved in. That is legislation. There will be no legislators in the millennial kingdom because the Lord Himself will give the law: ". . . the law will go forth from Zion, and the word of the Lord from Jerusalem" (Isaiah 2:3).

This point should be enough to motivate any Christian to shout, "Hallelujah!" Think of it — there will be no abomination known as the Texas Legislature or the United States Congress or the United Nations! The days of pork barrel legislation, graft, and waste will be ended.

The Lord will give the law, and He will not change it because of political pressure or public opinion polls. There will be no coddling of criminals and pandering to special interest groups.

The law will be given, and it will be enforced swiftly and decisively. As the Scriptures say, the Lord will rule with "a rod of iron" (Psalm 2:9 and Revelation 2:26-27, 19:15).

The Glory of the Lord

And what will be the purpose of all this? There are many reasons for the millennial reign of Jesus. God is going to use that period of time to fulfill promises He has made to the nations, to nature, to a remnant of the Jews, and to the Saints. But the fundamental purpose is to fulfill His promise to His Son that He will one day be glorified in history, just as He was humiliated in history.

This promise is a persistent theme of the Scriptures. It is the essence of the Father's promise in Psalm 2, and it is echoed throughout the Bible, in both the Hebrew Scriptures and the New Testament.

The prophet Isaiah says that when the Lord returns in "terror" and in the "splendor of His majesty," all proud men will be humbled, and "the Lord alone will be exalted in that day" (Isaiah 2:10-11). The Lord's name will be honored, and He will be called "Wonderful Counselor, Mighty God, Eternal Father, Prince of Peace" (Isaiah 9:6). He will return to manifest His glory before His saints (Isaiah 24:23) and before the nations of the world (Isaiah 66:18).

Paul affirms this purpose of the Lord's return in 2 Thessalonians 1:10 where he states that Jesus is returning "to be glorified in His saints" and "to be marveled at among all who have believed."

When Jesus came to earth, He surrendered His glory (Philippians 2:6-11). The book of Hebrews tells us that His glory has been restored as He sits today on the right hand of His Father on His Father's throne in Heaven (Hebrews 1:1-3).

Some of the apostles were given a preview of His glory at the Transfiguration (Matthew 17:1-8). Jesus revealed Himself in His glory to John on the island of Patmos (Revelation 1:12-18). All the Redeemed will see His glory when He returns, and — incredibly — we will be glorified with Him! (Colossians 3:4)

That means we will receive glorified bodies like the one He has now (Philippians 3:21), and we will receive honor and glory as we reign with Him over the nations of the world (Revelation 2:26-27, 3:21, and 5:9-10).

THE SPIRIT WARNS

Psalm 2 begins with David speaking as a prophet, lamenting over the way the world's rulers scoff at the Lord. It proceeds with the Lord laughing over the feeble attempts of men to frustrate His will. It is then punctuated by a proclamation of Jesus in which He announces His Father's promise that He, the Son, will one day triumph over all the kingdoms of the world.

The psalm concludes with a warning given by the Holy Spirit:

> **10 Now, therefore, O kings, show discernment;
> Take warning, O judges of the earth.**

> **11 Worship the Lord with reverence,
> And rejoice with trembling.**

> **12 Do homage to the Son, lest He become angry,**
> **and you perish in the way,**
> **For His wrath may soon be kindled . . .**

The Audience

The Spirit's warning is addressed to the kings and judges of the earth. It is a solemn call for the political leaders of the world to clean up their acts and submit themselves and their nations to the Lord's will before He bursts from the heavens in wrath.

Unfortunately, this stern warning seems forever to fall on deaf ears and hardened hearts. The warning was spoken 3,000 years ago, and power grubbing and political corruption continue unabated to this day. The world's political leaders continue to thumb their noses at God and mock His Anointed One.

But a "day of reckoning" (Isaiah 2:12) is fast approaching, and what a day it will be! The book of Revelation says that on that day "the kings of the earth and the great men and the commanders and the rich and the strong . . ." will hide themselves in caves and will cry out to the rocks of the mountains: "Fall on us and hide us from the presence of Him who sits on the throne, and from the wrath of the Lamb" (Revelation 6:15-16).

The Lord has delayed the outpouring of His wrath because He does not desire that any should perish but that all should come to repentance (2 Peter 3:9). But there is a limit to the Lord's patience, and while He waits, "He reserves wrath for His enemies" (Nahum 1:2). The Lord may be slow to anger, but "He will by no means leave the guilty unpunished" (Nahum 1:3).

But the political leaders of the world are not the only audience for the Spirit's warning. The warning is also aimed at the Redeemed, for — as I have already pointed out — we will one day serve as the kings and judges of this world. So, let the Redeemed take notice of what we are called to do as we await the Lord's return.

A Call to Worship

First, we are called to "worship the Lord with reverence" (Psalm 2:11). The actual Hebrew word here is "serve" rather than "worship." But I like the use of the term, worship, because it emphasizes that our ultimate worship of the Lord is expressed in how we serve Him.

We so often think of worship only in terms of what we do when we come together corporately as a congregation of believers. Don't get me wrong — corporate worship is extremely important. We were created to worship God (Deuteronomy 6:13), and God actively seeks people who are worshiping Him in spirit and truth (John 4:23).

But the ultimate worship is expressed in what we do when we leave the congregation and return to the world. Do those who come in contact with us recognize that we have been in the presence of the Lord? Do we return from worship "to bless our household," as was the case in King David's life? (2 Samuel 6:20)

The Role of Works

Ever since the Reformation, there has been a de-emphasis of works in Christian living. This was not the aim of the Reformers. Their purpose was to de-emphasize works in relation to salvation. Their clarion call was to return to the biblical injunction in Ephesians 2:8-9 which tells us that we are saved by "grace through faith, and not as a result of works."

But the very next verse in that Ephesians passage says that we are "created in Christ Jesus for good works which God prepared beforehand, that we should walk in them." The point, of course, is that although we are not saved by works, we are saved for the purpose of doing good works in the power of God's Spirit to bring honor and glory to Jesus (Colossians 3:17).

Thus, in Titus 2:14 Paul writes that the Lord redeemed us in order to purify for Himself a people who would be "zealous for good deeds." He therefore admonishes "those who believe God . . . to engage in good deeds" (Titus 3:8). This is the reason that James, the brother of Jesus, wrote that "faith without works is useless" (James 2:20).

The writer of Hebrews draws it all together in a beautiful summary that shows us clearly that both praise of God and service to

God are forms of worship:

> Through Him [Jesus] then, let us continually offer up a sacrifice of praise to God, that is, the fruit of lips that give thanks to His name. And do not neglect doing good and sharing; for with such sacrifices God is pleased. — Hebrews 13:15-16

Do you have a passion to worship God? Do you desire to celebrate Him for who He is and what He has done? And do you desire to express that worship not only with the praise of your lips but with the labor of your body and the money you have earned?

One other thing — Do you understand that one day soon You will stand before the Lord and be judged of your works?

A Call to an Unusual Form of Rejoicing

The future judgment which we face for our works is the reason that the Spirit expresses His next command in such an unusual way. He calls us to "rejoice with trembling" (Psalm 2:11).

Have you ever thought about what a strange command this is? A person normally rejoices with laughter, dancing, singing, or handclapping. How does one rejoice with trembling?

I think the command relates to the tension that exists in the Scriptures between grace and works. We are saved by grace, and we should rejoice over that and over the completion of our salvation (the glorification of our bodies) that we will enjoy when the Lord returns. But at the same time we should tremble over the prospect of standing before Jesus to have our works judged.

There is both good news and bad news about the Lord's forthcoming judgment of the Redeemed. The good news is so good that many Christians find it hard to believe, but it is true nonetheless. The incredible good news is that the Redeemed will not be judged of their sins to determine whether they will spend eternity in heaven or hell.

The reason, of course, is that we have already been judged of our sins. That judgment took place at the Cross when all our sins — past, present, and future — were placed on Jesus, and He received the wrath which we deserve.

That's why the Bible teaches that if you are covered by the blood of Jesus, your sins have been forgiven and forgotten (Isaiah 43:25 and Hebrews 8:12). They have been removed from the presence of the Lord "as far as the east is from the west" (Psalm 103:12-13). As Corrie ten Boom used to say, "The Lord has placed our sins in the deepest part of the ocean, and He has put up a sign that says, 'No Fishing!'" (See Micah 7:19.)

What does it mean for the Lord to "forget" our sins? It means they will never be held against the Redeemed again with regard to the determination of their eternal destiny. That's why the writer of Hebrews could confidently assert that when Jesus appears a second time, He will come "for salvation without reference to sin, to those who eagerly await Him" (Hebrews 9:28).

So, if our sins have been forgotten, what will be the nature of our judgment when we, the redeemed, stand before the Lord? This brings us to the bad news that should cause us to tremble. We are going to be judged of our works, not to determine our eternal destiny, but to determine our degrees of reward. And in regard to our works, our shortcomings and failures will be remembered.

This news comes as a great shock to most Christians for most seem unaware that their works have any significance, and others do not realize that there will be degrees of reward.

Degrees of Reward

The concept of degrees of reward is clearly spelled out in the Scriptures. In 1 Corinthians 3:8 Paul says "each will receive his own reward according to his labor." He then says that our works will be tested by the Lord to determine their quality (1 Corinthians 3:13). He indicates that some will, in effect, be saved with their tail feathers smoking! This is because their works will not stand the test of the Lord's "fire" (His judgment). He thus concludes, "If any man's work is burned up, he shall suffer loss; but he himself shall be saved, yet so as through fire" (1 Corinthians 3:15).

Some of the last words Jesus spoke on this earth had to do with degrees of reward. Those words are recorded in Revelation 22:12 —

"Behold, I am coming quickly, and My reward is with Me, to render to every man according to what he has done."

The Bible even reveals what some of these rewards will be. For example, "a crown of life" is promised to those who persevere under trial (James 1:12 and Revelation 2:10). An "unfading crown of glory" will be given to faithful elders and pastors (1 Peter 5:4). Soul winners will receive "a crown of rejoicing" (Philippians 4:1 and 1 Thessalonians 2:19). An "imperishable wreath" is reserved for those who exercise self control (1 Corinthians 9:25), and a "crown of righteousness" will be given to those who live their lives with the love of the Lord's appearing in their hearts (2 Timothy 4:7-8). We are also going to be given white robes that will be decorated in varying degrees to reflect "the righteous acts of the saints" (Revelation 19: 8).

The Judgment of Works

How will the Lord judge our works? What criteria will He use?

I believe the starting point will be the gifts of the Spirit which we received when we were born again. The Word teaches that at the moment of salvation every redeemed person receives at least one gift of the Spirit (1 Corinthians 12:7 and 1 Peter 3:10). Some receive more than one gift, and some may receive additional gifts as they develop in the Lord, particularly if they are good stewards of their initial gifts (Matthew 25:14-30).

I believe the Lord will ask each one of us how we used the gifts He gave us for the advancement of His kingdom. And then I believe He will test our works in terms of quantity, quality, and motive.

The test of motive should prove particularly interesting. I can imagine Him calling up some well known preacher and saying, "When you accepted Me as your Lord and Savior, I gave you the gifts of evangelism and teaching. How did you use these gifts to advance My kingdom?"

I can imagine the preacher responding with a lengthy recitation of his many meetings and all the souls he saved.

But then the Lord will stun the man by replying, "Yes, I am well aware of all that, but I also know your motive. You did not go forth and preach because you loved Me or because you had a passion for lost souls. You preached because you desired fame — and you received it. Your picture appeared on the cover of *Time* magazine, and that is your reward — your only reward."

And then I can imagine the Lord calling up some little old lady that no one has ever heard of and saying to her, "My dear, on the day you became an heir of salvation, I gave you only one gift, the gift of mercy. And every time someone you knew came down ill, you were the first to arrive with an encouraging word and a willingness to help in any way possible. When a death occurred in your church, you were the one who spread the word, called for prayers for the family, and organized the meals. When you saw the homeless poor, you were the first to invite them into your house for refuge and food. And when you did these things, you did them for only one reason — because you loved Me."

I suspect He will then give her a crown with so many jewels that she will have a neck ache for eternity!

What about you? Do you know what gifts you have been given by the Spirit? Are you using them to advance the kingdom? And are your motives pure? Are you serving the Lord in the power of His Spirit for the purpose of His glory?

A Call to Commitment

As we await the Lord's return, we are to "worship the Lord with reverence" and we are to "rejoice with trembling." The third thing the Spirit calls us to do is to "do homage to the Son" (Psalm 2:12).

What the Hebrew actually says here is very clear but is seldom literally translated because it sounds so strange. Literally, the Hebrew words say "Kiss the Son."

For years I wondered what those words meant. I consulted commentaries and found a lot of conjecture, but none of the answers seemed to click in my spirit. So, I continued to pray that the Lord would show me the true meaning of the words.

One day, as I was reading the book of Hosea, the Spirit suddenly impressed a verse upon my heart that gave me the answer I had been seeking. The verse is found in chapter 13.

As this chapter begins, Hosea has just completed his preaching tour of Israel in which he calls the people to repent of their idolatry. To his horror, when he arrives back home, he finds a neighbor bowing down before a silver calf, and he cries out, "Men kiss calves!" (Hosea 13:2)

When I read those words, the Spirit witnessed to my spirit. I immediately thought of the words of the psalmist: "Kiss the Son!" Suddenly, this strange statement made complete sense to me.

You see, if Hosea were alive today and could preach to us about America, I think he would say, "I have traveled all over your land to seek its spiritual temperament, and I say to you, everywhere I go I find men kissing calves!"

Except, I suspect he would put it in modern English: "Everywhere I go in this land I find men kissing CD's in the bank, chrome plated automobiles, and audacious houses. I see men in love with money, power, and fame. I say to you, take all that the world has to offer, set it aside in a junk pile, and put God first in your lives. Fall in love with Jesus!"

That's what it means to "Kiss the Son!" It is a call to commit your life to Jesus by falling in love with Him and putting Him first in your life — above career and family. It's a call to make Him the Lord of everything in your life — your family and job, your hopes and dreams, your thoughts and words, your music, reading material, food, drink, recreation — *everything!*

By making Him your refuge, you will be delivered from the wrath that is to come (Romans 5:9 and 1 Thessalonians 5:9), and you will come to know the full meaning of the last line of Psalm 2:

> ***How blessed are all who take refuge in Him!***

ARE YOU A CHRISTIAN?

If not, you need to receive Jesus as your Lord and Savior *now*, before it is eternally too late. God, in His mercy, has spared your life to this moment and has led you to this message because He loves you and desires your eternal salvation (John 3:16 and 2 Peter 3:9).

All you need to do is receive the gift of salvation which God has provided through the blood that Jesus shed for your sins on the Cross. You can do that by sincerely praying the following prayer:

> Dear Heavenly Father, I confess to you that I am a sinner. I believe that Your Son, Jesus, died on the Cross for the forgiveness of my sins. I now receive Him as my Lord and Savior. Please forgive me of my sins, give me the indwelling presence of Your Holy Spirit, and give me the hope of life everlasting with You. Thank You, Father. In the name of Jesus, Amen.

Now, you need to seek out a fellowship of believers where you can make a public profession of your faith by confessing the name of Jesus (Matthew 10:32 and Romans 10:9) and by being buried with Him in baptism (Romans 6:3-5). That fellowship will supply you with a community of faith where you will find prayer partners and teachers who can develop you spiritually through the study of God's Word.

One other thing — you need to make the daily reading and study of God's Word one of the top priorities of your life. Read Psalm 1 to see how much emphasis is placed on this by the Lord. We live in an age of spiritual deception, and the only way you can protect yourself against deception is to test everything by the Scriptures (Acts 17:10-12).

If you are a Christian, you need to examine your priorities to see if Jesus is truly first in your life. And you need to examine your heart to see if you have made Jesus the Lord of every aspect of your existence. I would suggest that you pray the following prayer:

> Heavenly Father, I love You and I thank You for the salvation I have through faith in Your Son. But I confess that I have often gotten my priorities out of order and have failed to make Your Son the Lord of every aspect of my life. I sincerely want to demonstrate my love for You by fully submitting my life to You. Shine the spotlight of Your Spirit upon my heart and reveal to me those areas where your Son does not reign as Lord of my life, and then give me the power to surrender them completely to You. Thank You, Lord. Maranatha! In the name of Jesus, Amen.

Let me challenge you to follow-up this prayer by making a commitment to set aside a period of time every morning to spend with the Lord in prayer and Scripture reading. If you are married, spend some of that time together with your wife, praying for each other and for your children. But also spend part of the time alone with the Lord, giving Him an opportunity to speak to you personally through His Word and by His Spirit witnessing to your spirit.

I would also suggest that you start keeping a spiritual journal to record your conversations with the Lord and His answers.

There is only one way that you can really come to know the Lord in a very intimate, personal way — and that is to spend time with Him, talking with Him, reading His Word, and worshiping Him.

Appendix 1

Recommended Books on Bible Prophecy

One of the best overall books on Bible prophecy that has ever been published is *Things to Come* by Dwight Pentecost (Zondervan, 1964). It is scholarly and comprehensive, written for serious, college level students.

Surveys

A comprehensive study concerning all aspects of Bible prophecy that is scholarly in its approach but easy to read is a book by Paul N. Benware entitled *Understanding End Time Prophecy* (Moody Press, 1995).

With regard to end time prophecies only, one of the best surveys for the more general reader is Leon Woods' book, *The Bible and Future Events* (Zondervan, 1973). Other very readable surveys are *The Final Chapter* by S. Maxwell Coder (Tyndale House, 1984) and *A Survey of Bible Prophecy* by R. Ludwigson (Zondervan, 1973). *The King is Coming* by H. L. Willmington (Tyndale House, 1973) presents an overview of end time events in a very unique and easy to follow outline form.

A spiral bound study guide which I wrote, called *The Christ in Prophecy Study Guide* (Lamb & Lion Ministries, 1987; 2nd edition, 2001), presents an analytical survey of all Messianic prophecies contained in both the Old and New Testaments. Another indispensable reference volume that presents an exhaustive survey is *All the Messianic Prophecies of the Bible* by Herbert Lockyer (Zondervan, 1979).

A survey book intended for the serious student is Arnold Fruchtenbaum's encyclopedic study of Tribulation events which bears the strange title, *The Footsteps of the Messiah* (Ariel Press, 1982; 2nd edition, 2003). It focuses on showing the sequence of end time events and their relationship to each other.

A brief and fascinating survey book full of penetrating insights is one titled *What on Earth is God Doing?* (Friends of Israel, 2003). It was written by Renald Showers, a gifted teacher and writer who serves the Friends of Israel Ministry. The book presents a capsule overview of God's purposes in history from start to finish.

Interpretation

Nothing is more important to the understanding of Bible prophecy than the principles of interpretation that are applied to it. An excellent introductory book for the general reader is *How to Study Bible Prophecy for Yourself* by Tim LaHaye (Harvest House, 1990).

The most profound book ever written on the topic is *The Interpretation of Prophecy* by Paul Lee Tan (Assurance Publishers, 1974). This book is an essential tool for any serious student of prophecy.

The history of prophetic interpretation is presented in great detail in the amazing, four volume, encyclopedic study called *The Prophetic Faith of Our Fathers*, edited by LeRoy Edwin Froom (Review and Herald Press). Volume 1 (1950) covers the Early Church. Volume 2 (1948) surveys the Pre-Reformation and Reformation periods. Volume 3 (1946) looks at the Colonial American and European Awakening. Volume 4 (1946) provides a look at the 19th Century. This great work of scholarship took years to complete. The first two volumes are based upon original research conducted throughout Europe in the 1920's and 1930's, utilizing ancient documents, many of which were destroyed in World War II.

Symbolic

Perhaps the least understood area of prophecy is symbolic prophecy, sometimes called prophecy in type. About half of Herbert Lockyer's book, *All the Messianic Prophecies of the Bible*, is dedicated to this important topic (Zondervan, 1979).

Two books concerning symbolic prophecy that are easy to read and are full of useful insights are *Christ in the Tabernacle* by Louis Talbot (Moody Press, 1978) and *Jesus in the Feasts of Israel* by Richard Booker (Bridge Publishing, 1987).

Old Testament Prophets

A magnificent introduction to all the Old Testament prophets is provided by Leon Wood in his exceptional book, *The Prophets of Israel* (Regular Baptist Press, 1979).

One of the finest commentators on the Old Testament prophets is Charles Feinberg, a Messianic Jew. His works include *God Remembers: A Study of Zechariah* (Multnomah Press, 1965); *Jeremiah: A Commentary* (Zondervan, 1982); and *The Prophecy of Ezekiel: The Glory of the Lord* (Moody Press, 1969). A good introduction to Isaiah can be found in the book by Herbert Wolf entitled *Interpreting Isaiah: The Suffering and Glory of the Messiah* (Zondervan, 1985).

An outstanding series of scholarly commentaries on Isaiah, Jeremiah and Ezekiel can be found in volume 6 of *The Expositor's Bible Commentary* edited by Frank E. Gaebelein (Zondervan, 1986). The commentary on Isaiah is by G. W. Grogan; Jeremiah is by Charles L. Feinberg; and Ezekiel is by Ralph H. Alexander.

There are a number of good books about the Minor Prophets. Two that are designed for the general reader are *Major Truths from the Minor Prophets* by John Hunter (Zondervan, 1977) and *Will We Ever Catch Up with the Bible?* by David Hubbard (Regal Books, 1977).

The best scholarly resource on the Minor Prophets is to be found in volume 7 of *The Expositor's Bible Commentary* edited by Frank E. Gaebelein (Zondervan, 1985). The authors of the commentaries on the specific books read like a who's who of Evangelical scholars. A fine single volume scholarly study is the one by Charles Feinberg entitled *The Minor Prophets* (Moody Press, 1976).

Israel

The best panoramic survey of Israel in prophecy is contained in Walter K. Price's intriguing book, *Next Year in Jerusalem* (Moody Press, 1975). Another very good overview is Richard Booker's outstanding study, *Blow the Trumpet in Zion* (Victory House, 1985).

An excellent book that relates prophecy to the history of Israel, particularly modern history, is called *It is No Dream* (The Spearhead Press, 1978). It was written by Elwood McQuaid, the former director of the Friends of Israel Ministry. Charles Feinberg has also produced an excellent volume that mixes prophecy with history. It is titled *Israel: At the Center of History and Revelation* (Multnomah Press, 1980).

Daniel

An outstanding verse by verse commentary on Daniel is the one by Leon Woods that is simply entitled, *A Commentary on Daniel* (Zondervan, 1973). The best one for the general reader is by Renald Showers. It is titled *The Most High God* (The Friends of Israel, 1982). A lighter book that is both fun to read and inspirational in character is *Daniel: God's Man in a Secular Society* by Donald Campbell (Discovery House, 1988). It is designed to serve as a study guide for Bible study groups.

No book of the Bible has been attacked as viciously by theological liberals as the book of Daniel. A tremendous defense of the book's integrity can be found in a volume called *Daniel in the Critic's Den* by Josh McDowell (Campus Crusade for Christ, 1979).

Revelation

Many excellent studies have been published about the book of Revelation. For the general reader, two of the best are *Revelation Illustrated and Made Plain* by Tim LaHaye (Zondervan, 1973), and *There's a New World Coming* by Hal Lindsey (Vision House, 1973). Lindsey's book is the best one he has ever written.

I have also authored a book about Revelation for the general reader. It is entitled *Wrath and Glory* (New Leaf Press, 2001). One of the most popular features of this book is a chapter that addresses the most commonly asked questions about Revelation.

For those who desire to dig deeper, *The Revelation Record* (Tyndale House, 1983) by Henry Morris presents a detailed verse by verse analysis. Dr. Morris is the distinguished founder of the Institute for Creation Research.

A very unique study of Revelation is the one produced by Salem Kirban, a born again Arab. The book utilizes hundreds of photos, charts and drawings to visually present the message of Revelation. It is titled, *Revelation Visualized* (Salem Kirban, Inc., 1978). What makes it even more unusual is that it is co-authored by Gary Cohen, a born again Jew!

An outstanding introduction to Revelation and the various methods of interpreting it is supplied by Merrill Tenney in his remarkably balanced volume, *Interpreting Revelation* (Eerdmans, 1957).

Millennial Viewpoints

The best introduction to the various and often confusing viewpoints of end time prophecy is a book by Robert Lightner called *The Last Days Handbook* (Thomas Nelson, 1990).

A very thought provoking book on the topic is one edited by Robert G. Clouse entitled *The Meaning of the Millennium* (InterVarsity Press, 1977). It contains four viewpoints presented by advocates of those viewpoints. A similar but more detailed presentation of the four viewpoints can be found in the parallel commentary by Steve Gregg called *Revelation: Four Views* (Thomas Nelson, 1997). A scholarly presentation and analysis of the various views is contained in John Walvoord's book, *The Millennial Kingdom* (Zondervan, 1959).

For a classic presentation of the fundamentals of premillennial theology, the book to read is *The Basis of the Premillennial Faith* by Charles Ryrie (Loizeaux Brothers, 1953). It is brief and incisive, and it is written with an irenic spirit.

The Antichrist

One of the most detailed studies of the Antichrist ever written is the book by Arthur W. Pink entitled, *The Antichrist*. It is thoroughly biblical and very thought provoking. It was originally published in

1923 but has been recently republished (Kregel, 1988). The best current day study is the book by Ed Hindson entitled, *Is the Antichrist Alive and Well?: Ten Keys to His Identity* (Harvest House, 1998).

The Rapture

The important controversy over the timing of the Rapture has been best addressed by John Walvoord in two of his books: *The Blessed Hope and the Tribulation* (Zondervan, 1976) and *The Rapture Question* (Zondervan, 1979). Walvoord is the former President of Dallas Theological Seminary. Another fine book on the topic is *The Rapture* by Hal Lindsey (Bantam Books, 1983).

Tim LaHaye has written a very powerful and exhaustive defense of the Pre-Tribulation Rapture entitled *No Fear of the Storm: Why Christians Will Escape All the Tribulation* (Multnomah, 1992, later re-published as *Rapture Under Attack,* 1998).

Signs of the Times

This is a field that attracts many sensationalist writers. There is an abundance of books, but few good ones. One of the most fascinating is *World War III: Signs of the Impending Battle of Armageddon* by John Wesley White (Zondervan, 1977).

A volume that is comprehensive in scope but exceptionally brief is *Signs of the Second Coming* by Robert G. Witty (Broadman Press, 1969). A more recent study, and an excellent one, is by Henry Morris. It is titled *Creation and the Second Coming* (Master Books, 1991).

One of the best prophetic writers to emerge in recent years is Ed Hindson of Liberty University. His books are solidly biblical, down-to-earth, and readable by the average Christian. He has written two outstanding studies of the signs of the times: *Final Signs* (Harvest House, 1996) and *Earth's Final Hour: Are We Really Running Out of Time?* (Harvest House, 1999).

Another excellent writer in the field of Bible prophecy is Dave Hunt of Berean Ministries. He has produced a very insightful study of the end time signs in his book, *How Close Are We?* (Harvest House, 1993).

Heaven

The Eternal State has been the most ignored area of Bible prophecy, probably because the Bible says so little about it. The best book on the topic — one that covers death, resurrection and eternity — is *The Future Life* by the Frenchman, René Pache, translated into English by Helen Needham (Moody Press, 1962). A very worthwhile, exhaustive study of the Eternal State can be found in Bob Chambers' book, *Heaven* (College Press, 1991). This is an unusual book because Chambers is an Amillennialist who spiritualizes the prophecies about the Millennium while interpreting the prophecies about Heaven literally!

Children

Only one book has ever been written for pre-school and elementary children concerning end time prophetic events. It is the one I wrote entitled, *Jesus is Coming Again!* (Harvest House, 1992). The book emphasizes the positive promises of God regarding the Millennium and the Eternal State.

Media

Chuck Missler and I have both produced cassette tape albums that contain verse-by-verse commentaries on the book of Revelation. My study, *An Overview of Revelation* (Lamb & Lion Ministries, 1987), contains 12 tapes. Missler's *Revelation Commentary* (Koinonia Ministries) consists of three albums with eight tapes each.

Jack Van Impe has produced an excellent series of video commentaries on Revelation called *Revelation Revealed* (Jack Van Impe Ministries). I have videotaped a 75 minute overview that covers the book chapter by chapter. It is also entitled *Revelation Revealed* (Lamb & Lion Ministries, 2003).

Ray Stedman's outstanding commentary on Revelation can be found posted on the Internet in 23 messages at www.pbc.org/ stedman (Peninsula Bible Church).

The best illustrations of Revelation have been produced by Pat Marvenko Smith. She has illustrated every main scene of the book and has made the pictures available in a variety of forms — slides, posters, overhead transparencies, video, and PowerPoint. You can find all her resources on the Internet at RevelationIllustrated.com.

Fiction

The "Left Behind" series of books by Tim LaHaye and Larry B. Jenkins present a fictionalized story about the Rapture and the Tribulation that is based upon biblical prophecies. This series is published by Tyndale House and has broken all sales records for prophetic books. The series of novels has become a best seller even when compared to secular books. The books have been made available on audio tape, and special edited versions have been published for teens. The first of the volumes, entitled *Left Behind*, was published in 1995.

Bibles

The very first study Bible ever published came out in 1909. It is still one of the best selling study Bibles in the world. It was produced by a Dallas pastor named C. I. Scofield and is called *The Scofield Study Bible* (Oxford University Press, 1998). It has been revised and updated regularly over the years by an editorial committee representing a premillennial, pre-tribulational viewpoint.

A newer study Bible that presents the same view of the passages related to end time prophecy is *The Ryrie Study Bible* (Moody Press, 1976). Both the Scofield and Ryrie commentaries are available in a variety of translations. The latest and most up to date study Bible that focuses on the interpretation of prophecy is *The Tim LaHaye Prophecy Study Bible* (AMG Publishers, 2000).

The Living Bible Paraphrased (Tyndale House, 1971), though not a typical study Bible, is nonetheless an interpretive Bible that reflects a premillennial interpretation of all key prophetic passages.

Classics

The greatest and most enduring classic on the return of Jesus is William E. Blackstone's book, *Jesus is Coming*. It was written in 1878. The third revised edition of 1908 has been recently re-published with an introduction by John Walvoord (Kregel, 1989).

A foreign book that has come to be considered one the great classics of end time prophecy is ***The Return of Jesus Christ*** by René Pache, translated into English by William S. LaSor (Moody Press, 1955). It is must reading for any Bible prophecy enthusiast.

The 20th Century American classic is, of course, Hal Lindsey's book, ***The Late Great Planet Earth*** (Zondervan, 1970). The New York Times has certified that it was the number one best selling book in the world (with the exception of the Bible) for ten years, between 1970 and 1980!

Perhaps the most unusual book ever published on Bible prophecy is ***Dispensational Truth*** by Clarence Larkin (Reverend Clarence Larkin Estate, 1920). Larkin was a draftsman who devoted his talents to illustrating prophetic concepts with fascinating charts and diagrams. This is a classic that will keep you up all night!

Note: Many of the books mentioned in this appendix are now out of print, but copies can usually be found on the Internet at a very reasonable price at www.abebooks. com.

Appendix 2

Recommended Prophecy Ministries

All the ministries listed below offer excellent study resources regarding Bible Prophecy. All the ministries are premillennial and pre-tribulational in their basic prophetic concepts. This is not an exhaustive listing of such ministries. These are ministries the author is most familiar with.

According to Prophecy Ministries
Don Perkins
P.O. Box 6
Lemon Grove, CA 91946
phone: 619/661-5913
email: don@according2prophecy.org
website: www.according2prophecy.org
Only Black evangelist in America who devotes full time to the teaching and preaching of Bible prophecy. Very balanced ministry with an outstanding website and many good study aids.

Ariel Ministries
Arnold Fruchtenbaum
P.O. Box 3723
Tustin, CA 92781
phone: 714/259-4800
email: homeoffice@ariel.org
website: www.ariel.org
Messianic ministry with a strong emphasis on Bible prophecy. Conducts in-depth tours of Israel and produces many publications, tapes and books.

Christian Jew Foundation
Gary Hedrick
P.O. Box 345
San Antonio, TX 78292
phone: 210/226-0421
email: orderline@cjf.org
website: www.cjf.org
Messianic ministry with one of the oldest continually broadcast radio programs. Presents a strong emphasis on Bible prophecy in its many tapes and publications.

Crown & Sickle Ministries
Don McGee
60498 Floyd Road
Amite, LA 70422
phone: 985/748-2943
email: csmin@bellsouth.net
website: www.crownandsickle.com
A new Bible prophecy ministry that specializes in conducting meetings and conferences. Produces a monthly newsletter.

Discovery Ministries
Gary Frazier
P. O. Box 13770
Arlington, TX 76094
817/275-1771
email: from website
website: www.discoveryministries.com
Dynamic teacher of Bible prophecy. Organizes tours to Israel for churches and ministries. Conducts prophecy conferences with Tim LaHaye and Ed Hindson.

Friends of Israel Gospel Ministry
William E. Sutter
P.O. Box 908
Bellmawr, NJ 08099
phone: 800/257-7843
email: foi@foigm.org
website: www.christianity.com/foi
Publishes an outstanding magazine called "Israel My Glory." Provides many tapes, videos and publications that relate to Bible prophecy. Produces a nationally broadcast radio program. Conducts tours to Israel.

God's News Behind the News
Joe VanKoevering
P.O. Box 10475
St. Petersburg, FL 33733
phone: 1-800/366-1463
email: mail@godsnews.com
website: www.godsnews.com
Provides a bi-monthly magazine and a weekly television broadcast. Sponsors a large national conference yearly.

Hal Lindsey Ministries
P.O. Box 1131
Murrieta, CA 92564
phone: 800/348-8735
email: hal@hallindseyoracle.com
website: hallindseyoracle.com
Website contains up-to-the-minute news reports from all over the world, written

from a biblical and prophetic perspective. Many prophecy study resources available through the website.

Jack Van Impe Ministries
Jack Van Impe
P.O. Box 7004
Troy, MI 48007
phone: 248/852-2244
email: jvimi@jvim.com
website: www.jvim.com
Produces a nationally broadcast television program, a bi-monthly magazine, and a monthly newsletter. Also produces a great variety of excellent video programs.

Koinonia House
Chuck Missler
P.O. Box D
Coeur d'Alene, ID 83816
phone: 208/773-6310
email: from website
website: www.khouse.org
Daily radio program and monthly newsletter. Produces books and excellent cassette tape programs.

Lion of Judah Ministries
Gary Fisher
P.O. Box 681505
Franklin, TN 37068
phone: 615/591-8036
email: garyfisher@bellsouth.net
website: http://sxws.com/LIONJUDH
Produces a bi-monthly teaching newsletter. Focuses on conducting home Bible studies and church meetings.

Maranatha Evangelistic Ministries
Al Gist
224 Al Gist Road, Longville, LA 70652
phone: (337) 725-6209
email: al_gist@hotmail.com
website: www.sxws.com/maranathaevangelisticministries
A new prophecy ministry headed up by a seasoned preacher who specializes in conducting evangelistic meetings, using Bible prophecy to call people to repentance.

Midnight Call Ministries
Arno Froese
P.O. Box 280008
Columbia, SC 29228
phone: 803/755-0733
email: info@midnightcall.com

website: www.midnightcall.com
Publishes a monthly magazine that is distributed worldwide in many languages. Heavily involved in book publishing and sponsorship of prophetic conferences.

Pre-Trib Study Group
Tommy Ice & Tim LaHaye
P.O. Box 14111
Arlington, TX 76094
phone: 817/861-9199
email: icet@711online.net
website: The group's membership consists of most of the premillennial, pre-tribulational preachers, teachers and college professors in America. It meets annually to discuss Bible prophecy issues. Publishes a monthly newsletter.

Prophetic Witness Movement International
P.O. Box 109
Leyland, Lancashire PR25 1WB
England
phone: 011-44-1772-452-846
email: info@pwmi.org
website: www.pwmi.org
Founded in 1917 by F. B. Meyer in response to the Balfour Declaration. Publishes a monthly magazine and conducts meetings and conferences throughout Great Britain.

Prophezine
John Terry
phone: unlisted
email: john@prophezine.com
website: prophezine.com
An excellent Internet magazine on Bible prophecy that is issued twice monthly.

Rapture Ready
Todd Strandberg & Terry James
1011 W. 31 Ave.
Bellevue, NE 68005
phone: 402/292-6167
email: todd.strandberg@adab.centaf.af.mil
website: www.raptureready.com
An Internet ministry that provides a rich variety of Bible prophecy study materials and links to other prophetic ministries. Keeps a unique, updated "Rapture Index" that analyzes the intensity of prophetic developments in the world.

Revelation Illustrated
Pat Marvenko Smith
1740 Ridgeview Dr., North
Huntingdon, PA 15642
phone: 1-800/327-7330
email: from website

website: www.revelationillustrated.com
Provides a magnificent series of illustrations of scenes throughout the book of Revelation. The illustrations are available in slides, prints, posters, and overhead transparencies. A CD containing all the illustrations has been produced for Power-Point presentations.

Sounds of the Trumpet Ministries
Richard Booker
4747 Research Forest Drive, Suites 180-330
Woodlands, TX 77381
phone: 281/469-1045
email: shofarprb@aol.com
website: www.rbooker.com
Conducts prophetic conferences, publishes books, and offers correspondence courses and tours to Israel. Runs an institute that teaches the Jewish roots of Christianity.

Thy Kingdom Come Ministry
Charles Pack & Phillip Goodman
P.O. Box 4414
Tulsa, OK 74159
phone: 918/835-6978
email: from website
website: www.prophecywatch.com
Produces a major prophecy conference each year and provides a bi-monthly prophetic newspaper. Also produces a weekly TV program called "Prophecy Watch."

World of the Bible Ministries
Randall Price
P.O. Box 827
San Marcos, TX 78667
phone: 866/604-7322
email: from website
website: www.worldofthebible.com
Produces books, videos, and tapes concerning biblical archaeology and its relationship to Bible prophecy.

World Prophetic Ministry
Ed Hindson
1099 N. Pepper Ave.
Rialto, CA 92376
phone: 909/825-2767
email: from the website
website: www.thekingiscoming.com
Sponsors a nationally televised program called "The King is Coming." Publishes a monthly prophetic newsletter.